SEÁN BOYLAN ON ...

The 1987 Final: After a gap of seventeen years in the wilderness, Meath were in an All-Ireland Final. It was a wonderful feeling. We were going to play against Cork, the new kings of Munster.

1991 Dublin-Meath matches: Suddenly this contest caught the imagination of a nation that had just come through the euphoria of the World Cup adventure in Italia '90. In the wake of all that, Gaelic games were perceived to be almost dead – and then these amazing games came along. They were very physical games – powerful football played with unrelenting intensity.

The 1999 team: The 1999 squad found that ingredient on the training field and went on to win the All-Ireland title ... We knew that they were going to come through. The memories were purged. The hunger was there. The sacrifices were made. The effort was put in. And it was especially nice to win the All-Ireland title fifty years after Meath had won their first title.

Managing: There is no magic formula in managing a team. It is largely a matter of being in the right place at the right time and creating the right environment for success. At the outset, you are looking for certain levels of skill, confidence and vision in a player.

Herbalism: Plants have a chemistry that works on the human body – favourably or not. It is a case of realising more what you cannot do than what you can do. Nowadays I am more at ease with what I do. I can explain to a client what will or will not work and why it may complement the modern treatment. It is a question of balance.

Seán Boylan was the Meath manager for twenty-three years. He runs a successful herbal clinic in Meath. He lives with his wife, Tina, and six children in Dunboyne, County Meath.

John Quinn was a broadcaster with RTÉ for twenty-seven years. He has published a number of books including five books for children.

SEÁN BOYLAN
THE WILL TO WIN

THE AUTOBIOGRAPHY AS TOLD TO

John Quinn

THE O'BRIEN PRESS
DUBLIN

First published 2006 by The O'Brien Press Ltd,
12 Terenure Road East, Rathgar, Dublin 6, Ireland.
Tel: +353 1 4923333; Fax: +353 1 4922777
E-mail: books@obrien.ie Website: www.obrien.ie
ISBN-10: 1-84717-004-8
ISBN-13: 978-1-84717-004-0

British Library Cataloguing-in-Publication Data
Quinn, John
The will to win : Sean Boylan
1. Boylan, Sean 2. Gaelic football managers - Ireland - Biography
I. Title II. Boylan, Sean
796.3'3

1 2 3 4 5 6 7
06 07 08 09 10
Printing: MPG Books Ltd

The herbal information mentioned in this book is not intended as medical information. No treatment or
therapies should be attempted without qualified medical advice.

Dedication

To my wife, Tina, and my children, and in memory of my parents, Seán and Gertie.

Acknowledgements

I would like to thank some of the people who helped and encouraged me over the years. Thanks to:

My children: Seán, Ciarán, Dáire, Doireann, Aoife and Óran.

My sisters: Frances, Pauline, Josephine, Gemma and Philo, and their families.

My friends: Noel Keating (RIP), Brush Shiels, Denis Murtagh, Owen Lynch (The Crow), and Tommy Reilly.

To all members of the Meath teams, managements, county board and clubs, and especially to Noel Keating (RIP) and Kepak.

To the people who work with me at home and the ones who have gone before us.

My preference would be to name everybody who travelled this marvellous journey with me. My nature would be to mention every person individually, from the man on the gate to the president of the association. For once I cannot do this as twenty-three years involves a lot of people, but I remember each person and the bond that we shared. This bond is sacred to us. What happens in the dressing room stays in the dressing room!

My publishers, The O'Brien Press, especially Michael O'Brien, Publisher, Íde ní Laoghaire and Síne Quinn.

Colm O'Rourke for his contribution to the book, and Liam Mulvihill for his quote.

Special thanks to John Quinn for making this book a reality.

And to all the supporters of the Meath team!

CONTENTS

'BOYLAN – THE MAN'

Colm O'Rourke

Seán Boylan is a complex man. He is a husband, father, devoted family man and a thousand other things as well. To understand the man, though, one must first of all know the importance of his roots. Seán's a country man with great pride in his home place. Then, of course, he is a product of that environment – Dunboyne, Meath and Ireland. His loyalty to old family friends and his practical patriotism were handed down from his father, who played an active role in the formation of the State in the years after 1916.

Values such as honesty, loyalty and common courtesy dictate his very existence – old-fashioned qualities that are not as important as they used to be but are nonetheless central elements of his personality. Seán's graciousness in defeat is often commented upon, but that is easily explainable in terms of his sporting principles. Football is not war; it is the embodiment of all that is good in the human condition. No matter how disappointing the loss, there was never any hint of bitterness or lack of sportsmanship from this exceptional manager.

As a team manager his greatest asset was the ability to create a type of team bond and unity of spirit where good players often became great and ordinary ones did extraordinary things on days when they were most needed. He told young men what was possible and they believed and delivered. And beyond the dressing room door, nobody mattered; he deflected criticism and always posted a reasonable response to the outside world.

Some sceptics believed that behind the veneer there must be some type of Machiavellian character. By the end of his twenty-three years everyone realised that the public and private Seán Boylan were the same.

Training players with strong and different personalities and egos was not always easy, and many players were dropped for various reasons. Of course this is no different from what happens on other teams, but this part of management never came easy to Seán; he preferred giving good news. Though plenty of players did not always see eye to eye with him, there are few who don't look on him with a favourable light and recognise what he achieved for Meath.

His conversations with players were legendary. The range of topics covered was wide and varied, but Seán often spoke in riddles and sometimes confused his listeners – this was the eccentric part of his personality.

His early training methods were considered revolutionary and at times quite bizarre. He allowed players to let their hair down occasionally, even encouraged it. Who else would bring a team away for weekends before big games, the last game in '91 against Dublin and the All-Ireland replay in '88, and let the players have a real knees-up? He trusted his players and the players trusted him that he would have them right on the day, both mentally and physically.

The extent of the change in Meath football during his time can be seen in one statistic: from 1970 to 1986 Meath won no Leinster title; in the next fifteen years eight were annexed. The only constant here was Seán Boylan.

What he did was to take over a county, which no one wanted to manage, a county low on self-esteem and confidence, and helped make Meath the leading power in football at that time. Even at the end Seán believed he could build another team which would challenge for an All-Ireland title if he was given sufficient time.

He was right, though, to get out when he did and now he moves on to another challenge at International Rules level – a fitting reward for someone who has given so much without ever looking for a red cent for doing the job; someone who simply felt it was a privilege to stir his county team towards success.

His legacy is one of total dedication to the people of Meath whom he served so well. I had the honour of playing under him longer than any other player and I enjoyed every moment of it. When we started off together in a tournament game in Longford in 1982 nobody could have foreseen where the journey would take us. We changed from losers to winners, and without the good and generous man called Seán Boylan, it would never have happened.

PREFACE

I first approached Seán Boylan about doing this book in 1999, but he was probably too busy winning an All-Ireland title then, something he made a habit of doing in his extraordinary twenty-three year career as manager of the Meath Gaelic Football team. Four All-Ireland titles, runners-up on three occasions, eight Leinster titles, three National League titles, a Centenary Cup and an armful of All-Star awards for his players – achievements like these lifted Meath out of the doldrums and made them one of the consistently potent forces in Gaelic Football over the past twenty years. Seán Boylan surely had a story to tell.

There is another side to the man, of course. Football management may be a passion of his but it is not the only one. He has a love and respect for the soil and the bounty it provides in healing and curing. This is born out of a family tradition that stretches back over five generations. When, as a seventeen-year-old student, Seán committed himself to helping his ailing father with his herbal remedy business, he set out on a path of learning and discovery that would lead to the development of a very successful and respected herbal clinic. This was the day-job. Gaelic football is an amateur sport. Combining those two passions is quite an awesome task. Seán Boylan surely had an even bigger story to tell.

The problem was that Seán does not like talking about himself, but after five years of reminding and encouraging, he finally agreed to 'give it a try' when Michael O'Brien of The O'Brien Press expressed serious interest in publishing Seán's story. Over a period of eighteen months I have been trekking to Dunboyne to record that story. That journey of itself would almost make another book. I kept a diary entitled 'Desperately Seeking Seanie' which outlined the ups and downs, stops and starts of the whole process – right from day one in late 2004 when we were to begin the story in a quiet corner of the lobby of the Burlington Hotel in Dublin, only to find ourselves in the company of several hundred doctors attending a World Congress on Cancer ...

For me it has been a fascinating journey. As a fellow Meathman who has savoured Seán's glory days, it was a labour of love. I emphasise, however, that this book is not my assessment of Seán. It is his own story as told to me. Seán Boylan is a gracious, talented and successful man, but he is equally a very private and complex man. His story is worth telling. I am honoured that he told it to me.

And to have it realised into these pages I am indebted to a number of people – all of them women ...

– to his wife Tina Boylanwho 'encouraged' him to persevere when Seán had doubts about the whole venture;

– to Íde ni Laoghaire and Síne Quinn of The O'Brien Press for their valued and valuable editorial judgement and advice, and to Emma Byrne for her work on the design of the book;

– to Máire Ní Fhrighilfor converting into type the work of a writer for whom the pen is the cutting edge of technology;

– and to my late wife, Olive, who, on hearing Seán speak at the Céifin Conference in 1999, said to me, 'You know, there's a book in that fellow!' Thank you, my love. As ever, you were right! I hope I have done your suggestion justice.

John Quinn

CHAPTER ONE

Steeped in History and Herbs

My Royal County roots go very deep indeed. My great-great-grandfather was also called Seán Boylan, as was my father, and now our eldest son continues the tradition. The first Seán (my great-great-grandfather) lived in Tara, the seat of the ancient High Kings of Ireland. There was a skirmish in Tara which was part of the ill-fated 1798 rebellion. For their involvement in that and for providing refuge for retreating rebels, my ancestors' home was burned to the ground by the British yeomanry. That original Seán Boylan married Elizabeth Glennon, whose family had come from Dunboyne. The Glennons and most of Dunboyne also suffered at the hands of the yeomen in 1798. It is said that eighty-four houses were razed in retaliation for the attempted rebellion. Elizabeth's brother, Peter Glennon, was among those deported to Van Diemen's Land (now known as Tasmania. Van Diemen's Land was the primary penal colony in Australia at the time) aboard the convict ship *Success*. Following their eviction from Tara, the Boylans moved to Dunboyne where they were given shelter by the local priest. However, his house was also razed, but he escaped on horseback. My great-great-grandfather built a two-storey thatched house where the rockery now stands in front of our modern home.

All that remains of the priest's house is a little stool that was handed down through the generations

Over the years the Boylans built up a farm and market-garden business here at Edenmore, just outside Dunboyne village. When Seán moved from Tara he had few material things to bring with him, but he had one gift which he had inherited from his ancestors – a knowledge of the healing properties of herbs. It was said that even in the eighteenth century, Seán and his brother Michael had original herbal remedies for four conditions: osteoarthritis, asthma, dropsy and tuberculosis. These remedies were handed down from father to son over the centuries. Who knows how far back the tradition goes? One theory is that these remedies were given to particular families by monks (whose monasteries were places of healing) in times of religious persecution. It is easy to be cynical about herbal remedies today, but long before the advent of a medical profession or a health service, people had little option. You went to a particular individual for a particular ailment.

Remedies travelled in strange ways. My grandfather, Edward, used a remedy called *Essiac*, a non-toxic herbal treatment for cancer which is made from four common herbs: sheep sorrel, burdock root, slippery elm and turkey rhubarb. It was developed in Canada in the 1920s by a nurse, Reneé Caissé, who had been given this remedy by a patient who had been cured of cancer. That patient had been given Essiac by a Native American herbalist. Reneé Caissé spent her adult life treating cancer patients in her own clinic until she died at the age of ninety-one in 1978. My grandfather died in 1910, so how did Essiac arrive in Edenmore? My theory is that it may have arrived in Ireland around the time of the Great Famine when the Native Americans sent help to this country. It is just a theory but a plausible one, I feel. In any event the herbal remedy tradition was carefully preserved and handed on by generations of the Boylan family. I joined my father in the business at seventeen and, ironically, the very first case I had to deal with involved the treatment of a man whose kidney had been infected with tuberculosis. I was using a remedy that my great-great-grandfather had used in Tara, so the tradition continued. For years my father provided remedies free of charge to the many people who came to him. The business gradually evolved and became a full-time operation which is now a professionally-run clinic here at Edenmore – but that is a story for another chapter ...

As with the herbs, a strong nationalist tradition was also passed down through the Boylan generations. My father would recall how his father insisted that 'nothing good ever came from England ... even the wind that blows from there is a foul one,' he would say. He was, of course, referring to the east wind! An uncle of my father's took particular pride in asserting that during his long life he never spoke to a policeman! That was the atmosphere in which my father was reared.

He was born in either 1880 or 1882 – there are two conflicting birth certificates – and so he grew up through the period of the Gaelic Revival. He left school at the age of nine to help out in the family farm and worked hard as a young man. He would drive a horse-drawn bogey of hay regularly to the Smithfield market in Dublin and bring home a load of coal on the return journey. He was a noted athlete and hurler. Dunboyne had a strong hurling tradition and my father captained the team which won five county championships between 1908 and 1914. The GAA would have been inextricably linked with the nationalist movement. Dunboyne hurling team accompanied the funeral of the Fenian O'Donovan Rossa in Dublin in 1915, carrying draped hurleys.

The growing strength of the Home Rule movement under John Redmond prompted Unionists to set up the Ulster Volunteer Force (UVF) in 1913. The Home Rulers set up the rival Irish Volunteers and although there was a corps set up locally in Dunboyne, my father had no faith in them. He reckoned that those involved would never fight for Irish freedom and so he set up his own maverick volunteer unit. Each man paid threepence a week towards the purchase of arms and equipment. They had a drill instructor, Larry Murtagh, from Dublin, whom my father would have met through his GAA connections. The Volunteer movement split in 1914 with the Redmondites becoming the National Volunteers and the Irish Volunteers, who were intent on rebellion, being controlled by the more extreme Irish Republican Brotherhood (IRB), a secret oath-bound organisation dedicated to the establishment of an Irish republic by physical force. My father joined the latter and was appointed by Patrick Pearse to organise the Meath area. He attended the General Council meetings of the IRB where he would be in the company of Pearse, McDonagh, Ceannt and McDermott – later signatories of the 1916 Proclamation. At the unveiling of the Parnell monument in Glasnevin, Pearse said to my father: 'You have done more for us than any man since Parnell … '

Volunteer meetings would be held in secrecy and often hurling matches and possibly the trips to Dublin market would have been used as cover for political business. I remember Jimmy 'Spuds' Kelly telling me how he was discharged from the Richmond hospital in Dublin with a broken leg in plaster on Easter Saturday and duly got a lift home from Hanlon's Corner with my father. What thoughts must have been going through his mind that evening, but he would have given 'Spuds' no inkling of what fateful events would unfold that weekend.

On the previous day, Good Friday, he had got written instructions from Pearse that the Rising would begin at 6.00pm on Easter Sunday. My father in turn sent orders to his men to mobilise at our house on Sunday afternoon. The plan was to seize Clonsilla railway station and prevent the movement of British reinforcements from Athlone.

My father rarely spoke of his military career in latter years. Nine days before his death, I met Seán McEntee in the Mater hospital, Dublin (he was visiting the dying Seán Lemass). McEntee told me he had been in our house on that Easter Saturday evening in 1916, when he was en route from Belfast to Dublin. Regarding that same evening, my father gave me a rare insight in 1967 when we were on our way to the Coombe hospital to see my newborn niece, Catherine, and her mother, Frances. Passing by Rialto church, he told me that he had gone to confession there on Easter Saturday, 1916. The priest, who obviously knew him, said 'I believe blood will be spilled.' The answer was a terse 'Yes!' 'Good luck to ye, then,' replied the priest.

Confusion reigned when Eoin McNeill countermanded Pearse's order and my father spent the next week trying to inform his men and ascertain what exactly was going on. On learning that the Rising had in fact started in the city, he mobilised his local Volunteers in an attempt to demolish the railway bridge beside our house until a signalman told him there was only a 'local row' in the city and they duly stopped the demolition! Eight days later, our house was surrounded by British lancers and my father, together with his brothers, Ned, Peter and Joe, were arrested and taken to Richmond Barracks in Dublin, where they were held in the company of the soon-to-be-executed Ceannt, McDermott and McBride.

From Richmond Barracks my father and other prisoners were despatched by cattle-boat to Holyhead and thence to the severe conditions of Wandsworth Prison in London. They were subsequently moved to Woking Prison and finally to Frongoch in Wales. Conditions were much better there for the hundreds of Irish rebels. There were language and educational classes and it was here that my father became friendly with the emerging rebel leader, Michael Collins. My father was eventually released from Frongoch when a Justice of the Peace, Laurence Ward, vouched for him. In an ironic twist of fate, the Wards had been given the land the Boylans had been evicted from many years earlier, but there had never been animosity between the families over the 'sins of the fathers'.

Following his release at Easter 1917, my father began re-organising the Dunboyne Volunteers straight away. In a drive to improve membership he organised an *aeríocht* (music festival) in the hurling field here on our land. Michael Collins and WT Cosgrave addressed the crowd and appealed for new members. The volunteers were now known as *Óglaigh na hÉireann* (the Irish Republican Army). My father became Brigadier of the Meath Brigade.

Sinn Féin, the political wing of the IRA, had a landslide victory in the general election of 1918 and set out on a campaign of civil disobedience, establishing alternative government structures to the British system. Whether it was disrupting and ultimately forcing the cancellation of the Ward Union Hunt's activities or directing the work of the Volunteers' own police force, my father was an absolutely fearless man.

The British General McCreevy said of him: 'We had to admire Boylan. He was ruthless, but if we had got him, he wouldn't have lasted long.' Following a famous raid on Trim Royal Irish Constabulary (RIC) barracks in 1920, when the barracks were burned down and a substantial amount of arms and ammunition were taken by Meath IRA under Brigadier Boylan, my father got a message from a priest that the Crown Forces intended to 'burn down Boylan's house.' My father let it be known that if his or any volunteer's house was burned, he would have 'every British loyalist house in Meath burned as a reprisal ... ' No action was taken.

My father and his Dunboyne volunteers were largely on the run during the 'War of Independence' as it became known, taking on the infamous 'Black and Tans'. In a restructuring of the *Óglaigh* in 1921, my father was promoted to the rank of General and was made Commanding Officer of the First Eastern Division. The Truce was called in

July 1921 and in December of that year the Anglo-Irish Treaty was signed. Michael Collins, who negotiated the Truce, had earlier said to my father: 'For what period will we be justified in carrying on the guerilla warfare? What will be the effect on the children unborn? There is a danger of going too far and giving the British an opportunity of committing her entire army to wholesale war on our people ... ?'

My father supported Collins and the Pro-Treaty side in the Civil War that ensued. When that war ended the new government offered my father the position of Commander-in-Chief of the Irish Free State army, but he declined. He had been badly injured in an accident and he wished to return to civilian life.

My father was an extremely strong and brave man who had always remained inconspicuous during his Volunteer days. He would never allow his photograph to be taken. In 1966 during the Golden Jubilee of the Rising, we searched in vain for a photograph of him in uniform. On one occasion while on the run, he hid under the Boyne bridge in Trim, staying underwater, breathing through a reed while the soldiers searched for him. He had unbelievable strength – strength which would be put to the ultimate test in 1919. Together with Matt Furlong and Peadar Clancy he was testing a gun on Menton's farm (where Sheikh Makhtoum has his stud now). One round of ammunition failed to go off. Someone touched the cap. The shell blew up in their faces. Furlong suffered horrific injuries from which he died on the following day. My father was hit in the jawbone. He was taken to the Mater hospital, but insisted on cycling that night to a meeting in Trim and subsequently to another meeting in Hollywood, County Wicklow.

Truly he was an iron man but ultimately he paid the price. The wound festered. He would suffer terribly for the rest of his life. In 1923 he was given a year to live as a result of his injury. In St Bricin's hospital he was given ether to drink, in an effort to ease the pain. Ultimately what saved him were his own remedies. He made an intense study of herbs and their application and he survived. Not just survived – he led a full life. Because of his military experience, he was called in to quell the Curragh Mutiny in 1924 when the Free State army of officers issued an ultimatum to the Executive Council, demanding removal of the Army Council and a declaration of the Government's intention to achieve an Irish Republic. He developed his farming and herbal businesses. He was co-opted as a county councillor and chairman of the Meath county board of the GAA. And he met and married Gertie Quinn, who bore him six children.

In 1958 my father contracted viral pneumonia and his health deteriorated. He took no antibiotics and cleared the pneumonia with herbal remedies. As children, we grew up seeing the best of modern medicine working in tandem with old remedies. He subsequently developed Parkinson's disease. He was given *Artane* for that, but he also took the old remedies to counteract the side-effects of that drug. He lived for a further thirteen years and all the time the inflammation from the 1919 explosion left his toes withered.

All through his life, he adhered to his old Republican values and bonds. In 1966 when ascending the steps of Dublin Castle to attend the Jubilee Commemoration of the Rising, he met an old colleague who had taken the anti-Treaty side. 'John, you were right and we never knew it,' said the colleague. 'I know, Ned, and we could never tell you,' my father replied. He was a deeply religious man. He always carried a relic of the True Cross in a little locket, which he claimed saved his life on many occasions. His name was read off the altar in denunciation after the Rising, but it never stopped him going to Mass and he never fell out with the priest. 'I'll lose my soul for no man – priest or otherwise!' he declared.

General Seán Boylan was a straight, uncomplicated man. An iron man. And I – his son – am steeped in history and herbs ...

CHAPTER TWO

Seán and Gertie

In 1926 my father married Teresa Doherty from County Leitrim, but tragically Teresa died within a few years. They had no children. Life went on in an independent Ireland … Thirteen years later my father travelled to Cloone, County Leitrim, to attend the funeral of a Fr Conifrey who had been supportive to the men during the troubles (after all, Cloone is the home base of Seán Mac Diarmada, one of the signatories of the 1916 Proclamation). Mrs Pope, her daughter Mollie and Gertie Quinn were among the women helping out in the priest's house after the funeral. My father stayed that night in the Popes' house. The next day, he went to visit Sister Philomena Doherty, a sister of his late wife Teresa, in the Convent of Perpetual Adoration in nearby Drumshanbo. The three women, Mrs Pope, Mollie and Gertie, accompanied him to pray at the convent, but things were happening – and not unnoticed. Sr Philomena is supposed to have said to the Mother Abbess that Gertie would be very suitable for Seán. A fortnight later, Gertie travelled to Dublin and came home with an engagement ring! A month later my father asked his brother Joe if he would 'drive him down the country.' My uncle Joe was a rate collector and one of the few people in the locality to have a car. He acceded to his brother's request without question. They drove to Cloone where Seán Boylan and Gertie Quinn were married on 29 June 1939. Whirlwind would hardly even describe their romance!

Gertie Quinn came from a family of nine children. Together with her brother Joe she ran the family farm in Leitrim. It used to annoy her greatly when people said you couldn't make a living on a farm in Leitrim! Herself and Joe proved it could be done. She was thirty-one year's old when she married my father.

They did have a practical reason for a hasty marriage. My father felt there was going to be a war and he wanted to visit Lourdes and Rome. And after a few days in Galway the honeymooners travelled to Lourdes and Rome – fulfilling my father's dream. So Sr Philomena's judgement was right. (She and Gertie corresponded every week until Philomena died. They were almost closer than sisters.) My father was twenty-five years older than Gertie but they were married for thirty-two years. She bore him six children in ten years. I was born in December 1943, coming after twins Frances and Philo, then Gemma and succeeded by Pauline and Josephine. Frances was born on 20 February while Philo waited until 22 February – so they celebrate their birthday on 21 February! On the night I was born my parents were due to go to an operetta in Castleknock College, but could not travel due to snowy weather. Instead I arrived out of the blue! I came in a hurry and have been in a hurry ever since – I am noted for never being on time for anything!

As well as being a busy and devoted mother, Gertie was very much involved in the herbal remedy business. The herbs were grown in the front garden and stored in the sheds. Brews were made up every day. The herbs were washed and boiled up in seven-gallon pots in the kitchen and strained off in the scullery, where the remedies were cooled and filled into bottles. The Boylan children were involved in a total apprenticeship, charged with washing bottles, filling and wrapping them. The house was the clinic. The diningroom was the waiting-room. People just came as they pleased and sat there, waiting. There were no 'hours of business'. They came at all hours – even on Christmas Day – just as farmers tended to do with the veterinary surgeon. The farmer would never call a vet in the morning. (Wait and see. And then it gets dark and worries grow – we had better call the vet!) Gertie eventually put a structure on the operation of the clinic.

Seán was the man of the house, but Gertie was the head of the house. Seán only told you once and you did what you were told, but he was incredibly fair and generous. He ceded the ultimate sanction to Gertie: 'Ask your mother!' She brought her own talents and wisdom to Dunboyne. I recall being down in the fields harvesting herbs when news came that one of the workers had scalded his foot while straining off the boiling brew. Indeed, when he pulled off his sock, the skin came with it. Dashing across the yard to treat the injury, I was held up by my mother reminding me to wrap the scalded area with a cabbage leaf. My reaction was 'Don't be bothering me now, Mother.' I applied an ointment to the burn and did not bother with a cabbage leaf. The next day the pain had gone and the foot eventually healed. However, my mother reminded me that my father had got that particular cabbage leaf remedy from her. The healing was on her side of the family too – her brother Joe had remedies for verrucas and warts. Yet here was I dismissing her with 'Don't be bothering me' ... I had a lot to learn.

For all their 'busyness', my parents still found time for a social life. Card playing was a huge part of their lives and it became equally big in our lives as children. Through his treatment of Dr Donal Cregan, then president of Castleknock College, my father struck up an extraordinary friendship with Brother Peter D'Arcy who would cycle down from the college to collect his herbal remedy and then stay for the card games. Brother Peter did this for years every Wednesday and Sunday and later, as he grew older, my parents would collect him and return him to the college. They would be joined for the card games by Mattie Pierce, my uncles Ned and Peter, Johnny Cannon, Willie Lynskey, Paddy Mulcahy (brother of General Richard Mulcahy) and his wife Pauline. There would be serious rows over 'penny' games of '25' and '110', but it was all good fun, with lots of chat – and supper provided by Gertie. It was a way of life and it is said that during the war years the games often went on all through the night.

As Seán's health declined through the 1950s and '60s, Gertie tended to his needs heroically, bathing and dressing his arms and legs daily, as the poison resulting from the 1919 explosion continued to ooze from his limbs. My father died in 1971 at the age of ninety-one – not bad for a man who had been given a year to live nearly fifty years earlier. Gertie survived him by eighteen years. The whirlwind romance had blown strongly for over three decades. My parents complemented each other in many ways. She was very competent, a great mother and cook, an organiser and a counsellor. She had her own share of ill-health: rheumatic fever and a shattered knee following a fall from a bicycle. In 1957 the thatched house in which we were born and reared was badly damaged by fire. They built a new house where I now live. My mother would have had to oversee that while tending to her husband's illness and rearing six children.

When I look back now, I wonder how they coped at times. Ours was a busy, often crowded home. Often on Sundays, between card-players and visitors, there might be up to twenty people for tea, and callers day and night looking for 'a bottle'. And amid all that, they managed to send all six children to Dublin for their secondary education. My mother was an extraordinary woman. My father was an iron man. Seán and Gertie I owe them both so much!

CHAPTER THREE

A Village Childhood

Dunboyne in the 1950s was a quiet rural village. There were a number of big farms (Brutons, Wards, Buckleys) outside the village and there was always great bustle on a Tuesday night when cattle were being prepared for the Dublin market on the following day. There was also a cattle-fair held at the bullring in Dunboyne, where the Garda station is now.

Gaelic games dominated our social and sporting lives. Dunboyne was traditionally hurling country. Bob O'Keefe (later President of the GAA) had helped set up the hurling club when he came to Dunboyne as a teacher at the turn of the twentieth century. (Every chance you got you went to the village green for a puckaround – not something you could do now!) Football made a breakthrough in 1949 when Meath won their first All-Ireland Senior title. I still have a memory of the crowded train stopping beside our house on that day. I remember – as a mere five-year-old – kicking a ball around the garden to shouts of encouragement from the fans all bedecked in their paper hats and scarves. When Meath won the National League in America in 1951, I remember cars crossing the railway bridge sporting stars and stripes flags!

We had our local heroes, like Jimmy Reilly who won a League medal in 1951 and was centre-half-back on the All-Ireland winning team in 1954. Another local, Bobby Ruske, played in goal for Meath. Then the great Brian Smith, captain of the 1949 team, came to live in the village. These men were our idols and our neighbours. It was a great thrill to kick a ball around with Brian in the run-up to the 1954 final. There was always a great sense of community: people had time for you. Ray Conroy brought me to under-fourteen training on the bar of his bike. Wonderful men like Pat Kelly, Tommy Ruske and Kevin Breslin gave their time freely to look after us youngsters. And Frank Deanes and Barney Reilly knew nothing of health and safety regulations when they packed ten or twelve of us into a car to bring us to a match – we survived. They were heady days!

Going to Croke Park was always a big thrill. I missed the 1954 final – I couldn't get in! My first visit is not a happy memory: the Leinster Football Final of 1955, when Kevin Heffernan and his fellow-Dubliners tore us apart. Our day would come – eventually. I was privileged to be at the Cork-Wexford Hurling Final in 1956. I was right behind the Wexford goal to see Art Foley make a wonder save from Christy Ring and spur the 'Yellowbellies' on to a famous victory. In the following year I witnessed my first Meath victory when the Minor footballers won the All-Ireland title as a curtain-raiser to Louth's great – and only – Senior victory. I was behind the goal at the Canal End – I can still see it as if it only happened yesterday. And if you couldn't get to Croke Park there was always Micheál O'Hehir on radio. He had his unique way of telling the story of a game: a 'schemozzle in the square' covered a multitude of sins, and sendings-off were always anonymous – 'Someone has been sent to the line for a transgression ... ' We knew so much about games we never saw, and later when we saw archive film clips of those games they weren't half as good. It was the way Micheál told it!

Ours was always a busy house. It would be busy enough with six children, but then there was the steady stream of callers coming and going. It was normal to come out of the kitchen and find people sitting on the couch in the hall waiting to see my father. You learned the social graces: how to converse with neighbours and strangers. Initially they came at all hours looking for remedies, until my mother organised hours of business. Even then it took them a while to learn! They would climb over the gate (which was meant to signify 'Closed for Business') and bang on the door. In the early days my father did not charge for remedies. It was only when the business grew and the herbs had to be grown commercially that he began to charge for 'a bottle'. Even then, if there was a good herb-crop, the price might drop from four shillings a bottle to two shillings a bottle. They might not teach that at business school, but my father was ever-conscious of his own health situation and also firmly believed that 'The Lord will provide'. In reality, of course, there was very little money around in the forties and fifties.

The traffic through the house grew even more complicated when it was decided that those involved in the national movement were entitled to a pension. To qualify for this they had to get their Commanding Officer to sign the requisite form. As a result the queue grew longer in our house. If you weren't here for a bottle you were here for a pension! Trouble was, when old comrades get together they have to talk about the old days, irrespective of which side they took in the Civil War. So, if you were looking for a bottle and the man ahead of you was looking for a pension, you might have a bit of a wait.

From an early age I was involved in the work of the farm or the herb-gardens, working alongside wonderful men like Jack Moran, Paddy Woods, Mick Reilly, Jim Caffrey and others. I would have my own herb-patch to look after and occasionally I would unearth a half-crown in the soil. Jack and the boys would grumble: 'How come we never find money?', but it was, of course, an 'incentive' planted by my parents. There was wonderful learning to be had from those men. Sitting up beside Christy Kelly on the old David Brown tractor as he did the ploughing, you learned about life and nature, place and its importance. There was a great sense of community and neighbourliness.

Our lives were dominated by religion – its practice and the observance of rituals. I received my First Holy Communion at the age of five – hardly attaining the 'use of reason'. Those were the days of the Latin Mass and I absorbed the responses so well (I always liked Latin at school) that I decided that I would be an altar-boy. The timing of my request was unfortunate for some. I made my pitch as a nine-year-old to Father Murphy during Christmas Eve confessions. He insisted on taking me though all the responses, much to the annoyance of the big queue outside. I landed the job and was told to report for duty on Christmas morning – much to the exasperation of my mother who had to find a surplice and soutane at short notice. Being mother, she did find them.

Being an altar-boy could be a busy life. At one time in the mid-fifties during the course of a bad 'flu, there were seventeen funerals in eighteen days ... I remember when Dick Reilly died, my father and Nick Moran went to Jervis Street hospital to coffin him. (Mick Reilly, Jack and Nick Moran would have dug all of the graves at that time.) On being presented with the remains, Nick announced: 'That's not Dick Reilly. He's a much bigger man!' It turned out that Dick had been mistakenly sent to Waterford, so we had to go to Kevin Street Garda Station to retrieve him. In life, Dick could be awkward at times, so 'as you live, so shall you die ... ' I was reared with the maxim: 'Mind the sick and bury the dead'. It was considered a honour and a privilege to look after the dead.

Ours was indeed a busy house – day and night. Every Wednesday and Sunday night the card-players came. And of course the great and the good visited at one time or another – WT Cosgrave, Lemass, De Valera, Seán McEoin, McEntee. On such occasions 'little boys should be seen and not heard' was very much the rule. As a result I think I am a much better listener than I am a talker.

Ours was also very much a house of women – my father and I ranged against six women. Although I had three sisters older and two younger than me, I like to joke that I reared them all. People will say I was spoiled, but I don't accept that. I never missed having a brother – Josephine was an excellent goalkeeper! And I was never short of male pals – down to the village green and there they were.

In 1948 my mother contracted rheumatic fever and was confined to bed for three months. As a result, her children were 'farmed out' to relatives for the duration. I was despatched to Cloneycavan, near Ballivor, to my Auntie Maggie and Uncle Liam Murphy. They were very kind to me, but it was a traumatic experience for a five-year-old. I often wonder if it affected me subsequently. I know that as a youngster I always wanted to be going home – even when pals would be going to a show in Dublin. Certainly in my first ten years of working at home I never went away on a holiday.

Our year was marked by a cycle of rituals, most of them related to religious practice. There was the excitement of Christmas Eve allied to the spiritual preparation of going to confession (and becoming an altar-boy). My father had siblings living in Harold's Cross in Dublin, so on St Patrick's Day we would then meet them, travel up by bus for Mass in Arran Quay and go on to see the parade in O'Connell Street. On Easter Saturday I would travel with my father to Gloucester Street in the city, to visit Sister Eithne, Michael Collins's former secretary. What a wonderful privilege it was for a young boy to meet such people. At Halloween the apples were brought from our orchards to the Capuchin friary in Church Street to be distributed to poor people who could not get fruit. (My father often had a wonderfully practical and lasting gift for a couple who were getting married – he would plant them a little orchard.) Our lives seemed to revolve around churches. Every November we would do the rounds of city churches: St Peter's in Phibsboro; Gardiner Street, Clarendon Street, Whitefriar Street – with our List of the Dead. I think that is how I got to know the city so well.

Overall, mine was a happy childhood, nurtured by a loving family and a wonderful community. Discipline was strict but fair. I can only remember one physical punishment – when I crossed over the border of acceptability and at the age of ten was caught using a stream of bad language. I was out in the fields with a donkey and cart pulling rag-wort weeds – you had to pull them or they would simply grow again. The old donkey was in a typically stubborn mood and wouldn't go where I wanted him to go, so I told him what I thought of him in a string of curses I had obviously learned at school. This was not accept-able in the Boylan household. My backside was tanned, I was told to say an Act of Contrition and ultimately was taken out of the local school and sent to the nuns' school in Eccles Street, Dublin (where my older sisters were attending secondary school). Later I would move to the Jesuits in Belvedere College, but all the time there was constant involvement with the farm and the herbs. Ultimately it would become a total involvement.

Growing up in Dunboyne was a full life: gaelic games, religion, politics, farming, herbs, people and enjoyment. I thought there was no place like it and I suppose in truth there wasn't.

CHAPTER FOUR

Schooling and Ambitions

I graduated from Eccles Street convent school to the Jesuits, Belvedere College (Dublin) primary school before moving on to secondary level. It meant catching an early bus from Dunboyne but in all that time, apart from absence through illness, I never missed the bus, even though I have a reputation now as a bad timekeeper. I really liked Belvedere and, being a sport-mad youngster, I availed of the many facilities the college offered. Gaelic football was not on the menu, although I did play hurling there. However, all that was to change one summer when I returned from Irish college in Carraroe, County Galway. My parents informed me that I would not be going back to Belvedere. Instead, I would be going to Clogher Road vocational school in Crumlin.

It was a bombshell. I never got a real explanation for the change. My parents would have wanted me to be 'good with my hands' and avail of the vocational training, but in hindsight I would say the reasons were financial. My parents had built a new house, my father's health was poor. Things were tight enough and the fees for Belvedere were an added strain on their finances. I would have been unhappy to be leaving Belvedere but I accepted my lot. It was a huge transition for me, a culture shock in many ways. I never regretted my two years there, but I always felt unfulfilled through not having finished the course in Belvedere. I felt at the time it was partly my fault. Maybe I had not put in enough effort. Maybe I spent too much time on the sports field. I now had even further to travel. Clogher Road, being on the south side of the city, necessitated two long bus journeys twice daily. I was something of an 'outsider' as the other boys all lived locally and, coming from County Meath, I was seen as a 'bogger'! It was a very difficult adjustment to make, but I made it gradually. The reason my parents chose Clogher Road was that the principal, Gearóid Ó Broin, was an old friend of theirs.

I made friends there and often at lunchtime I would borrow a bicycle and go exploring the surrounding areas, Crumlin, Drimnagh, the South Circular Road, until I knew that part of the city really well. I remember Tommy Blake, a good friend of mine, contracted polio. He just collapsed on the street one day. We thought he was play-acting but he ended up doing a long spell in Cherry Orchard hospital. Years later I recall our religious instructor Fr Joe Dunne (later to become a member of the *Radharc* television team) bringing Tommy, now recovered fully, down to see me in Dunboyne on the back of his motorbike. In Clogher Road I learned to get on with people and that interest in people has stayed with me all my life. I spent many happy moments in the 'shop around the corner' which was owned by Jim O'Keeffe who later became Lord Mayor of Dublin.

One major attraction of the school was its concentration on Gaelic football and hurling. Our PE instructor was Jim McCabe who would later become CEO of County Sligo Vocational Education Committee and later still held an important position with the World Bank. His importance for me then, however, was that he was centre-half-back on the last Cavan team to win an All-Ireland Senior Football title, when Jim was only nineteen. Every Wednesday afternoon Jim and another

Cavan star – the late Charlie Gallagher – would practise their football and I would go along just to kick the balls back to them. Charlie was the first player I ever saw practising free-taking. No wonder he became so unerringly accurate with that skill. My own football skills improved a lot just by being in the company of these two great players. I ended up playing centre-half-back for Dublin Vocational Schools in hurling and football. Pat Dunne (later of Manchester United) was goalkeeper on our football team.

Academically I did well in Clogher Road. I was 'good with my hands' too but even though I loved the land, I never really wanted to be a farmer. My main ambition from a young age was to be a priest, probably as a result of my altar-boy days. I was particularly interested in the Cistercian order and as a youngster I spent a few days in their monastery in Roscrea, County Tipperary. It wasn't that I was particularly pious. I just felt I needed God in my life. From a young age I was always conscious of a Higher Power and the order of things in the world. I had always felt that whatever talents I had were God-given and – for me – that came with a price. That price was a very strong belief that I had somehow to pay for those talents in the service of God. Other people were obviously aware of this, including my parents. I remember being told as a young lad: 'You should join the Benedictines, Seán. They make their own wine!' They obviously saw that as the best compromise – a priest who would still be 'brewing' the fruits of the earth!

I had an uncle who was a priest: Fr Willie Quinn. When I was in my late teens he spoke these words of wisdom to me: 'Even though it is a great honour and privilege to be a priest, sometimes you can do better work in the world – but it never settles until you get peace of mind with the decision yourself.'

I struggled with that decision right through my twenties and thirties. I had a normal social life. There were lots of girlfriends but whenever I got close to anybody in a relationship the priesthood thing always held me back. I could never explain to girlfriends that it had nothing to do with them and I am sure it was very frustrating for them. I wouldn't say I was thinking directly about the priesthood, but it was hovering in the background. I always had a huge concern about wasting people's time, so when a relationship reached a particular stage I would just stop and end the relationship and walk away. Mind you, the decision was sometimes made for me. I was 'given my cards' on a number of occasions by women who were understandably frustrated.

Eventually, the moment of revelation came – many years later. I was treating a client in Northern Ireland: a young girl who was very ill with psoriasis. She had reached the stage where she was using eight tubes of cream a week when the normal application would be one tube a month. Her skin had become wafer-thin and she developed persistent infections which I was treating with herbal remedies. I would visit her when I finished work at home and, in fact, I went to see her fifty-seven times in all. On one particular weekend she was very poorly and seemed near death. I saw her on the Thursday night, came home and worked all day Friday before returning to her that evening. I stayed with her until four o'clock on Saturday morning. Back home again, I couldn't rest and went back on Saturday evening. I rang my mother who said she could manage at home, so I stayed the night. On the Sunday morning the young girl at last turned the corner and thankfully she is hale and hearty today. I remember that morning so vividly. It was a beautiful spring Sunday with the fields glistening with frost as I headed for home. I turned off at Collon, County Louth, to catch Mass in the Cistercian monastery at Monasterboice. It was there that the 'revelation' struck like a bolt from the blue. I realised I needed God – but I needed God in the world, not in an enclosed order. The struggle was over.

My other great ambition was to study medicine. It is an ambition that has always haunted me. There were doctors and a dentist on my mother's side of the family, which may have been the root of that ambition. I was intent on pursuing a medical career but fate would intervene and point me in a different direction.

Warrenstown agricultural college is set among the lush rolling grass-lands of Meath, not far from the town of Trim. It was set up and run by the Salesian order. It now functions as a horticultural college, but in the sixties it attracted young men from all thirty-two counties who wished to pursue farming as a career. At that time it would not have been my intended career, but as far as my parents were concerned it would have seemed a natural progression for a young man to know about the earth that gave us all a living. They were not forcing me to work on the farm or with the herbs – they just thought I would benefit from the two-year course the college offered. I was a only sixteen and a half when I sat the entrance examination, having been given a 'grind' by Billy O'Neill, whose son Pat later played football for Dublin. I did well in the examination and interview and won an entrance scholarship. I remember coming home that evening. My father met me on the road and put his arms around me. There were tears in his eyes. He knew his son was moving away (I would be a boarder in the college, even though we lived a matter of miles away) but in truth I was only moving away to come home again ...

Later, I won the Lynch Trust scholarship which would help ease my passage through the college. It helped boost my ego too, as I had won it in the face of opposition from all over Ireland. I got on extraor-dinarily well with the Salesians – Fr Pat Collins, the Rector; Br O'Hare, Fr Corcoran, Br Chambers, Br O'Reilly and especially Br O'Sullivan, the Gaelic games man. All of them had a huge influence on us students but Br O'Sullivan was exceptional. He was a wonderful natural footballer, one of the greatest half-backs ever to come out of Kerry, but he had to give up playing football when he joined the Salesians. Years later he went to study for the priesthood in Maynooth College. Shortly before he was due to be ordained, he picked up a virus and died. The Lord ordained him Himself ...

There were 140 students in Warrenstown – a wonderful cross-section of young Irishmen. Even though I was much younger than most of them I was very much at home in their company. It is amazing the bonds of attachment you can form at that age. I am still close to many of them.

Gaelic games were a big part of college life. We played against other agricultural colleges, but we also played in the Meath club championship at intermediate level. We were a force to be reckoned with, featuring many inter-county players: Raymie Aylward and Peadar Murphy from Wexford; Liam Caffrey from Sligo; Pat and Willie McGrath from Dublin.

I loved every single minute in Warrenstown and loved every inch of the place. I found a new confidence there. Prior to that time I would always have felt inferior, feeling I was less talented or knew less than others. I would never talk about myself. On the sportsfield, however, I felt I could express myself in a different way. On my very first weekend in there I was cycling home to play for Dunboyne hurlers. It was a wild day so I abandoned the bike in Dunshaughlin and thumbed a lift. A car pulled up. 'Hop in,' the driver called. 'Good lad. It's great to see the *camán* [a hurley].' It was none other than the great Des 'Snitchy' Ferguson on his way from Kells to play for Dublin hurlers. The following year, 1961, Des was centre half-back on the Dublin team that lost the All-Ireland final narrowly to Tipperary. Later, when his playing days for Dublin were over, he trained the Meath hurlers and I played alongside him. Later still, his two sons would win All-Ireland football medals under my tutelage, but what stays with me is the affirmation and encouragement given to a sixteen-year-old by a sporting hero on a wild Saturday in Dunshaughlin.

I made the college team and was chosen to play for Meath minor hurlers. No less a man than Seamus Murphy, another sporting icon from Kerry (who taught Veterinary Science in the college), brought me to football trials. On my seventeenth birthday in December 1960, my sister Frances drove my father down to the college. He presented me with a driving licence. Even though I had been driving tractors as a youngster it was now official, and it gave me a great thrill.

I was only six weeks there when the Rector, Fr Collins, came to me and the conversation went:

'It's Seán, isn't it?'

'Yes, Father.'

'Are you getting those remedies from your Dad?'

'I suppose so, Father.'

'Well, I'll have to talk to Br James about that.'

And from the following week onwards, I was doing three days agricultural studies and three days horticultural studies per week. Apart from him actually knowing his students personally after only six weeks, this man had the vision to change the curriculum to suit my needs.

One evening in 1961 I rang home. An old man answered. It was my father, but I had never pictured him as 'old' until then – even though he was eighty years of age. Initially I thought it was somebody messing, but cold reality dawned on me. I was frightened. I went back to the study hall and thought about things in a way I had never done before. Here was an old man enfeebled by Parkinson's disease and a lifetime of pain, struggling to keep going. He was helped greatly by his wife who had her own share of ill-health and still had young children to rear. And here was I – the only boy – away from them in college. Within an hour I was asking for permission to use the phone again. I rang home.

'It's me, Daddy,' I said. 'I don't have exams until next year. I'm coming home.'

'Very good,' was his simple reply.

Purely out of concern for my parents, I was coming home to give a hand for maybe six weeks ... I'm still here! No wonder I have a reputation for bad timekeeping ...

It was a brave decision but the best one I ever made. My father was over half a century older than me. We would never have kicked a ball together as father and son might normally do, but we had ten great years together until he died in 1971. I learned more from him than I did from any man. He had great wisdom that he had absorbed from his forebears as you would absorb music and poetry. He had great presence. And he had incredible faith in me – far more than I ever had in myself. I never thought in those days that people would ever want to come to me for remedies.

People were coming to my father for a bottle for a variety of ailments. I asked him so many questions and got the classic Irish answer:

'That's the why ... '

'If you don't tell me why how can I learn?'

'You'll learn.'

Being a quick thinker – it dawned on me after about six weeks. He didn't want me to be a parrot. He wanted me to observe, to read, to study. It has been a lifetime of study ever since. At the same time, all my life I have been haunted by medicine. At times I wanted to stop doing what I was doing and concentrate on studying medicine. Yet if I hadn't learned from my father, all that wisdom would have been lost. That would have been a far greater tragedy.

CHAPTER FIVE

Hurling and Football

Working at home soon became a very full life. I was developing my interest in and knowledge of the herbs as well as keeping the general farm and the fruit farm going. Social life was hectic too. I was involved in several organisations and went here, there and everywhere to club meetings, dances, films. I was young and fit and active and I needed the company of young people after a long day at home. My social life usually started about eleven o'clock at night when I had put my father to bed. Brendan Crawford used to say, 'Seán is going out when the rest of us are going to bed.' It was true. The boss had to be looked after first and then I had my freedom. And I had a car. 'Never go on your own – always bring someone with you,' my father urged. My good friend, Micky Kenny, usually came with me and we travelled the country together. It was good to be young and to be alive. All that and Gaelic games too ...

I was particularly passionate about hurling. I had been selected for Meath minor hurlers during my days in Warrenstown, and in fact I played senior hurling for Meath before I got on the Dunboyne senior club team. I started out as an ordinary player but improved rapidly. Every day at lunchtime I would be out in the front field at home pucking around with Jack Moran and Mick Reilly. At club level I won medals in both football and hurling for Dunboyne at all levels up to senior grade, but senior medals always eluded me. Dunboyne were beaten in three senior county finals.

I played for Meath senior hurlers until 1981, usually at left-half-back or centrefield. We won Division Two of the National Hurling League twice. Meath had won the All-Ireland Junior Hurling title in 1970, but I was one of four players who had not been regraded to junior level at that time. In 1982 – approaching my fortieth year – I was selected at centrefield to play for Ireland against an Australian selection. The late Micheál O'Hehir was very much involved in this. He was very keen to develop Gaelic culture and games among the diaspora in Australia. He had approached me to go to Australia for three months to train their team and while it was an inviting prospect I had to decline because of work commitments. The Australians came here to play in 1982. This was long before, and had nothing to do with, the Compromise Rules that later materialised in football. It was simply O'Hehir's dream to have teams from Australia and the US competing in the Centenary championship in 1984. We won well, but the concept never progressed from there. At least I can say I won international honours for Ireland in hurling. There aren't too many players who can boast of that.

I was player-manager of Meath senior hurlers in 1981-82, but in fact I never picked myself to play. Hurling in Meath is confined to a relatively small number of clubs but we did well that year in both league and championship. I have always felt, and still feel, that given the right support, Meath hurlers could make the breakthrough, but in 1982 I experienced serious disillusionment.

I was attending a World Health Organisation meeting in Cambridge and left early to come home for a hurlers' training session. There was a strike at the airport in London so I had to travel overland to Liverpool to catch the ferry. After all my trouble only seven lads turned up for training. There was a disagreement at hurling board level and some clubs would not allow players to attend for training at county level. I was absolutely furious and walked away from management. It wasn't a matter of my giving in to the hurling board. To me it did not matter what my club said: if I was chosen to train with Meath, I would have trained with Meath. You have to be above pettiness if your aim is to play for your county. When I took over as manager of the football team I made that very clear at the very first meeting with the players. 'Lads,' I said, 'you may have beaten the daylights out of each other at club level last Sunday, but when you come in here on Tuesday evening you are coming in as Meathmen. It doesn't matter whether you are from Oldcastle, Dunboyne, Ballinabrackey or Bettystown – you are coming in as Meathmen and that is the only way it can be ... '

The hurling years were glorious years for me. Ironically, despite my 1982 walkout, I was asked by 'Snitchy' Ferguson to play for Meath in the 1984 junior final against Kilkenny. I was by now coach/trainer of the senior football team and I was forty-years-old, but thankfully I was in great health and very fit. I remember ringing Des Ferguson before the match and saying how committed I was to managing the footballers and regretfully I could not risk playing hurling the day before we played Dublin in a Leinster football final. But it was nice to be asked.

I have always felt there was plenty of hurling talent in Meath, but I was totally opposed to the idea of separate hurling and football boards, as we have in Meath. There should be one board with equal treatment for both codes. I pleaded for that at the Annual Convention in 1972. There should be co-operation not division. The games complement each other. I abhor the idea of a 'football Sunday' and a 'hurling Sunday'. If Meath are playing a National Football League match, why not have Meath hurlers playing on the same bill, thus guaranteeing them support? It happens rarely, but when it does, it gives the hurlers a lift. In 1975 when Meath won the National Football League, Meath hurlers played in a curtain-raiser to the football Semi-Final. It was some thrill for them to be playing in front of possibly 40,000 spectators. There might not be a football fan who remembers it, but the hurlers remember it. People will ask what good does it serve Meath hurling to be beaten by Kilkenny by twenty or thirty points, but you have to aspire to the top. If the preparation and support are right and the resilience is there to do it, who knows ... ?

On a lighter note, I remember another kind of 'compromise rules' being proposed in 1996. Wexford won the hurling title that year and on a visit to Meath, Martin Storey and Larry O'Gorman, who fancied themselves as footballers, suggested playing Meath in a 'half and half' match (one half of hurling and the second half of football). I thought it was a great idea because Meath (who were football champions) had great hurlers in Conor Martin, Mark O'Reilly, Darren Fay, Enda McManus, Jim McGuinness, Tommy Dowd, Brendan Reilly and Jody Devine. But as the night wore on, Martin was having second thoughts and at about 2.00am he said: 'Jaysus, I don't know. You'se Meathmen are dangerous enough without hurling sticks ... !' But it would have been great to try it.

Whatever about hurling, football in Meath was at a low ebb during the seventies. The one high tide was in 1975 when Meath beat Dublin in the National Football League final. My outstanding memory is of Ken Rennicks running at the Dublin defence and scoring six points. It was an amazing performance. Pat Reynolds was mighty at centre-half-back. It was my last time to see Pat and the great Jack Quinn play for Meath. However, the League victory was a false dawn – in 1976 and 1977 Meath were beaten in the Leinster championship final by the mighty Dubs. At that time I would not have been all that close to the

Meath football scene. I would have known who the players were but I would only have seen them playing whenever Meath hurlers were not playing – so that ruled out most National League matches. When it came to the championship I always went to see the footballers play. It was something that was weaned into me from childhood. Everything revolved around the championship, even if Meath had not won a Leinster title since 1970. In the late seventies and early eighties I was occasionally asked to give a helping hand with injured players. In 1981 I had to look after a young player, Liam Hayes, who was injured in his championship debut against Wexford.Wexford won that day. It was a low time for Meath football and it was no better the following year (1982) when Longford knocked Meath out of the championship in Tullamore. I was otherwise engaged – playing hurling for Dunboyne – but it was a dark time. How much lower could we go? Earlier that year (1982) I had watched Meath play Down in a League match in Dundalk. After the match I had a chat in the Imperial Hotel with Colm Coyle, JJ McCormack and Liam Hayes. I told them that in general the footballers had no idea of the level of fitness that was required for the game. If you play well for five minutes, then with practise you can play well for seven or eight minutes and gradually progress in that way. It was a question of getting the body physically ready and then getting mentally tuned to be able to concentrate for a particular length of time.

Those were some of the incidental connections with the football team. It may seem a 'back-door' way into management but that is how it happened – just by helping out on a very occasional basis. When the call eventually came, it was out of the blue. Gerry McEntee, Mattie Kerrigan and Mick O'Brien had all been nominated for management by the team but for various reasons none of them could take it on. Somebody then nominated me – to this day I don't know who it was. Liam Creavin, the county secretary, rang me to know if I would be interested. I went up to Brian Smith to talk it over, from there to Eamonn O'Farrell and back to Brian again. We teased it out until two o'clock in the morning. Brian was a great friend of my parents. He played 'devil's advocate' – he knew my lifestyle and the demands the herb business would make on me. It would be a big risk for me to take on the management job but it was equally a big risk for the county board to take on a relatively untried manager! I know there were those who would have said – 'Sure he's a hurler – what would he know about football?' In the end I decided to take the job on – for a few months, until they got somebody more qualified. What swung the decision for me was that someone from within the county had to take the job. At that time it would have seemed very strange to have to go outside the county for a manager. It was as simple and straightforward a reason as that. So I took on the job as 'coach/trainer' – for a few months – until the county board would find 'somebody else' ...

CHAPTER SIX

The Man Who Inspired Me

In 1979 the World Health Organisation convened a conference on traditional cures and remedies at Cambridge University. The conference was prompted by the rising cost of modern drugs, the side-effects of those drugs and the recognition that traditional cures and remedies had been beneficial to many people for a long time. Each country (twenty-nine in total) was invited to send two delegates to the conference. Professor Geary and I represented Ireland. I was both surprised to be invited and honoured that the traditional world I represented was being recognised in this way.

Even though I was one of the Irish representatives, I felt like a fish out of water. Most of the delegates came from the academic world. The university atmosphere was wonderful and people were friendly, but I kept thinking to myself – realistically, what can I contribute here? I felt overwhelmed and overawed. Then Conrad Gorinsky spoke and everything changed for me ...

Dr Conrad Gorinsky was creator of the Foundation for Ethnobiology in the UK. He was then Professor of Medicine at St Bartholomew's hospital in London – specialising in the area of ethnobiology (the study of people's interactions with organisms and ecosystems).

Gorinsky spoke of his experiences in the Amazon where he had made a study of traditional cures. He then spoke about the foods we eat and the plants we use. Gorinsky mentioned that there was a cut-off point in the sixteenth century when medicine received its Charter and that anything used before then is now considered taboo. He challenged this by asking: Why should this be so? Nobody knows it all.

His words fascinated and energised me. He was a man at the fore-front of modern medicine, but he recognised the value of traditional ways. I remember in particular one statement he made: 'We owe more to our heritage than to walk away from it.' Those words had a huge effect on my life. Prior to this I would never talk about what I did at home – even to people I would pal around with. Maybe it was because I was young and relatively inexperienced or felt unable to explain my work with confidence, but from that day when I listened to Conrad Gorinsky I felt a new impetus to study, to delve deeper and learn more about traditional remedies. A whole new vista opened up for me. Of course, modern medicine offered much, but there was also another world that I had inherited and that was valuable as well. I couldn't walk away from that heritage. There is so much out there that we don't know about. Plants have a chemistry that works on the human body – favourably or not. It is a case of realising more what you cannot do than what you can do. Nowadays I am more at ease with what I do. I can explain to a client what will or will not work and why it may complement the modern treatment. It is a question of balance.

There is a wealth of knowledge available regarding traditional remedies. In the University of Kew (in the UK) alone there are mono-graphs on some four thousand plants. I use at least fifty different plants in my work. Many of them we cultivate commercially for the clinic, some are found growing wild in the woods and hedgerows, though you have to be particularly careful with the latter nowadays as pesticides can make them unusable.

Traditional cures are more and more coming into their own because modern methods of extraction and analysis enable us to be more confident in their use and to dispel old myths and folklore regarding some remedies. I never actually spoke with Conrad Gorinsky, but his words at that Cambridge conference in 1979 changed my life. I am reminded of the old Apache saying: 'We are what we are, but we are what we were also.'

CHAPTER SEVEN

Learning the Trade

The late seventies and early eighties were very lean times for Meath football. There was no tradition of winning anything. Players of that era will tell you of the apathy towards training. The successive defeats in the Leinster championship by Wexford (1981) and Longford (1982) – neither of which would be reckoned as a footballing force – were the lowest ebb a proud county could reach. So when I took over as coach/trainer in 1982 there was really only one direction we could go. Yet there was obviously great potential with footballers like: Colm O'Rourke, Gerry McEntee, Joe Cassells, Padraig Finnerty, Phil Smith, Finian Murtagh, Liam Hayes, Martin O'Connell, Liam Smith, Willie Rogan, Padraig Lyons and Tom Duff – there was the nucleus of a fair team in that lot alone! The problem was they had not been used to winning and they would have to learn how to win. I would have to get their fitness levels up; get them to believe in themselves and get them used to winning. The players needed to make their own luck and create their own tradition, forgetting all talk about the 'greats of the past'. Not exactly a small order, but a great challenge!

I remember my first meeting with the squad in September 1982 – under the stand in Páirc Tailteann, Navan. I was naturally a little bit in awe of the situation. I shook hands with each one of the lads – some of whom I knew well, like Coyle, Hayes, Murtagh, and some I didn't know at all. When the meeting started, some players had not arrived. They came in later, making, I suppose, a statement, like,'We are the men'! I heard one of the early arrivals mutter: 'Who do those so-and-sos think they are?' I pretended not to hear, but I made things very clear to them all that night. They might have played against each other at club level on Sunday (and might have kicked the daylights out of each other) but when they came in to me on Tuesday it didn't matter whether they came from Oldcastle or Bettystown, Ballinabracky or Dunboyne – they came in as Meathmen and that was it. All equal, all with one goal: to do their best for Meath. End of story. It was extraordinary the way they did learn to pull together. They made huge sacrifices and it was so satisfying to see that effort rewarded ultimately with success at the very top level.

There is no manual of football management. You learn to write your own manual with a lot of help and no little pain along the way. It is a long learning curve. I never called myself 'the manager'. The term was relatively new at the time. There were managers in the seventies like the great rivals Kevin Heffernan of Dublin and Mick O'Dwyer of Kerry, and in the year I took over with Meath, Eugene McGee managed Offaly to a sensational All-Ireland victory. I just fell into the 'manager' bracket, but I was essentially 'the coach/trainer', answerable to the county board and six selectors (a cumbersome arrangement which would ultimately cause problems). At the same time the county board was taking on a big risk, appointing an untried and relatively unknown man to look after their senior football team. It was news at the time. I recall Micheál Ó Muircheartaigh ringing me for a radio interview on the morning after my appointment. Little did I realise it was the start of an endless succession of interviews, but it did confirm something for me. Meath were still seen as an important footballing force. Meath were newsworthy.

My initial aim was to get to know the players and to get the show on the road with a settled and balanced team. I had to do some serious trawling for players. Every minute of my spare time seemed to be taken up with looking out for players. Catch half a match here, half a match there. During the summer, I would see club championship matches on Thursday, Friday, Saturday, Sunday – sometimes a couple of matches in one day. That remained the case throughout my managerial career. You can play all the 'challenge' matches you want, but in the heat of championship you find out things about players: their temperament, and their ability to cope when things are not going well. It is not always about who is brilliant on the day. It is more about consistency. You may have all the skill in the world, but if you don't have application and consistency then it's an uphill battle. This is particularly true for young players trying to make it into the senior ranks. They may have shone at under-age level, but when they progress to the adult stage everyone is trying to put them in their place. Consistency and application – they were the traits I was looking for. And eventually found in a bunch of lads that went on to bring glory to their county five years later.

My first match in charge of Meath was a tournament game – the O'Reilly Cup versus Longford in Edgeworthstown. It clashed with club championship matches at home and we were missing players, so I drafted in a young fellow called Colm O'Rourke as captain for the day. We won, gaining some revenge for the Leinster championship defeat. We had won a trophy. It was a start. We played Cavan in the first round of the National Football League in Kingscourt and got a draw out of it. We did well in the League, eventually beating Roscommon to gain promotion to Division One. After the Roscommon match, Colm O'Rourke made the famous remark that 'if we have Boylan around for long enough we will make a manager out of him!' Mick

Lyons was sent off that day for the newly-introduced 'personal foul' (only one of two sendings-off in his entire career, despite the hard man image he was portrayed as having). The O'Byrne Cup, a tournament for Leinster teams, was played between the League and the championship and when we won it in 1983 – defeating Longford again – under the captaincy of Mickey Downes (who had also played for Clare) there was great excitement. Another trophy – we were acquiring the winning habit – but the real test would be the Leinster championship of 1983. Joe Cassells was interviewed after the promotion-winning match against Roscommon and uttered the prophetic words: 'Promotion is great but if we are beaten in the first round of the Leinster championship, we won't be forgiven. '

Unfortunately for Meath, we were drawn against Dublin in the first round of the championship. We did very well, being denied victory by Ciaran Duff's last-minute equalising point. We drew again in the replay (shades of the saga that would unfold eight years later) but a Barney Rock goal in extra time finished us off. Dublin went on to win the All-Ireland title that year, beating Galway with the 'dirty dozen'. We were making progress, with regular visits to Croke Park. Earlier in 1983 I made my debut as manager there, when we played Armagh in the League Semi-Final. The weather was atrocious: incessant rain and sleet. We lost by four points, but the 8600 brave souls present were privileged to witness one of the greatest goals ever seen in Croke Park. Colm O'Rourke won the ball at centre-field, went on a solo run and unleashed a rocket of a shot from forty yards. It was certainly one of the greatest goals I have ever seen. Fr Sean Hegarty was in charge of Armagh, a man of low stature. When he came into our dressing room afterwards, Joe Cassells was heard to remark: 'I thought Seanie was the smallest manager in Ireland – until now!'

To repeat: there is no manual of football management. There are things you learn to do and not to do. I learned fairly quickly how I could be put in my place. Late in 1983 I attended a conference in Rome. I came home to attend what I assumed was a meeting of the Meath players. It was a circuitous journey, via London and Manchester, and when I eventually got home, I drove straight to Navan. Only then was I told that the meeting was concerning the finance committee of the county board. I had called the meeting of players, but somebody had changed the agenda in my absence. I was very vexed but said very little because I knew if I opened my mouth I would certainly have said too much. The finance committee was querying the amount of money that 'training' was costing the county board. I was costing nothing and all I ever wanted for the players was what they were entitled to have. The bottom line was that the bills had to be paid and these were lean times economically – and pre-sponsorship days. It was, I suppose, a way of telling me my place – a statement that 'you are the coach/trainer and we are the county board'. I did not need to be told that, however. I was always respectful of people's positions and the sacrifices they were making in the service of their county.

It was never a sacrifice for me, but simply a labour of love. I loved the *craic* of it all. I loved to see fellows developing and blossoming. I loved being able to help them out in that regard. It was, I suppose, hard for people to visualise then that in a few years (and I knew it would take a few years) these lads would become kingpins of Gaelic football. It takes hard work to win respect!

Managing a football team (any football team) presents a huge challenge. You are confronted with a bunch of lads from different clubs and different walks of life. They have different backgrounds, different personalities, different attitudes, and different personal stories. Some players are working, some are not, some are students, some are married, and some are single. It can be an enormous task to mould them into a team, but the one thing that unites them is that they want to play football and are prepared to make huge sacrifices to win. And in

Meath's case they had won nothing for a long time. My attitude was very simple: put the effort in. Once you make an excuse for not being there, for missing training, it becomes very easy. I told the players I would never ask them to do something I wasn't prepared to do myself. That entailed being there (even if, in my case, it might be at the last minute) and doing the training. It meant that no matter what pressures you were under at home – when you got to training, we were all the same. That was it.

Another thing I learned was how to deal with fellows socially. During the League run we might go for a drink after the match. We wouldn't go mad but I would be there with them. However, when it came near championship time, players would never be all that close to you, for fear of not being selected. Also, being a Pioneer, I realised the difference between drinkers and non-drinkers in the squad. Drinkers felt there were things they could 'get off their chest' among themselves after a few drinks, but when they said things to me, I would remember them! That wasn't fair, in my opinion. I won't say I distanced myself, but I had to make sure I would not want to take advantage of a situation where someone said something under the influence of a few drinks. I would be there watching them however, minding them. Lads who play on a county team become fair game for everyone when they go out socially. I would be mindful of that, keeping people away from them when necessary. I would have talked to an awful lot of people over the years. People might say: 'What's he talking to that guy for?' If I felt I could shield a player, I took the necessary steps.

As a manager you are coach and trainer, but you are also a father-figure, a boss, a motivator, a counsellor and a friend. People might say to me about a player: 'I wouldn't bother with him! He gets sent off in club matches. He will only cause you hassle!' But if he is one of the best footballers around, it is up to me to get around him to play, even if it means putting his personal issues in his back pocket ... Whatever was best for the team – that's what I had to aim for. If a fellow has personal problems I have to make a call as coach. He might have to miss a few training sessions with my blessing. If someone genuinely needed a break (maybe a week in the sun) I would make that call. I would say that only twice was that position challenged by other players (who weren't doing great themselves at the time). It is very easy for people to say: 'I wouldn't put him in the team', and ten minutes into the match they are screaming: 'Put him on! Put him on!' If I am going to play a player, I play him from the start. Sometimes the communication can break down, of course.

My basic rule has always been: never lose sight of what is best for the team. When we made the big breakthrough by winning the Leinster championship in 1986 the main thing I had learned was the importance of having everyone tuned into the same wavelength. I could stand in front of a bunch of players and tell them I want this, that and the other done, but if the players had not bought into my thinking I would be talking to myself. Instead I arranged the chairs in a circle around the room and let the lads have their say. I was taking the risk of being undermined, but sometimes what may seem like your weakness is your strength. I was confident that that approach would work because our common ultimate aim was to bring success back to the county and there was no point in having lads out on the field not fully tuned in to what I was thinking.

So we talked things out – another part of the long learning curve of football management!

CHAPTER EIGHT

Building a Team

When the National Football League resumed in the autumn of 1983, we faced the 'auld enemy' – Dublin – in the opening match. Our players lined up to applaud the All-Ireland champions in Páirc Tailteann and then proceeded to draw with them once again. We thought: would we ever beat the Dubs? We had a good League campaign, drawing also with Cork, beating Kildare and Armagh, and losing narrowly to Kerry. We made it to the League Semi-Final against Galway, built up a big lead, but squandered it and Galway came back to draw. They beat us by a point in the replay, but in between we beat them by thirteen points. This was in the quarter-final of the Centenary Cup – a special tournament set up to mark the centenary of the GAA. We went on to beat Monaghan in the final. It meant an awful lot to the county to win a national trophy. We were back up at the top table – even if it all fell flat the following year (1985), but sometimes you have to take a step back in order to make a major step forward ...

Once again we made it to the Leinster final in 1984, eliminating Louth and Laois on the way. Once again we faced Dublin in the final. And once again we lost – by four points: 2:10 to 1:9. The rivalry was intensifying each year – 56,000 people watched that final! We may have lost that match, but it brought to a head the thorny problem of the Meath selection team, which comprised the county chairman, the county secretary, four selectors and myself. It was far too cumbersome. On the day of a match, I had to seek half a dozen opinions and reach a majority decision before I could do anything. It was like having a board meeting on the sideline. It was a crazy situation where a player from a selector's club might not be picked. The selector might be petty enough to say: 'Well, I wanted to pick you, but so-and-so didn't want you.' I wanted none of that. In the Leinster Final of 1984, John Caffrey of Dublin was sent off in the first half. I wanted to bring on one of our substitutes, Neil O'Sullivan, to exploit the extra-man situation. I warmed him up three times, but couldn't bring him on because I couldn't get agreement at the sideline board meeting. It was totally frustrating and made me feel foolish. There were things I would like to do on the sideline, but didn't because I was possibly not strong enough to push them through at that time. When I was with the lads at training, I would see things that the other selectors would not see. Also, I felt I had to be allowed to make my own mistakes, because that is another way of learning. For all these reasons I put the case for a three-man selection committee: myself and two others of my choosing. It was both a comical and a controversial time. It took three meetings of the county board to decide on the change, but I suppose that is part of the democracy of the GAA – that the delegates have their say. Finally Colm Cromwell and Jack Fitzgerald proposed giving me a chance with my own selection team. It was accepted and we faced into 1985 with two Meath veterans – Pat Reynolds and Tony Brennan – as my co-selectors.

I may have got my way with the selection process but on the field things went badly awry. In our very first National League match Galway hammered us by eleven points. We recovered to beat Cork in the next match, but struggled all through that League, avoiding relegation only by scraping past Tyrone in the last match. Then came the Leinster championship. We got past Kildare in the first round and then faced Laois in the Semi-Final. This was a disaster! A very good Laois team, which had in fact won the National League earlier in the year, beat us off the park by ten points. I think we only scored seven points that day. I was very down. For all the world, it seemed as if I had made a bags of the managership. I realised that day in Tullamore that we needed more players from other levels – intermediate and junior. It wasn't that the boys we had were not putting in the effort. Some of them were just not good enough at this level. I knew we would have to travel the highways and byways of Meath to find players. The trawl began.

'STAFF'

I know there were eyebrows raised when we introduced Brian Stafford from Kilmainhamwood. People looked at him in his 'civvies' and said: 'That fellow will never make an inter-county footballer!' What I loved about him was the way he could kick a ball. He could do amazing things with his feet – he seemed to be able to twist his ankles any way he liked. He could stand one way and make his feet go the other way. This gave him an incredible ability to 'sell a dummy' as many an opposing back would find out! It was a game against Armagh, played under lights in Carrickmacross that convinced me of his worth. He had a smashing game that night. I saw another great potential trait in him – that of free-taker – an invaluable asset in Gaelic football.

I asked Ollie Campbell (one of the great point-kickers in Irish rugby) to talk with Brian and they built up a great relationship. We tried Brian as a free-taker in a challenge match against Cork. It was played in torrential rain in a college ground, as Páirc Uí Chaoimh was unplayable. Every free he took went wide. Afterwards, I said to him: 'Fair play, Brian. That was great!' 'What do you mean?' asked a puzzled Brian, 'I missed them all!' 'Don't worry,' I reassured him. 'The important thing is you addressed the ball in the same way each time. You made up your mind and never changed it. It will come right in time.' And it did. Brian became such a prolific scorer. If you look back over the records of the late eighties, Brian's contribution was amazing.

'Staff' was a most amenable man with an incredible footballing brain. When Brian came in he was his own man. He would weigh things up and measure them before he spoke. When he did speak, he was a man of few words. When we played Dublin in the quarter-final of the League in 1986, Brian said at half-time: 'Come on lads, these fellows are no use. They are there for the taking!' We lost by a point that day.

'Staff' would not have been the fastest man in the world, but what people did not realise was the phenomenal strength he had in his legs. He had an incredibly long stride. Once he got going you would never see anyone pass him. He also had tremendous positional sense on the field. You cannot instil that in a player – it is a natural gift. When he settled as full-forward with Colm O'Rourke on one side and Bernie Flynn on the other, they were a fairly lethal line. The amount of space 'Staff' would create for the others around him was astonishing. He was also a very laid-back character. I remember listening to an audio-tape of Micheál Ó Muircheartaigh's commentary on the 1987 All-Ireland Final. Mick Lyons and I were driving to Ballinamore, County Leitrim, to present some medals and we listened to the tape. In his inimitable style Ó Muircheartaigh remarked: 'Brian Stafford has the ball. They say when he is training at home in Kilmainhamwood he brings his dog along to dribble the ball back to him!' That was true, but what a footballing brain 'Staff' had! At the celebrations following our win in that final, the first man to shake Brian's hand was Ollie Campbell, his place-kicking coach. Ollie would not go to the final because he had not been at matches during the year and did not want to deprive a genuine fan of a ticket. He was so thrilled for Brian. And hadn't he coached him well.

PJ

PJ Gillic from Carnaross had been a great minor footballer, although that is never a guarantee of success at senior level. He had great hands and an incredible kick of the ball. At the age of eighteen he had the footballing head of a thirty-year-old. He knew that nothing moved quicker than the ball, but that ball must be delivered into the right place – to the best advantage of the recipient. That is why you would see him in Croke Park delivering balls along the sideline to colleagues sixty metres away – each ball perfectly judged. Also at under-age level he had been an excellent freetaker, so whenever Brian Stafford was injured PJ could step into the breach. He was simply an amazing player: powerfully built with powerful awareness and powerful loyalty. He gave us another string to our bow in that he could win 'hard' balls on the wings and deliver them to the forward line. PJ was a wonderful find in our trawl for new players.

'JINKSY'

The first time David Beggy featured in our plans, we were playing a match in Walterstown. 'Jinksy' arrived on a motorbike. Colm O'Rourke looked up and roared: 'No! No! No! This has to be my worst nightmare!' Colm had taught young Beggy in St Patrick's Classical School, Navan, and some fierce slagging ensued between them. 'Jinksy' had never played at minor level and had only played occasionally at senior level with Navan O'Mahonys. I had seen him kicking around one day and that was all I needed to see. My fellow-selector Pat Reynolds (one of the greatest half-backs of his era) also described Jinksy as 'a worst nightmare', because you wouldn't know what he was going to do next. Mind you, Jinksy might not always know himself – or at least he could give you that impression. He had lightning pace going at a defence and he was very brave in going in for a ball. The amount of tackling he would do was phenomenal. He quickly became a huge part of the jigsaw that is a winning team and became a wonderful player, winning All-Ireland medals and an All-Star award.

'Jinksy' was a great character – born to boogie, as he would say – and he loved to show off. The late Mick Dunne interviewed him before the Leinster Final in 1986 and it went something like this:

'David, this must be a great occasion for you. Playing in a Leinster Final in Croke Park – your dream realised! All the times you have been in Croke Park dreaming of this day ... '

'Actually, I've only been in Croke Park once before – for a U2 concert ... '

Again, before the All-Ireland Semi-Final against Kerry, Jinksy's response when he was asked how this Kerry team compared with others he had seen: 'I never saw Kerry play in my life ... '

For all his fun and playful nature, Jinksy was incredibly serious about his game. He made great sacrifices to play for Meath. He eventually ended up working in Scotland, but he worked hard to have himself right for games and then would have to travel over and back. He never shirked a challenge. He may not have been a great club player but he was an outstanding county player. He was aptly named 'Jinksy' – what he could do with a ball was amazing. Sometimes he would lose the ball, but more often than not he would win it back. He had the great ability to mesmerise and baffle opponents. There was an excitement about him and combining that excitement with the solid Joe Cassells behind him and the inventive Colm O'Rourke (the old 'master') inside him made for a great set-up. And we all remember who scored the winning point against Dublin in the four-match saga of 1991 – the man who was 'born to boogie'.

LIAM HARNAN

Liam Harnan came from Moynalvey club. He had played at minor level for Meath at the age of sixteen. Another man of few words, who did his 'talking' on the pitch! He had a great belief in his own ability and was subservient to no one. What struck me about him, physically, was that he had a very long back. At centre-half-back he had a presence that we had not seen in that position since Bertie Cunningham in the sixties. People said Harnan was a hard man, very tough – 'uncompromising', to coin a cliche – but he was a great footballer. His distribution of the ball was tremendous – just ask Bernard Flynn. The amount of ball that Liam would deliver, giving Bernard space to come on to it, was immense. I suppose Liam went back to an era when you tried to get by the centre-half-back on your hands and knees. He was a powerful footballer and everything he did was on the ball. He took a lot of stick from opposing players and fans but he was well able for it. He was another of those lads who came onto the team from nowhere. In 1985 both Harnan and Stafford were injured for the Laois match, which we lost heavily, so when they got their chances in the League later that year and in the 1986 Leinster championship, they certainly were not going to throw those chances away. With Liam Harnan in command at centre-half-back, in behind Gerry McEntee and Liam Hayes and in front of Mick Lyons, things were falling into place. Now we had a resilient spine in the team.

TERRY FERGUSON

Terry had been better known as a hurler, like his dad 'Snitchy'. He was a very ordinary footballer when he came onto the panel but he developed into an All-Star. Terry was 'Mr Versatility' – he could play at wing half-back or corner-back. He had tremendous energy: you just wound him up and he would go and go and go. No one could ever convince Terry that he wouldn't get the next ball and he would do it without fouling. He had very long arms and very quick hands in the tackle. He did the simple things well: get the ball away quickly out of the danger area and on to someone who could make better use of it. Terry was the ultimate team player.

MICKEY MCQUILLAN

We had had problems in 1983 with goalkeepers. In their day Greg Twomey and Sean Briody were good 'keepers but things had not gone well for them that year. We had turned to the veteran Jimmy Fay in 1984 for the Centenary Cup and the championship. Fay did well, but he was getting on in years as a footballer and we were on the lookout for someone new. Mickey McQuillan had played for Meath at a very young age, but had been dropped off the panel because he was playing soccer. In 1985 Pat Reynolds said that we had to get McQuillan back on the side. So we approached Mickey and he came straight in and settled in the last line of defence without a problem. His first match was against Galway in the 1985 League. Meath were hammered by eleven points, but Mickey made a number of great saves. We had found our man! Jimmy Fay had been a great keeper, but Mickey McQuillan brought goalkeeping to a new level for us.

KEVIN FOLEY

Although Kevin had played some football in University College Dublin (UCD) where he was studying veterinary science, he had been away from the game for some time before we approached him. His brother Frank was a better-known footballer and had played for four years at minor level for Meath before going off to Canada. When he returned and joined Kevin on the panel in 1988, we had six sets of brothers on the panel: the Foleys, the Fergusons, the Gillics, the Lyonses, the Coyles and the McEntees. The Foleys played for Trim but when Kevin qualified, his veterinary work took him to Wexford and later to Limerick and Cork. Over the years he made an inordinate number of trips back to Meath for training. Very often we were fortunate enough to have a helicopter pick him up, courtesy of our sponsors Kepak, but Kevin put in a lot of driving as well.

There is a great story concerning one of those helicopter rides. In 1991 we had a young player, Hugh Carolan, on the panel. He had been on the Meath All-Ireland Minor winning team in 1990 and played rugby with Blackrock. A lovely guy and a great prospect at senior level, Hugh's career was ultimately cut short by injury. One Friday evening in 1991 Hugh had gone to a friend's twenty-first birthday party in Galway. It was arranged that the helicopter would pick up Kevin Foley in Cork, divert to Athenry to collect Hugh on the local hurling pitch and bring them both to training in Gormanstown in Meath. However, when Hugh turned up in Athenry the gates of the GAA pitch were locked so Hugh, being a sensible young man, went to the field next door and stood in the middle of it to await the helicopter. A local farmer, checking out his cattle, noticed him and walked over to Hugh. The conversation went something like:

Farmer: 'Are you all right there, *a mhic*?'

Hugh: 'Yeah, grand. Just waiting for a lift.'

Farmer: (after a pause) 'Right. Well, God bless ye, son. I'll see you around.'

He walked off, feeling sorry, I'm sure, for the poor confused young fellow standing in the middle of a field 'waiting for a lift' ...)

Kevin Foley had amazing application to the game and soon became an integral part of the team. He would always want to pick the best opposing forward to play on – and that is how he learned his trade at half-back. He was incredibly focused, hard as steel and fearless. Kevin would put his head in where you wouldn't put your boot and took some fierce knocks as a result. He was subjected to an immense amount of ridicule and criticism from the media and his opponents' fans. He was often branded a dirty player, but I don't accept that. He was a very laid-back character, but he was fiercely competitive. He just never held back and never gave up. He was the type of player your opponents love to hate, but your supporters just love him for his commitment.

Kevin of course immortalised himself in the last minute of the four-match saga against Dublin in 1991, when he popped up to finish off that amazing eleven-man move to the net, having been also involved in the move further out the field. Even the Meath supporters scratched their heads – Foley scored the goal! What was he doing up there? In fact, during the previous weekend when we were away in Scotland, we had spent a full seventy minutes in training doing nothing else but practising that type of sweeping move up and down the park. Nothing else. Up and down the park for seventy minutes. So the Foley goal didn't exactly come out of nowhere.

And of course Kevin Foley never scored for club or county before or since that memorable Saturday, 6 July 1991. But what a time and place, after five hours and forty minutes playing your deadliest rivals, to notch your only score ...

It was quite extraordinary that all these lads came through at the same time, in the space of a year. There were others, like Stan Gibney from Ratoath. A great character and a very fine footballer, Stan was unfortunate to get a back injury that ended his playing career. He had a great footballing brain and played a huge part in Meath's League campaign in 1985/86 and in winning the Leinster championship in 1986.

Being a manager is a voyage of discovery – about yourself and about your players. The players shape you as do the backroom men. Before 1984 selectors like Liam Creavin, Brian Smith, Mattie Gilsenan, Jim Curtis, Tony Creaven and Paddy Cromwell had contributed to my education as manager. Then Paddy Reynolds and Tony Brennan came on board. They were members of the last Meath team to win an All-Ireland in 1967 and of the first Gaelic football team to go to Australia. Tony had made a huge input into under-age level, while Pat was very involved with Walterstown club. They knew their football and were good decision-makers. The most important thing for me was that they were new and fresh in their thinking. I had not palled around with them prior to 1984, but we worked very hard together. It was all very fairly done but we put in incredible hours picking teams, because there were hard decisions to be made.

For all that, the wheels nearly came off straight away! After a poor League campaign in 1985 and that disastrous loss to Laois in the Leinster championship, there was growing frustration that Meath had gone so long without winning a major title. I was opposed by Paul Kenny for the managerial position that autumn, but a few of the old hands, mainly Colm O'Rourke and Joe Cassells, put the case for me and I survived. But I know that people were grumbling: 'Sure Boylan's a hurler, what would he know about football?'

I may have been a hurler, but I was fortunate enough to build a great football team.

CHAPTER NINE

Those Training Methods

An awful lot has been written and spoken about our training methods, but my basic approach was simple. I had to look at the players I had, where they stood in fitness terms and what facilities were available. These facilites might include the Hill of Tara, Bettystown beach, Gormanston swimming pool or the Grand Canal all of which we used for different purposes and at different times. There has been a lot of talk about the work we did on the Hill of Tara – how fellows vomited their guts out, nearly died and so on. It had nothing to do with playing football, but everything to do with stamina, with fellows finding inner strength – because the first thing to go under pressure is 'the gut'.

There were fellows who were great footballers but hopeless runners, yet they would persevere and run up and down that hill or sand dune. The natural athletes like Liam Smith, Joe Cassells and Terry Ferguson would be up front striding out like gazelles. They would go forever like the battery bunnies. Others found it a chore. Bobby O'Malley hated training, but he always did it. Likewise with Gerry Mac and 'Staff'; they hated the training but they did it and they all did it together.

The spring of 1983 was my first one in charge and it was an

extraordinarily wet spring. The playing-pitches across Meath were soaking. Croke Park would be a lot drier when we got there in the summer, so we went to Bettystown beach for training – it was a much better surface. When we were there we did a lot of stamina work on the sand dunes – again to keep going, to be able to sustain playing good football for sixty or seventy minutes. It was simply a matter of using the facilities that were available.

At the start of 1990 things looked bad for us. We had been beaten by Dublin in the 1989 Leinster Final. A new 'four-quarter' League was introduced for the 1989-90 season. We beat Mayo easily in our opening match of 1990 and then faced Roscommon in Kiltoom. There was an incessant deluge all that day and we were absolutely hammered by sixteen points. 'Junior' McManus gave an incredible display for Roscommon, whose supporters gave Martin O'Connell a rough time. Some of the Meath fans could not take any more and huddled behind the goal, shouting: 'Show them your All-Ireland medals, Marty.' A fortnight later we travelled to Belfast to Casement Park where Antrim put four goals past us, and walloped us by ten or twelve points. Our feelings of dejection were soon lifted when we heard the results of the Roscommon-Tyrone match. A draw. It meant a lifeline for us, as we were back in a three-way play-off. Amazingly, we went on to beat Donegal, Cork and Down to win the League title. It was a long road from the deluge at Kiltoom. It had been a much longer road than that, of course.

This bunch of lads had put up an awful lot of mileage and played a lot of top-level football. They had:
- won the Centenary Cup in 1984
- were humiliated by Laois in 1985
- won the Leinster Final in 1986 –
- only to be beaten by Kerry in the All-Ireland Semi-Final
- won successive All-Irelands in 1987 and 1988

- won the National League in 1988
- lost the Leinster Final to Dublin in 1989
- won the National League in 1990
- and lost out narrowly to Cork in the All-Ireland Final of that year!

Even away back in 1984 we had played on nine successive Sundays because of the way the League and the Centenary Cup had been structured. Something would have to give. Something would have to be done.

I spoke with Jack Finn, our team doctor, on our way out of a Dalgan Park training session one evening in 1990. I told him I could not do stamina work with the lads that year, because so many of them had problems with ligaments and knees. They could run up hills all right but could not run downhill for love nor money. I told Jack that I had been reading about Joan Benoit, the American long-distance runner. Six weeks before the Los Angeles Olympic Games in 1984 she underwent an operation on her knee. After the operation she did all her training in water, right up until eleven days before the games began. She went out and won the Women's Marathon. Jack's reply was: 'You're right, Seán. We're in the nineties now. We must look at different ways of doing things.'

I put an idea to the county board at the end of 1990. I also made contact with Gerry O'Reilly, a fifteen-hundred-metre runner from Dunboyne who had represented Ireland in two Olympic Games. He and a promising young athlete called Sonia O'Sullivan sourced wetsuits for us with Glenn McWalter in Atlanta, Georgia. At the time the wetsuits were very expensive. It cost us three thousand pounds to import them. The fact that the county board considered the idea showed a huge vote of confidence in me. That was only the start. We now had to get access to a swimming pool and convince the lads of the worth of this training. Gormanston College provided the pool. The players reaction was hilarity, accompanied by mutterings of: 'This is absolutely ridiculous!'. They eventually got the hang of the suits, and even our sponsor Noel Keating (RIP) gave it a go. He claimed he lost four pounds in weight in just one session.

Everyone was scared that word of water-training would get out, but thankfully it never did. We trained for weeks and weeks in water. We had been drawn against Dublin in the first round of an open 1991 Leinster draw. If we had been beaten then – and the word got out that we had done most of our training in water – I could imagine the comments:

'Boylan has surely lost it this time ... '

'His head is gone ... '

'Definitely, the marbles are gone ... '

Three weeks before the Dublin match in June 1991 we put our feet on the training pitch. The injuries had all repaired by then. Little did we or anybody guess that it would take four epic matches to beat Dublin. Whereas in 1996 we won an All-Ireland title using nineteen players over the entire series, in that four-match epic against Dublin in 1991 we used a total of thirty-one players! They were four matches of fierce intensity, so if ever there was a year for water-training 1990-91 was surely it. My training advice is: look at where your players are in fitness terms and at what facilities are available to help achieve the fitness levels that are required.

We had already tried something else over the 1989-90 season. We had been beaten in the 1989 Leinster Final by a very strong Dublin team trained by Gerry McCaul, which had a powerful new half-back line of Keith Barr, Eamonn Heery and Tommy Carr. They were very unfortunate against Cork in the All-Ireland Semi-Final and should possibly have won an All-Ireland title that year. For Meath to come back again and beat Dublin in 1990 would be a huge task. We were fortunate in the way the League had worked out for us and went on to win it, which gave us a boost for the championship. The competitive edge was back, but the lads were tired and we needed to build up our upper body strength.

I knew some fellows who were involved in rowing in Bullock Harbour in Dalkey, so I got the loan of some boats and put them in the Grand Canal between Summerhill and Kilcock. As it happened, there was a training stables right beside the canal, which happened to have a five-furlong 'gallop' covered in wood-shavings. So we used both facilities. Again, it's important to make use of what is there to reach your goal. It was amazing the number of lads who weren't happy in the water, even though it was only waist-deep ... As a group we all had to row on the same stroke. Everyone had to do it right or else it would have been a disaster. Pulling together, literally, brought unity back into the squad. When a group has been together for a long time, it is only natural that things will become brittle and fragile, so the Grand Canal sessions were not just about upper body strength. On top of that, the last furlong on the racing gallop was uphill, so the going was tough all around.

In 1996 we had put together a very young team. Even in January the team were shaping well and we thought we could win a Leinster title with them, maybe even more, even though they had taken a ten-point walloping from Dublin the previous year. Our feeling was right – they went all the way to win an All-Ireland title. This young team were, in fact, a tribute to the great 1987-88 heroes. They were the new kids on the block, wanting to do the same as their heroes, proud to do the same. Everyone was saying: 'These lads could win three All-Irelands in a row.' It was never going to be that simple. They were beaten in the 1997 Leinster Final by Offaly, having survived another three-match epic with Kildare. They lined out against Offaly having lost the entire full-back line and the centre-forward due to injuries and suspensions. We gained a handsome revenge against Offaly the following year (1998) but again fell short against Kildare in the Leinster Final.

When 1999 came around there were a lot of bad memories to be cleared – two successive Leinster Final defeats. I remember looking at the squad one night in training and saying to myself: 'I don't know what I'm going to do … ' I thought about it for a long time and finally brought the lads together in Dalgan Park. 'Listen,' I said, 'if we're going to win the first round of the Leinster championship against Wicklow, we're going to have to train every night for two weeks … ' Between day and night sessions we did eleven sessions on the trot. It had nothing to do with ability. It had to do with getting their heads right, each individual finding that ingredient within himself and asking: 'How much am I prepared to put into this effort? How much do I really want to win?' It's a cliché nowadays to talk about 'having the hunger' but it is still true. Each player had to answer those questions, make the necessary sacrifices and put himself about. In a group dynamic, both good and bad things rub off players. My target was to win that first-round match, then win back the Leinster title and see if we could go a stage or two further. The 1999 squad found that ingredient on the training field and went on to win the All-Ireland title. In fact, they were never really in danger in any match in the series. We knew that they were going to come through. The memories were purged. The hunger was there. The sacrifices were made. The effort was put in. And it was especially nice to win the All-Ireland title fifty years after Meath had won their first title on a day when the five-year-old Seán Boylan was showing off his skills on the front lawn to the fans on the train at Dunboyne …

Sport is also about networking – helping each other out. I remember sitting in the VIP box in Croke Park at the 2000 All-Ireland Final between

Galway and Kerry. Sonia O'Sullivan was the special guest, following her silver medal at the Sydney Olympic Games. She did a lap of honour and then came up to the VIP box. She was, of course, besieged by autograph-hunters but when she saw me, she came over and threw her arms around me. 'Seán, it's a long time since we got the wetsuits for you in Atlanta!' she laughed. How she even remembered that just amazed me, but that is what sport is all about – making friends and contacts. When we began using the sand dunes in Bettystown, the local golf club allowed us to use their changing facilities, and Mrs Crinion gave us the use of the Neptune Hotel. So many people have been good to us over the years.

On one occasion, Gerry O'Reilly from Dunboyne came with me to Bettystown. He was a personal friend and a very good athlete who was home on holiday from Villanova University. We did some stretching exercises on the hotel lawn and Gerry joined in. Gerry McEntee was very curious about this intruder and said to Joe Cassells beside him: 'Who's the big blondie fellow?' Joe, never a man to miss an opportunity to jibe a colleague, replied: 'He's the new midfielder!' 'I didn't ask what he was. I asked who he was,' McEntee snapped.

Later, running along the beach, I asked Gerry O'Reilly to lead the lads out. He did so, along with Little Liam Smith. Gerry, of course, had been running with the likes of Eamonn Coughlan and very soon left the lads trailing. It was so comical, but it is always good to bring some-one into training from an other discipline. And, of course, a bit of humour never goes astray either. We had no scarcity of comedians among the panel, especially when they had a few drinks on them.

Again, I recall an incident in Bettystown. On our first visit there, we changed in the golf club. Finian Murtagh raced up to the top of the dunes, shouting excitedly to the following Lyons brothers and Liam Harnan.

'Mick! Mick! Padraig! Padraig! Liam! Liam! Come here – QUICK.'

The boys ran over to him in great anxiety. 'What? What is it?'

'Look!' Finian cried. 'That's the SEA!'

The implication was that fellows from Summerhill and Moynalvey wouldn't know what the sea was like. Being a smart lad, Finian took off at a fast pace.

CHAPTER TEN

The Clinic

When I made the decision in 1961 to leave Warrenstown College and come home to help my ageing and ailing father, my intention was to lend a hand for a few weeks or months at most. I was an exuberant seventeen-year-old with my life ahead of me and I certainly did not envisage spending my life dealing with herbs. Within six weeks of coming home, however, I was beginning to realise what knowledge and wisdom my father possessed and the effect he had on his clients. I realised that I could not and would not walk away from that tradition.

We had cattle on the farm and also did an amount of market-gardening: fruit, vegetables and flowers. We grew herbs in the front garden, but there was little difficulty in getting herbs then. Many of them grew wild and free, but the advent of pesticides would ulti-mately change all that. To this day there are people who might have an abundance of ox-eye daisy growing on their land and would tell us about it. With their permission we would harvest it. As a herbalist you are always looking out for virgin (uncontaminated) seed, so I could be driving along somewhere and see a lovely healthy plant, which I would bring home for its seed.

Jack Moran and Mick Reilly worked on the land for us in those early days, but the herbal side of things was very much a family affair. It was part of life. It was simply what was done in our house, but it was never a 'business'. People came for 'a bottle' – mostly on word of mouth – a remedy for rheumatism, a chest complaint, a skin problem. They came from all parts and would even approach my father when he was selling cattle in Dublin Cattle Market.

The herbs were brewed up on the big range in the kitchen, strained off in the scullery and cooled off in the pantry. The patients waited in the hall and my father saw them in the dining-room. For nearly thirty years, my father provided this service without charge, probably mindful of his own suffering and pain. The number of clients increased over the years. People mostly came on Sundays until one Sunday in the late fifties. On this particular Sunday, sixty-three people turned up – twenty-seven of whom got off the 2.45pm bus from Dublin and raced each other across the field in order to be out in time to catch the return bus a few hours later. What a sight that must have been, considering their varied incapacities. (It was known that the bus drivers would drop them off at our gate and often wait for stragglers on the return journey.) My mother called a halt to all of this. There would be official opening hours on week-days and everything would be properly structured. But often the, 'Closed' sign on the gate did not deter many from climbing over it and coming in anyway – just for 'a bottle' ... And I would often hear 'the boss' in the small hours, as he washed herbs out in the yard, in anticipation of a busy day at the clinic. Structure, indeed!

Those ten years I had with my father until his death in May 1971 were an extraordinary apprenticeship – the most influential years of my life. My father never wrote anything down about the remedies. I simply absorbed his knowledge as you would do with traditional music or storytelling. He would tell me a thing once and after that he would expect me to study it further. As time went on I expanded my knowledge through attending courses and conferences. Even though he now had Parkinson's disease on top of his earlier health problems, my father never complained. He was now seeing fewer people as I was gradually taking over, but he would still come down to meet people and was still involved up to six months before his death. In the late sixties we had moved the clinic out of the house to two cedarwood cabins in the garden. I don't think I ever took a holiday in those ten years nor was I paid a wage. If I needed money it was a case of: 'Take what you want out of the wallet.' They were very different times. I also had the use of the car to go out socialising, which was important in those days.

After my father's death, Paddy Mulcahy said to me: 'Your mother is head of the house now, but you are the man of the house.' The numbers of clients continued to grow. We never advertised – it was simply 'word of mouth'. People came from different areas. People came with skin problems, like dermatitis from Drogheda where the cement works, as well as Irish Oil and Cake Mills were located. Blood pressure was a recurring problem in the Kingscourt-Cavan area, and chest conditions were a problem in the midland areas. We were a bit like the hedge school of old, where people came for learning on the basis of the master's reputation.

I was growing in confidence in my work. The important thing was to know my limitations – to know what not to do. I built up a list of people to whom I could refer clients that I could not help. That, in turn, helped the clients because they appreciated that I was not wasting their time. I personally had never spoken in public about my work, but the opportunity arose in the early seventies when Vivian Murray of the Irish Goods Council asked me to speak during a vegetable promotion week. He wanted me to talk about the use of nettles, wild turnip and carrot, and how, for example, people would use nettles before spring cabbage came in season. Conscious of my father's wish that 'people would go back to nature more', I agreed and spoke to a packed audience. It was an important step for me.

From there, my horizons expanded. I attended meetings of the Herbal Society in London with George Rennick, the Meath Horticultural Adviser. In 1979 the World Health Organisation initiated research into medicinal plant cures, following the difficulties that had emerged with drugs like thalidomide. Professor Geary and I represented Ireland. I interpreted this as a tribute to our forefathers who had cared for the natural world. And even though I sat in the corner of Christ the King College, afraid that anyone would even look at me, it did give me a massive boost in confidence.

From there, I travelled all over the world attending conferences, often as a guest speaker, meeting a huge cross-section of academics and practitioners. This education brought things to a new level for me and prompted me to keep searching for higher standards in my work. Meeting with people like Professor Desmond Corrigan of Trinity College Dublin (TCD) led to the university becoming involved with us in research projects. Education and awareness had affected clients as well – where once people came for 'a bottle', now they rightly wanted to know exactly what it contained and what it would do for them. While the conferences were interesting, the minute a conference was over, I went straight home because I had a business to run. The balance to all of this was my involvement in sport: hurling, football or go-karting. It worked both ways. I might be feeling down over losing at sport, but when I opened the clinic door the next morning to someone with a serious illness, everything was put into perspective.

In 1995 I returned from Noel Keating's anniversary Mass to find the County Fire Officer on the premises. The news was not good. The cedarwood buildings were a fire risk and would have to go. We had already started a business expansion scheme for the development of our products. We now had to build a new clinic.

The modern clinic has five treatment rooms, a waiting room and office and reception space. Attached is the dispensary which incorporates a production area for both aqueous production (the traditional water-based method) and concentrate production (based on industrial alcohol or glycerine). Thus the products we sell are manufactured here in the clinic, which is very important. Outside is the drying-plant, which is in use from February to November, as we harvest the plants according to season. Finally there are the stores for the dried herbs, where the temperature is regulated to prevent damp affecting the herbs. The farm is entirely devoted to herb production and we also buy in non-native herbs. We have three people working on the herb production outside; three people work in the laboratory preparing the remedies, and another two manage the dispensary. Two consultants work with me in assessing clients. There are other practitioners here working in areas like Chinese medicine, acupuncture, homeopathy, massage and reflexology. These are people who I feel could benefit our clients and they have their own patients attend separately. All of this, together with office staff, could bring the full complement up to twenty people. We also have a strong liaison with chiropractors, osteopaths and physiotherapists outside the premises.

Our client range is very diverse. Most people might associate us with sports injuries but they only form a minor part of our work. We deal a lot with viruses, respiratory illnesses, allergies, skin problems etc. Most of our clients would have gone to a medical practitioner first but, for whatever reason, feel they are not getting satisfaction. Everybody who was ever sick wants to be better yesterday, but we have to be extremely cautious that we do not interfere with their prescribed medication. For some people we can do nothing. At least twenty per cent of clients are referred to other practitioners.This causes disappointment but it also assures them that at least they are not being used.

Alternative medicine has come a long way. From being dismissed at one time it has now become popular – witness how heavily the pharmaceutical firms have become involved in alternatives. More and more medicines are being made from plant extracts once more, but with vegetable matter, as opposed to synthetic products, it is difficult and costly to stabilise these medicines. Orthodox medicine has made amazing progress in areas like surgery and antibiotics but there is still a huge dependence across the world on traditional medicines. Somewhere in between must lie a sensible combination of the orthodox and the alternative. For our part we who are involved in alternatives must be open and transparent and we must heighten awareness of the potential of our products. In recent years I have been asked to make presentations to various medical schools – this is a breakthrough for alternative medicines.

As for the future, there is a major move by the EU to legislate the co-ordination and control of alternative medicines. The whole area is subject to so many regulations and rules already that I worry about over-legislation. I feel that trying to legislate for so many different traditions across Europe will be very difficult.

As for the Boylan tradition, my children are interested in what I do, but they are very young and who knows if they will pursue that interest and continue our inherited tradition. I would like to hope that the opportunities will be there for them. For myself, of course there are times when I might be tempted to say 'why bother?' or 'why me?', but then I open the clinic door and someone is looking for help ...

This is the talent I have been given. This is the work at which I have spent all my adult life. I owe it to those who went before me, who cherished and nurtured and cared for the natural world, to continue that tradition. In the words of my great mentor Conrad Gorinsky: 'We owe more to our heritage than to walk away from it.'

CHAPTER ELEVEN

Sacrifices, Decisions and Abuse

As a manager I've been lucky to have dedicated players who will do just about anything to play an important match including flying from different parts of the world to play.

Picture the scene: it's 16 September 1990, the All-Ireland Football Final has just concluded and Meath have lost to old rivals, Cork. A helicopter waits to whisk Gerry McEntee away to Dublin Airport. Within minutes of the final whistle he is up and away, heading to catch a transatlantic flight. Gerry was working as a surgeon in the Mayo Clinic in Rochester, USA. In the Clinic no one would understand the significance of an All-Ireland Final and why one of their surgeons would make such sacrifices to be a part of it. Gerry had flown in only a few days before the final and was injured in the match itself. It was typical of the efforts Gaelic players make to play the game they love – amateurs who will give their all on football's biggest day (and lose!) and yet will turn up for work the next morning four thousand miles away.

When Kevin Foley first came on our panel, he was working as a veterinary surgeon in Wexford. He would still turn up for training a few times a week in Dalgan Park, Navan. Later he moved to Fermoy, County Cork. Occasionally he came up by helicopter, thanks to our sponsor, Noel Keating, but most times he would drive and have to be back for work the next morning. I remember we played a League match in Armagh once. Kevin got concussed and had to go off. He was driven back to Meath, but then had to get into his own car and drive back to Wexford, where at eight o'clock the following morning he performed a Caesarean operation on a cow! The experiences of Gerry and Kevin might seem exceptional, but they are in fact a reality for inter-county players today.

Many players have long distances to travel to training and games. David Beggy worked as an auxiliary administrator of a conglomerate of nursing homes – in Scotland! It meant endless trips home at weekends. When he would return he might have to travel on to Ayr or Dundee or Perth. He could be posted to any one of those areas, which could mean a further few hundred miles of travel. And then, of course, he had to train on his own and hold his fitness levels in order to keep his place on the team. He just wanted to play.

When as All-Ireland champions we travelled to the US to play the All-Stars, Liam Hayes broke off from his honeymoon to play in the second match in San Francisco and then two days after returning from Los Angeles he lined out against Dublin in the replay of the League Final and scored a wonder goal. He just wanted to play.

When Darren Fay was captain in 2003 his wife gave birth to their baby three months prematurely. He was over and back to the hospital in Drogheda every evening, yet he only missed one training session. He just wanted to play.

When I first became associated with the Meath football team, it was to give massages and generally help out with injuries. Pat Reynolds and Tony Brennan changed all that. They were soon saying to me: 'That's not right. That work is a job for someone else. Your job is with the team.' It was Pat and Tony who really pushed me to the forefront, because initially I would have been very content to stand back. That gave me a boost, I suppose. After that, it's just the sheer honesty of the players and team commitment that lifts you. I remember in one match in 1996 when one particular player wasn't going well. We warmed up Jody Devine to come in as a substitute and he was almost on the field of play when suddenly things came right for the other player. Then Jody made his own decision, and said: 'Will we leave it for a while?' That, for me, is the magic of players – this man deprived himself of getting on the field of play for the greater good of the team.

When lads start to play at inter-county level it's very different from the club scene. They are into a whole new training regime, under a new coach. They are good footballers who can play well, but not for long periods. The aim is to go from five minutes of good play to ten minutes, then fifteen, then twenty and sustain that. This can mean training on Tuesday, Thursday, Saturday and Sunday, and doing that week-in, week-out over a long period can put severe strain on personal relationships and work arrangements. They may have to pass up the opportunity to work overtime and so they are making financial sacrifices too at a crucial period of their lives. A number of our 1987/88 team were married with young children. The players and their partners made massive sacrifices. We as selectors knew that, but the fans do not always realise it.

Colm O'Rourke was thirty years old when he won his first Leinster medal. He had been in the team since he was eighteen then he got a serious knee injury, he came back and aggravated that injury again, and came back again. It cannot have been easy for his girlfriend, who is now his wife Trish, but she was always supportive of him. Otherwise he could not have stayed at the top for so long. It was a similiar situation with Joe and Louise Cassells. They had a large young family and Joe was building up a business as an electrician, but there was never a question as to his commitment. Once I gave the panel a Sunday off. Some of the wives rang me during the week: 'Why did you give them a day off?' was the unanimous cry. 'The boys were unbearable at home. Don't EVER do that again!' The boys just wanted to play.

Decisions often have to be made on the sideline in the heat of a game. They can be difficult to make and often difficult for the punters to understand. 'What's Boylan at?' they will say. Sometimes you're at nothing at all, but generally you are trying to make things 'right' as best as you can. And, of course, sometimes things go hopelessly wrong and you are the worst in the world, but you can only do what you think is best. Half the training you do is to help fellows absorb the intense pressure on match-day – I have to train myself to absorb the pressure as well.

When we ran out on the pitch for the 1999 All-Ireland Final against Cork, I realised the Meath dug-out was surrounded by Cork supporters. I took my sweater off and left it on the bench. The tirade of abuse from one Cork individual began: 'Go away out of that, ye little bollix!' I ignored him and went out on the pitch to do my pre-match business. When I came back, the abuse resumed. It was outrageous stuff. I could well imagine what Larry Tompkins, the Cork manager, was getting at the other end from some Meath fanatic! During the parade our Cork friend never let up. Denis Murtagh turned to James Reilly, the assistant secretary of the Meath county board, and said: 'James, the next time your man says anything to Seán, I want you to say something to him.' (Whispers).

James: 'I couldn't say that!'

Denis: 'Say it!'

I knew nothing of this at the time. The match began. A few minutes in, Cormac Murphy of Meath and Philip Clifford of Cork went for a ball. It came off Philip and went over the line. Meath ball! I happened to catch it and threw it to Cormac. Our friend exploded into unrepeatable language behind me. Denis Murtagh, pointing with his big hand, turned to James Reilly and said: 'James, say it.' James turned to our friend and said: 'Shut your f$%*! mouth!' From then on, of course, our Cork friend gave all his attention to poor James. There are different ways of diverting pressure and – in this instance – Denis Murtagh's decision paid off.

Other people's decisions – particularly those of referees – can also affect you as manager. I may be there on the sideline, sitting on a football, looking totally unruffled, but at times daft decisions can ruffle you greatly. I hate injustice. You know your own players can do wrong just like the opposition can, but when you don't get the fairest crack of the whip from the referee, that can get to you. You have put lads through intense preparation and training, sent them out expecting a level playing pitch – and then an injustice is done. That is very hard to take. You understand that referees are human and have a huge rule-book to implement, but it is still hard to take. You have to remain above it and try not to let it get to you, but sometimes it does.

As regards abuse, when it comes from the opposition or their supporters, you can deal with it. But when it comes from your own side it is very hard to take. Supporters can be very fickle. When you run out on the field with your players, you are the greatest in the world. Twenty minutes into the game and things are not going so well – your supporters can turn on you too. When it happens it's not pleasant. I remember coming across an inebriated Meath supporter in a hotel in Malahide on the evening of the 1988 All-Ireland Final with Cork when a last-second point from Brian Stafford earned us a draw. This fan wanted to meet 'Staff' because his score had saved our friend £18,000 in a bet ... I had to be restrained from chucking him out because I knew if we won the replay, he wouldn't give a damn about 'Staff'. I know the punters pay their money and have the right to criticise, but sometimes their reactions can be hard to take.

One of our hardest decisions in my early years as manager caused major drama on the eve of the Leinster Football Final in 1984. Eamonn Barry was captain that year but he had been injured during the Centenary Cup run and had been off the team for a long time. We as selectors felt that, although Eamonn had recovered, he would not be able to live with the pace in the white heat of the first twenty minutes of a Leinster Final. Maybe when the game settled into a pattern he could come on and make a contribution, but he would not be in the starting fifteen. Eamonn seemed okay about that early in the Saturday afternoon on the pitch, but at six o'clock that evening in the hotel he announced that he felt our decision was unfair and he was pulling out of the squad – less than twenty-four hours before the match. He was clearly upset, but it was his choice and I am sure it was a hard decision for him, just as our decision to omit him had been hard. I said to the lads: 'Does anyone else want to go? Because now is the time, if you do!' People might say you should have gone after Eamonn and tried to talk him around, but of course I did not. I wouldn't go after anybody in a situation like that. To me, a Leinster Final is one of the biggest days you can have as a player. Naturally, as captain, Eamonn would want to lead the team out, but if he wasn't fully fit, it just wasn't going to happen. That's the way it is. Misfortunes happen. Eamonn never played for us again.

On the other hand, when we faced Carlow in the first round of the Leinster championship in 1986, Colm O'Rourke was recovering from an operation on his knee and Colm Coyle was coming back following an operation on his elbow. In this instance, we took a chance and played them both, because we felt the game would bring them on in terms of recovery and fitness. We also gave David Beggy his first game and he scored a goal and two points.

Circumstances will vary from match to match and you make your decisions accordingly. As selectors we had to be at one about those decisions and equally – if the decisions weren't working out – the lads would have to come off pretty smartly. The fans might not always agree with our decisions but that was not the point. Nobody knew the players as well as we selectors did. We had been at all the training sessions and we saw what was happening: who was showing well, who needed time, who wasn't 'right' and so on. What might happen at club level was important, and that was what the fans saw, but what we were seeing at the training sessions would be what would ultimately inform our decisions, and those decisions were not reached lightly – we spent many long hours picking teams.

CHAPTER TWELVE

The Old Hands

While our trawl for new players in 1985 was successful, the trick was to find the right blend and balance of the new boys with the older established players. I will call them the 'old hands' rather than the 'old dogs' as they might take exception to that phrase, but in truth we needed those old dogs, because the road to All-Ireland glory is certainly a hard road ...

'ROURKEY'

When the script is finally written about Meath football, it will probably state that Colm O'Rourke could have played in any position: full-back, full-forward, corner-forward, even in goals! If you talk to the 'greats' of the game, they will all agree that Colm was the MAIN MAN. When he got the ball, it electrified the place. He never lacked self-confidence, but people might not realise how hard he worked on the field. A lot of things were very natural to him but when you have a lot of natural skill and ability everyone wants to put you in your place, especially if you are a cocky youngster. Colm started his senior inter-county career at the age of eighteen and he had to contend with a lot of abuse from the start. There is no comparison between the Gaelic football of the seventies/eighties and the modern game. Some referees came up with an expression about Colm: 'He invited the foul', because whereas most forwards had to be given the ball, Colm would go out, win the ball, turn and take on the defenders. How could you 'invite the foul' when you win the ball, play with it and are then pulled down? Either he was fouled or he wasn't. 'Inviting the foul' was the greatest nonsense.

Colm had tremendous pace and speed, even though he had trouble for nearly all of his playing career with an injured left leg. I think he still holds the 'Superstars' record for one hundred metres. There was never a surrender in 'Rourkey'. The only time he might not play well was when he had the 'flu or some such ailment. He went out to play with injury problems, but once the game started, the adrenalin would begin to pump. 'Give it in to me, lads, any way you like. I'll win it!' he would say. That was his way. He was a phenomenally strong player. I have seen him take impossible scores with defenders hanging out of him. He formed a perfect combination with Stafford and Flynn. 'Staff' was so clever at creating space for 'Rourkey'. Colm O'Rourke was a very fair player. There was not a dirty stroke in him, but naturally he could get frustrated if people were messing him around. His football was a cross between the traditional 'hard' game and the modern movement game. The bigger the opposition the more it brought the best out of him. His duels with Mick Kennedy and Gerry Hargan of Dublin are legendary.

'Rourkey' was the Daddy of Meath football. In the 1988 All-Ireland final Gerry McEntee was sent off for striking a Cork opponent. For Rourkey this was more than Gerry McEntee being sent off. This was his pal being sent off. He looked over at me on the sideline and just nodded. He came out from his corner-forward position and played all over the field: half-back, centre-field, centre-forward, full-forward. He was everywhere and damn near refereed the match as well. If responsibility needed to be taken, RRourkey was the man. That was the tragedy of 1991 when after playing an incredible nine matches (including four draws) we reached the All-Ireland final against Down. A few days before the final, Colm fell ill with pneumonia. I always remember him coming in to us on the Thursday before the final. He had been told by his doctor that he could not play and was not even supposed to travel to Croke Park on the day. He broke down ... Mick Lyons spoke up: 'Lads, Rourkey has pulled the plough for us for long enough. It's time for us to do it for him now!' And of course Rourkey did travel and did come on in the second half, defying all medical advice, when we were eleven points down. He was an inspiration but unfortunately we just failed in the end by two points. It was a tragedy but that's how life goes. It was an extraordinary compliment to Colm that he won the Texaco Gaelic Football Award in 1991 – coming from a team that had lost the All-Ireland Final. An incredible honour, but richly deserved.

GERRY MAC

Gerry McEntee had been on the Meath team since 1975. He was one of the first midfielders in Gaelic Football to play as a seventh defender. Gerry would always make himself available. Considering his 'real--life' occupation as a surgeon, he had an extraordinary first touch. He just needed to get his fingers to the ball and he had it. Nobody, but nobody, would prise it from him. Gerry punished himself so much to get things right. As a young doctor working all sorts of hours – including night-shifts – he would still come straight from Tyneside, Limerick or wherever, to play a match or do training. Our driver James 'Scubs' Whyte would collect him and Gerry would grab some sleep in the car. He had an extraordinary presence and a terrific influence on every other player. One thing was certain – he would always be battling with you. He might feel differently about something and he would say what was on his mind, then get on with the play. Gerry Mac was Gerry Mac. It is hard to quantify his contribution to the team, but in many ways he was the soul of the Meath team. I really mean that. He was the soul of the team.

LIAM HAYES

I had come across Liam Hayes as a minor footballer when I would occasionally help out with injuries. In fact, my introduction to Liam as a senior player was when he lay unconscious under the Cusack Stand in Croke Park, having been knocked when playing in his senior debut against Wexford in the 1981 Leinster championship. I had to do what I could for him because the ambulance could not gain access to that side of the ground. We eventually got him to hospital in the back seat of a car. He played again when we lost to Longford in the following year, came on as a substitute against Down in the League play-off and from then on he was a regular on the team. Liam was phenomenally strong and a powerful footballer. He had all the skills and could turn on the proverbial sixpence. He was the ideal midfield partner for Gerry McEntee and scored some great goals for us, notably a screamer from twenty yards in the 1988 League Final against Dublin. Liam was also a fearless player. Mick Lyons used to say to his colleagues in club matches: 'Whatever you do, don't hit Hayes!' If you got Liam vexed, nobody could play him. Liam thought a lot about the game, maybe too much at times, but generally, when Liam Hayes played well, Meath won. He had a great ability to put personal problems aside when he went on the field. He was particularly helpful to new players coming onto the team. It can be a very daunting experience for young players to come into an established panel, but Liam always made them feel welcome. Brendan Reilly would always say that of him.

MARTY

Although he would ultimately achieve fame as a defender, Martin O'Connell started out as a wing-half-forward with his club, Saint Michael's from Carlanstown. This was a junior club and Marty was one of those players for whom it was imperative to get experience at a higher level. He had talent in abundance. He had great balance, was two-footed and a great fetcher and kicker of a ball. He was unbelievably competitive in training. Initially we played Marty all over the field. He was full-forward in the 1986 All-Ireland Semi-Final against Kerry, having scored an impressive six points in an earlier challenge match against Cavan. He was in and out of the squad for a time but always showed amazing discipline. The important thing about Marty is the player he eventually became at left-half-back. An awful lot of nonsense was spoken about that. It was said that Pat Reynolds didn't want Marty in that position because Marty was a greater player and Pat was jealous. Anyone who knows Pat knows that that is nonsense. It takes time to adjust to being a back. It's not just about winning the ball but about 'marking' the forward and Marty had seen the abuse some forwards had to take. Marty developed into one of the greatest defenders of all time and won recognition of that when he was selected on the Millennium Team in 1999.

BIG JOE

When we made the breakthrough and won the Leinster title in 1986, Jinksy Beggy had his first Leinster medal after being on the panel for a few months. It was also Joe Cassells's first medal – and he had been on the panel for thirteen years. Big Joe was one of the truly great servants of Meath football and was one of the most amazing athletes I have ever come across. He was very well known in athletics before he ever made his name in football. He was very competitive and yet he was such a huge man that many people found it hard to believe that he was

one of Meath's greatest athletes. He excelled at basketball and bad-
minton and also played hurling for Meath, winning a Leinster
Under-21 medal. In football he ended up winning all the awards that
were going. He was an outstanding club player and won a hatful of
Meath championships with Navan O'Mahonys. He was such a clever
and versatile player. He played for Meath as a defender at centre-field
and ultimately as a forward. When we won the 1987 All-Ireland title
Kevin Heffernan said to me: 'If someone were to tell me at the beginning of the year that Smoky Joe (as Heffo called him) would be the
missing link in the Meath forward line, I wouldn't have believed
them.' But that's what he was. He was the link man that held all the
others together. If Joe wanted to know something, he would quiz you
upside down and inside out until he understood it and then he would
practise it.

Joe did indeed play a pivotal role in the winning of All-Ireland
titles in 1987 and 1988. In the '87 final he covered every blade of grass.
Conor Counihan of Cork told me afterwards that when we eventually
took Joe off his reaction was: 'Thank God. That's him gone.' And then
Colm Coyle came on. He won the first ball and breezed past Counihan
as if he weren't there. 'Oh no,' thought Conor, 'not another one.'

Joe was made captain of the 1988 team but was injured on the 1988
All-Star Tour in Boston – on the very first night of the tour. It turned
out to be a pelvic injury but we didn't know what it was for ages. Joe
kept pulling muscles all year and it looked like Old Father Time was
catching up on him. He came on as a substitute in the Leinster Final
and Mick Lyons, who was captain for the day, wanted Joe to receive
the trophy. Joe refused and Mick was so frustrated that he went up,
took the trophy before Jack Boothman formally presented it, and
made what I am sure is the shortest victory speech on record. I can still
see Joe down on the pitch, arms folded, smiling away at Mick's frustration. His injury eventually came right and his first full match that

year was the All-Ireland Final replay against Cork. When he went up the steps of the Hogan Stand to receive the sparkling new Sam Maguire Cup, there was no prouder man in Ireland – and none more deserving than Big Joe.

COYLER

Colm Coyle was already playing for Meath before I came in 1982. He was another 'Mister Versatility'. He could play in any position and was a terrific reader of the game. Wherever Coyler would be the ball would be there too. Reputations meant nothing to Colm. We were playing Kerry in Tralee once when Kerry were still the kingpins of Gaelic Football. We were short a few players so I asked Colm would he play on Jack O'Shea. 'No problem,' was his reply. 'It'll be a change for Jacko to have to follow someone else around.' Brilliant! Coyler did, I suppose, have a 'hard man' reputation. He wasn't a big man but no one would convince him that he couldn't win a ball. Anything you got from Coyler, you earned it.

BOBBIE AND BERNIE

Bobbie O'Malley and Bernie Flynn could not be termed 'old hands' but they were babies who grew up very quickly. They were brought into the county senior team at eighteen from minor level with a view to reaching football maturity in two or three years. They had been playing with a junior club (Saint Colmcille's) and even though they were both very classy players, I was afraid that if they only got experience at junior level, they would develop bad habits. In the event, Bobby made the grade after a few weeks and Bernie made it after a few months. They had made the positions of corner-back and corner-forward there own. Both of them won Centenary Cup medals in 1984. Bernie was probably the most natural two-footed player that ever stood on a Gaelic football field. He had the most extraordinary balance. He was small compared to the other forwards but Bernie thought he was seven feet tall. He would simply point to his chest, as if to say: 'Put it into me lads. I can do it.' And he did – over and over again. In the National League Final replay of 1988, he gave one of the finest displays I have ever seen. He scored five wonderful points. Again in the 1991 All-Ireland Final against Down he kicked another five points, off both feet. I remember Mikey Sheehy saying that Flynn's display had to be one of the best ever seen in an All-Ireland Final, even though he ended up on the losing side. Fellows like Bernie were so consistent over years, not just over any one year. A knee injury eventually cut short his playing career, but he was simply a phenomenal player who had all the skills.

Bobbie O'Malley was a great servant to Meath football. He might have come on to the team at the tender age of eighteen, but his football thinking was of a man ten years older. He got a serious knee injury in 1985, underwent surgery, came back and went on to win every honour in the game: All-Ireland medals, Footballer of the Year, All-Star awards, captain of Meath and of the Irish team that won the Compromise Rules series in Australia. Whether it was football, singing or golf – Bobby was a perfectionist. He was another great reader of a game, but his greatest asset was his ability to isolate himself, even amongst a crowd. He could keep his energy levels up even if opponents were pulling and dragging at him. Sometimes he became frustrated and there would be a bit of 'slapping', but in the tackle he would cut you in two. He was quite fearless – going down on the ball, coming up with it, rolling with it before delivering a great pass. He was totally unselfish as a player. I loved to see him moving with the ball, head up to see who he could give it to. He was just a 'natural' who happened to have fair old company around him in the shape of Mick Lyons, Terry Ferguson, Kevin Foley, Liam Harnan ...

Above: First Communion Day. *Back:* Mother, Stephen Kelly, Aunt Jenny, Fr Ignatius's driver, Father.
Front: Gemma, Pauline, Fr Ignatius, Philo, me and Frances. Note: stool at front, taken from the priest's house, burned in 1798.
Below: A meeting of Church and State. L to R: Bishop Fogarty of Limerick, WT Cosgrave, Desmond Fitzgerald, Ernest Blythe and my father.

Left: Confirmation Day.
In my Belvedere College uniform, with my father.

Below: Indulging in one of my other passions! Leading the field in a go-kart race, Prosperous, County Kildare.

Above: Early appearance in Croke Park with Meath minor hurlers. Seán fourth from left, front row. Meath vs. Wexford, 1961.
Below: Seán sharing the Meath Millennium Award with his wife and sisters. *Back:* Frances, Pauline, Josephine. *Front:* Gemma, Tina, Philo.

Left: Wedding day, 22 December 1990.

This page: The Boylan Meath All-Stars! *Front:* Ciarán, Oran, Aoife, Doireann, Dáire. *Back:* Seán Jr, me and Tina.

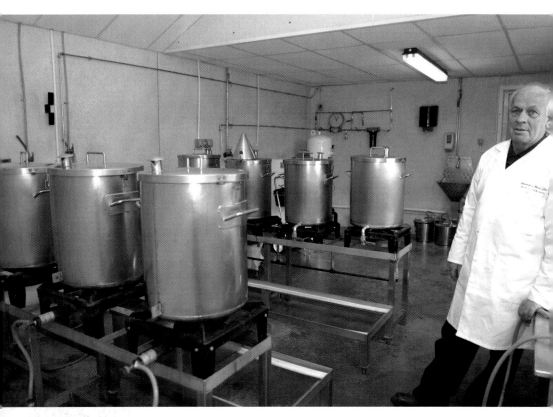

Above: Martin Reilly oversees the herb-brewing process in the clinic.

Below: My favourite herb, parsley-piert, growing in a plastic tunnel.

Seán accompanying his good friend and neighbour, Brush Shiels, on the mouth organ.

Getting the feel of the newly-laid pitch at Páirc Tailteann, Navan.

MICK LYONS

Mick had been playing at full-forward for his club, Summerhill, but we converted him to full-back at county level. Some conversion. An extraordinary presence in the 'square', or as the fans put it, 'The Lyons Den!' He was regularly the subject of some fierce slagging (and worse!) from opposing fans. Some players might find that hard to take but Mick used it to his benefit – They might think I'm a fool but ... He was very uncomplicated in his assessment of those around him and could read situations to perfection. He knew where to be and what to do, as evidenced by his brilliant block on Jimmy Kerrigan of Cork in the 1987 All-Ireland Final. It was the turning point of the game – the ball went to the other end of the field and Rourkey stuck it in the Cork net. It was just the perfect timing of the 'block', as cool as could be. Of course, Mick Lyons had a 'hard man' image but those of us who worked closely with him knew him as the original 'gentle giant'. I know some of the Dublin fans will find that hard to swallow, citing his sending-off against Dublin in the third match in 1991. Television replays subsequently showed it was a joke – he should not have been sent off at all. Other players might have walked diagonally to the dug-out but, typical of the man, Mick walked straight off without pro-test at the Hill 16 end – the Dublin fortress – and was promptly show-ered with coins and fruit. He never flinched – just walked off and sat down beside me.

'I didn't do anything, Seán,' he said.

'I know, Mick,' I replied.

That, and his dismissal against Roscommon in 1983 (when he was a victim of the newly-introduced 'personal foul' rule), were his only sendings-off under my stewardship. Two dismissals in ten years of football at the highest level – some record for a supposedly 'hard man'. I suppose one of the places he would have acquired that reputa-tion was in Cork in 1984 when representing Ireland against Australia in the first Compromise Rules Test. He was unmercifully flattened by an Australian 'tank' known as 'The Dipper'. There was a lot of controversy about that match and the media hyped up the publicity for the second Test in Dublin. Result: three thousand people had attended in Cork but forty-six thousand turned up in Croke Park, anticipating fireworks. Early on in the game Mick went for a ball, 'accompanied' by two Aussies, one of whom was The Dipper. We all thought: Lyons will be killed STONE DEAD. Mick emerged with the ball, leaving the two Aussies to collide with each other ... It was the beginning of a legend and the start of an affinity, even with the Dubs. Fathers would supposedly threaten unruly sons with: 'If you don't behave yourself, I'll get Mick Lyons for ye!' There is a wonderful anecdote told about All-Ireland Final Day in 1988. As the fans were streaming down Clonliffe Road to the match, an ambulance wove through them, siren blaring. A couple of neutral fans tried to 'rise' the Meath followers. 'Make way for that ambulance,' one called. 'Mick Lyons is after running into a telegraph pole.' 'If that's the case,' came a gruff Meath voice in reply, 'it's the f@*&£n' telegraph pole that's in the ambulance!' Mick's a legend among his own.

Mick was an inspiring captain and a great leader, yet he was a man of few words. When we went on the All-Star Tour to the USA in April 1988, we were faced with the dilemma of having to play the replay of the League Final within days of our return. I asked Mick if he would say a few words to the team before we set out. He did and he put it simply:

'Lads, we had our holiday in January. This is a football tournament, not a holiday. If Seánie says we have to train every day, we'll train every day. We'll have a good time, but we'll train. And then we'll come back and win the League ... ' And that is exactly what happened. The captain said what he had to say and got on with the job. Mission accomplished.

ON THE FRINGE

There was, of course, a whole raft of players on our panel who played important roles in our progress to ultimate success. They might not always make the first fifteen but very often it was the quality of the substitutes that brought the best out of the team – even though at that time only three substitutes were allowed.

Liam Smyth from Saint Mary's Club was in the squad when I came in. He played a major role on the county team between 1982 and 1984 and later came on against Laois in 1986. A tremendous club player, 'Little Liam' may have been diminutive in stature but he had terrific energy and was one of our greatest goalgetters. He was a thorough professional in his approach and was tremendously fit, giving his all in training sessions. He was great at drawing backs out of position, and brilliant at solo runs and 'selling dummies'.

The same applies to **Finian Murtagh** from Navan O'Mahonys, with whom he had won several club championship medals and who was there for ten years of my reign. He was in and out of the team, scoring regularly. He kicked eight points in the draw with Dublin in the Leinster championship of 1983. Both Liam and Finian were power-ful and committed players. You would see them giving their all in backs versus forwards at training and they had huge roles in the team. Yet they found it hard to stay on the team because other players were just so good and offered a better balance overall.

Mattie McCabe was in the same position. He had silky skills and extraordinary vision and was something of a 'supersub'. He could come in every time and change the game. Some players just cannot get into a game if they don't play from the start, but not Mattie. In the 1987 Leinster Final he came on for Joe Cassells and scored a goal and three points. In fact, Mattie's record of goals against Dublin is amazing. He scored a goal in each of the Leinster Finals 1987, '88 and '89, but he was competing with PJ Gillic's extraordinary strength which could deliver a sixty-metre pass with such precision, while on the other wing, Jinksy had the ability to do the unexpected at a phenomenal pace. At times Jinksy might even bamboozle himself, but his work ethic and his scoring rate were remarkable. It was always a question of team balance. And all of them were so keen to play. Having done so well in the Leinster Final of 1987, Mattie was up for a place in the All-Ireland Semi-Final against Derry, but he wasn't looking right in training. We took him to Blanchardstown hospital to have a suspect leg X-rayed. The radiologist stunned us by saying: 'That man can't be playing football. He has a broken leg!'

Mattie had broken a bone in his leg. He could remember how it happened but he wanted so much to play. It was typical of the man. Mattie was no show off, but with his extraordinary natural vision, he had more to show off than most players.

There were a lot of other 'fringe' players who in their day contributed to the development of Meath football: Gerry Cooney, Frank and Neil Sullivan from Walterstown; Aidan Crickley from Moynalvey; Des Lane from Slane; goalkeeper Donal Smyth, Mick McDonnell from Summerhill; Padraig Finnerty from Skryne; JJ McCormack from Walterstown; Johnny McEnroe from Oldcastle and of course Padraig Lyons from Summerhill. **Padraig Lyons** who owned the corner-back position for so long and was also our penalty-taker – with mixed results. In the League match against Galway in Navan in 1984 we were awarded a penalty. At the other end, Jimmy Fay leaned against the goalpost and said to the umpire: 'This will end up in the back of the net – or else in the hospital swimming pool.' Padraig duly buried it in the net but later that year in the Leinster Final against Dublin he missed a penalty. It is difficult enough to score a penalty in Gaelic Football and it's a long journey back after missing it – especially if you are a corner-back – but you just have to get on with it.

Padraig Lyons was a powerful corner-back and a great reader of the game. He was unfortunate to get a leg injury in the club championship final in 1986. He got a lot of treatment for it as four days later he flew out with the Compromise Rules team to Australia. As it happened, that was a frustrating month away for Padraig, as he never got a game, but between the intensive treatment and the long journey out, the injury never healed properly. It was a case of bone building up on bone. He lost muscle power and that led to a loss in acceleration in that vital four- or five-yard burst that a corner-back needs. On top of that, Padraig tore a thigh muscle one night in training and never got the same power back in his leg. From then on he was competing with Terry Ferguson for the corner-back position. In the drawn All-Ireland Final against Cork in 1988 he played very well in the first half but had a torrid time in the second half. He told me subsequently that he wasn't well. Anyone else would have come off at half-time but Padraig didn't. If we had known in time, he probably would have started in the replay, but instead we gave a start to Terry. What an important player to have on your panel, though. Padraig fought so hard to get back after that original injury. He was still there in 1991. Terry pulled a muscle in his back when togging out for the last game in the four-match saga against Dublin. Padraig started but was off after ten minutes with a torn hamstring. He played on for his club, ending up in goals and indeed became a phenomenal keeper for Summerhill.

They may have been in and out of the All-Ireland winning teams but without the fringe players – particularly players of the calibre of Padraig Lyons and Mattie McCabe – Meath would never have reached the pinnacle of success in 1987 and 1988.

CHAPTER THIRTEEN

The Book that Became
My Bible

Some years ago, in gratitude for my treatment of her condition, a nun from the US gave me a present of a book. It was entitled *Fearfully and Wonderfully Made* – a collaboration between Philip Yancey, a writer, and Paul Brand, an orthopaedic surgeon, on the miracle that is the human body. The title is taken from Psalm 139, verses 13-14: 'You created my inmost being; you knit me together in my mother's womb. I praise you, because I am fearfully and wonderfully made ... '

Dr Paul Brand spent a lifetime treating leprosy and studying and observing the human body. He wrote: 'I have come to realise that every patient of mine, every newborn baby, in every cell of its body, has a basic knowledge of how to survive and how to heal, that exceeds anything I shall ever know. That knowledge is the gift of God, who has made our bodies more perfectly than we could ever have devised.'

Philip Yancey, an eager young journalist, learned about Brand in the seventies. Brand was then a distinguished surgeon, working in the only leprosy hospital in the US, where Yancey accompanied him on his rounds and then recorded conversations with him on subjects ranging from leprosy and theology to world hunger and soil conservation. The resultant book, *Fearfully and Wonderfully Made,* had a profound and lasting effect on my professional life.

Paul Brand was born in India in 1914 and educated in England before returning to India in 1946. He intended to stay for a year but stayed for seventeen years with his wife Margaret, an eye specialist, treating leprosy patients. He made an amazing discovery when he shook the hand of a leper whose grip almost crushed the surgeon's hand. This totally confused him until he realised he was experiencing power without sensitivity. He began researching the subject and discovered that all the manifestations of leprosy – missing toes and fingers, blindness, ulcers and facial deformities – all trace back to the single cause of painlessness. Leprosy silences nerves and as a result its victims unwittingly destroy themselves, bit by bit, because they cannot feel the pain. When he left India and continued his research, he then applied his knowledge of painlessness to other diseases such as diabetes, thus helping to prevent tens of thousands of amputations each year.

It was in India that Paul Brand honed his skills as a surgeon and gathered his knowledge as a researcher. While his physician friend treated the leprosy and brought it under control, Paul and Margaret Brand worked surgical miracles: restoring rigid claws into usable hands through innovative tendon transfers, remaking feet, transplanting eyebrows and fashioning new noses. Brand worked tirelessly with the very fine and tender skin tissue until power eventually came back and then sensitivity. He became a sort of cobbler, inventing special shoes with a heel bar that exercised the feet. He himself would surprise everyone in the hospital in the US by walking around in his bare feet. Brand's extract on feet is fascinating:

I find bone's design most impressive in the tiny jewel-like chips of ivory in the foot. Twenty-six bones line up in each foot – about the same number as in each hand. Even when a soccer player subjects these small bones to a cumulative force of over one thousand tons per foot over the course of a match, his living bones endure the violent stress, maintaining their elasticity. Not all of us leap and kick, but we do walk some sixty-five thousand miles, or more than two and a half times around the world, in a lifetime. Our body weight is evenly spread out through architecturally perfect arches which serve as springs, and the bending of knees and ankles absorb stress.

Think of the stress that Brian Stafford and Colm O'Rourke's feet have endured in their footballing careers!

Page after page, chapter after chapter of this remarkable book pay tribute to the miracle of the human body – a miracle we forget about in our daily lives. Brand quotes Saint Augustine to make this point:

Men go abroad to wonder at the height of mountains, at the huge waves of the sea, at the long courses of the rivers, at the vast compass of the ocean, at the circular motion of the stars; and they pass by themselves without wondering ...

In my work I treat a lot of skin conditions and marvel at how versatile skin is and how well it can react to the right treatment. For someone like myself, dealing with the ailments of the human body, *Fearfully and Wonderfully Made* gives wonderful insights into the working of that body. Brand's extract on skin is brilliant, he quotes Richard Selzer:

What is it then, this seamless body stocking, some two yards square, this our casing, our facade, that flushes, pales, perspires, glistens, glows, furrows, tingles, crawls, itches, pleasures and pains us all our days, at once keeper of the organs within and sensitive probe, adventurer into the world outside!

Skin is a window on which we read the health of the activities within. It is a source of ceaseless information about our environment – touch is one of our most complex senses. Brand believes that waterproofing is skin's most crucial contrition to the human body. Sixty per cent of our body consists of fluids and these would soon evaporate without the moist, sheltered world provided by skin. Skin is also a frontline defence against the hordes of bacteria that attack the human body.

It is a rough world out there, and the epidermis provides a continuous rain of sacrificed cells ... People who count such things estimate that we lose ten billion skin cells a day. Up to ninety per cent of all household dust consists of dead skin. Just shaking hands or turning a doorknob can produce a shower of several thousand skin cells; one trembles to calculate the effect of a game of racquetball.

Or for that matter, a game of hurling or Gaelic football! And, of course, as the former manager of a football team, I am interested in Brand's treatment of muscles and their role in movement and balance: 'Six hundred muscles, which comprise forty per cent of our weight (twice as much as bones) burn up much of the energy we ingest as food in order to produce all our movements.' And it was muscles that started Brand on his journey, when his own hand was almost crushed by the grip of a leper's hand.

Somewhere in that severely deformed hand were powerfully good muscles. They were obviously not properly balanced, and he (the leper) could not feel what force he was using. Could they be freed? That single incident in 1947 changed my life.

The other aspect of *Fearfully and Wonderfully Made* that resonates with me is Brand's concept of service. When he looks back over his life it is not the greatest meals, amazing holidays or award ceremonies that bring him pleasure. Rather is it his work as part of a surgical team in the service of others, often in primitive conditions, working in intense heat with the help of a flashlight.

Our culture exalts self-fulfilment, self-discovery and autonomy. But according to Christ, it is only in losing my life that I will find it. Only by committing myself as a 'living sacrifice' to the larger Body through loyalty to Him will I find my true reason for being.

This book, a chance gift by a patient, to whom I am eternally grateful, has practically become my bible. At times I might feel I know everything, when of course I know so little. Just a glance through *Fearfully and Wonderfully Made* will always bring something home to me and will especially remind me of the greatest healer of all: Jesus Christ. It has been and is a huge and ongoing influence on my life and work.

NOTE

Dr Paul Brand died in 2003. In 2004, Zondervan Books (USA) published a tribute volume *In the Likeness of God* which incorporates *Fearfully and Wonderfully Made* and its sequel *In His Image*, by Philip Yancey and Dr Paul Brand.

CHAPTER FOURTEEN

The Road to Sam

By the end of 1985 we were finding a balance in a team that would hopefully achieve success. I had been under pressure that year, but some of the senior players had a certain amount of faith in me. I am by nature a shy person and would be a better listener than a talker, but a number of the old hands – the Lyons brothers, Rourkey, Big Joe, Gerry Mc and Liam Hayes – put it bluntly to me and said, 'Stick your shyness in your arse pocket!' And as Padraig Lyons said later,'By, £$%^&, did he!' A few of the old hands also pleaded my case to the county board when I was opposed as manager and I duly survived. It was now or never.

During the 1985-86 National League Campaign we experimented with a lot of players in an attempt to find the right balance. We reached the quarter-final of the League and were up against the 'old enemy', Dublin. We were six or seven points down at half-time. There were six lads on the team that day who had not been involved the previous year: Terry Ferguson, PJ Gillic, Brian Stafford, Liam Harnan, David Beggy and Stan Gibney. It was a huge task for them but they were not in any way overawed. In the dressing room at half-time, 'Staff' spoke out: 'Come on, lads! We can win this. These guys [Dubs] are no use!' He was nearly right. We lost by a single point (2-8 to 1-10) but it had become clear to me that we had the potential to win the Leinster championship. Brian Mullins, the Dublin manager, put his arm around me after the match and said: 'Look, Boylan. You lot can win the League and we will win the championship!' But what transpired in 1986 was exactly the reverse!

After that defeat by Laois in 1985, we knew we needed new talent and it seemed we had found it. PJ Gillic was maturing from being a great underage player. Terry Ferguson was a good defender who would develop into a great one. Liam Harnan had been on the minor team at a very young age but was away from the scene for a while and both he and Brian Stafford had been injured in 1985. David Beggy had come from nowhere. Most unfortunate of all was Stan Gibney, a fantastic footballer who had also been a great minor, but sadly had recurring back trouble during the League campaign and subsequently slipped from the first team back to the substitutes for the championship.

We got past Carlow in the first round of the 1986 Leinster championship by a few points. But it was an unusual match. There was a championship debut for a lot of players but we also took a calculated risk with two more seasoned warriors. Colm O'Rourke and Colm Coyle were recovering from surgery. We played them in order to get them up to match fitness. In the event, Jinksy Beggy saved our bacon that day, allied to a bit of luck that is often needed in the championship. Next up were Wicklow. On paper this seemed a handy run to the Leinster Final, but only on paper. Laois had been National League champions in 1985 (and had, of course, demolished us in the championship) but Wicklow dumped them out of the 1986 championship in the first round at Aughrim. Fortunately we had Wicklow's measure and so the scene was set for a Meath-Dublin Leinster Final.

The weatherman played all sorts of tricks that day. It started off as a lovely day. Jinksy opened the scoring with one of his blistering runs, fell over, got up again and kicked a wonderful point. We moved into a four-points-to-two lead in the sunshine and then the heavens opened. The newspaper analysts said that the rain suited Meath, but in fact we were doing very well before the deluge. We had fallen behind by two points (0-6 to 0-4) at half-time. Crucially, for Dublin, Barney Rock had felt the steel of Liam Harnan's shoulder at the end of the first half and retired with a serious shoulder injury. Dublin only scored one point in the second half. We scored five. I can still see Colm O'Rourke sending over the 'insurance' point. Finian Murtagh had clipped over three lovely points with his sweet left foot. 'Mister Versatile' Joe Cassells played at right corner-back in place of the injured Bobby O'Malley, and when Tommy Carr was deployed as a third midfielder for the Dubs in the hope of drawing Mick Lyons out of position, it was Joe who followed Carr. It suited Joe perfectly, being a natural midfielder himself.

Meath 0-9, Dublin 0-7. The rain poured down but Meath hearts were elated. It was a wonderful day for the county – a milestone. It was our first Leinster title in sixteen years. After all the heartbreak of years in the wilderness, it was an amazing experience to see Joe Cassells lift the Leinster trophy. And, of course, there was the possibility of further glory.

Kerry unfortunately had other ideas, beating us in the Semi-Final by 2-13 to 0-12. People say we lost it through that calamitous first-half goal when Joe Cassells, Mick Lyons and Mickie McQuillan all went for the same ball and ended up in a heap, leaving a bemused Ger Power to tap the ball over the line. It certainly was a disaster as we had been playing very well – and leading – up to then, but it is often forgotten that we came back immediately with successive points to lead 0-7 to 1-2. There was some fantastic football played in that match but what really changed the game for us (and we learned a huge lesson from it) was another collision, this time between Colm O'Rourke and Tommy Doyle of Kerry. It was a complete accident but Tommy sustained a cut over his eye, which necessitated a lengthy stoppage for stitches. We seemed to lose our concentration and momentum. Kerry, on the other hand, scored four points on the trot and had the lead at half-time – a lead they were never to relinquish, even though our lads fought very hard. One abiding memory of that day was our concern for Joe Cassells. He came out to midfield to contest a ball with 'Bomber' Liston and went down under a heavy tackle. Afterwards in the dressing room he began to lose power in his hands and feet. We rushed him to the Mater hospital for a check-up and, thank God, he was fine. Joe is a big man, but he had us worried.

After that defeat it was clear that if we wanted to go further in 1987 we would have to be a better team by at least seven points. That became our target and the lads worked hard at achieving it, through preparation, application and dedication. There were things they had to be prepared to do and things they had to be prepared to forego. Sacrifices would have to be made right from the start and not just a week before a match. These lads could party with the best but from now there would be only the occasional party night. As far as they and we were concerned there was only one party that mattered: bringing Sam Maguire back to Meath after an absence of twenty years!

The players knew that having run Kerry close in 1986 they had the potential to go all the way, but everyone would have to buy into the plan: players, clubs, county board and, of course, ourselves in management. Winning a Leinster title had given us a great boost, as up to then Dublin and Offaly had dominated it for so long without a break. It had taken Offaly a long time to break through because Dublin had been so professional in their approach. Under Eugene McGee Offaly had become equally professional – so for Meath to make the breakthrough would take a huge effort.

We met in September 1986 and talked about what would be needed and then started on the training programme that would hopefully bring us to the top. The first rule was: don't assume anything. We had no God-given right to success, so the focus would be on the first round of the Leinster championship. I knew that the long-starved supporters also felt we could achieve success and would be looking ahead, but we had to earn that right. If you underestimate the opposition for one minute, you are in trouble. The sacrifices demanded of these amateurs were huge. A lot of them were married with families and mortgages, yet they had to make time available for training on three or four nights a week. These were the eighties, long before Celtic Tiger days. They were hard times with unemployment running at over twenty per cent.

A problem arose with training facilities – Páirc Tailteann was undergoing refurbishment. We needed a training ground that would be independent of the clubs so as not to interfere with club training or underage matches. Dalgan Park, the home of the Columban Fathers just outside Navan, came to mind. It had two fine playing pitches. I remembered being there at huge *Muintir na Tíre* gatherings under that organisation's founder, Canon Hayes. I spoke with the county board chairman, Fintan Ginnity, and with the Columban Fathers, and a deal was done. Dalgan Park was just ideal for us, there were beautiful extensive grounds with a fenced-in pitch. There were a lot of old priests, retired from the Far East missions. There were people there on retreat. The neighbours came and watched too. The training sessions became huge family and community occasions. It was central and it became our place – our spiritual home.

Training expenses became another problem. Success brings additional expenses and because of our good run the previous year, the word came down from the finance committee that expenses would have to be scaled back. No more steaks in expensive restaurants! I needed to find a solution. I thought of the Convent of Our Lady of Sion in Bellinter (down the road from Dalgan Park). I met two remarkable women: Sister Máire Clune from county Clare, the prioress, and Aileen Collins, the administrator. I explained to them that I was looking for a place that could provide meals for the players after training. Sister Máire and Aileen welcomed us with open arms. The nuns at Bellinter looked after us so well.

The Daughters of Sion had been founded in the nineteenth century to help reconcile Christians and Jews and here they were – one hundred and forty years later – feeding hungry Meath footballers. We availed of Bellinter for six weeks before we played, and lost to, Galway in the quarter-final of the National League. Having lost our base at Páirc Tailteann, it was fantastic to have our own 'home' and then to be able to leave there and relax and dine in the privacy of Bellinter. Both places made a significant contribution to our ultimate success.

During those six weeks, no one from the county board had ever asked about the players' meals. I spoke with Aileen about the bill, which I was prepared to pay from my own pocket. 'Is the season over?' Aileen naively asked. 'No,' I said. 'It could be over in June or it might run until September!' 'Oh, give me that bill then,' was Aileen's reply. That was the last I heard of it, as the county board settled it when we had won the All-Ireland Final. I had spoken about it with Jack Fitzgerald, our representative on the central council and one of the fairest and most respected figures in Meath GAA circles. Jack could not believe the situation that had arisen. Even in 1949, when Meath won their first All-Ireland, the team had always been well-fed after training. Moreover, after a match they had always ensured that wives and girlfriends were entertained. Jack's philosophy was that if you have a happy home, there will be no problem with fellows going training or playing. I thought – fair play to Jack. Whatever ensued, I heard no more about the cost of meals again.

We may have sorted out the training facilities but other problems were beginning to emerge. We did reasonably well in the National League before and after the Christmas break in 1986, with wins over Dublin, Kerry, Roscommon and Monaghan, but I was not happy. From my point of view the players had not settled down after they had won the Leinster championship. They needed to be 'earthed'. Suddenly they had become heroes, but at a certain point you have to stop and ask: what made me what I am? I believe that the way you apply your skill, mind your talent, and pull together is crucial. I was getting annoyed at the way the players were carrying on and things came to a head in March 1987.

We went to Charlestown to play Mayo and were soundly beaten, managing to score only three points in an hour's football. I remember John Maughan (who would manage Mayo against us in an All-Ireland final nine years later) had a fantastic game against us at centre half-back. It was a bad day all round. Even the restaurant where we had a meal left a lot to be desired. When it was time to set off home there was difficulty in rounding up some of the lads who had gone drinking. Some fellows were annoyed at the carry-on and drink was spilt. There was more 'aggro' when we stopped in Edgeworthstown on the way home. It was a bad, bad day and I had had enough!

I summoned the players to training in Dalgan Park, which had no floodlights, on a winter's evening! I'm sure they were saying: 'What is Boylan up to? Is he mad?' I let them change in the dressing room but told them not to put on their boots. We were just having a meeting. They waited. I spoke: 'This is the way I see things. No one is taking this seriously anymore. There is nothing worse than wasting time. Have a look outside. It's pitch black. How many supporters do you see? None. How much cheering do you hear? None. In other words, we are right back down to earth. Do you want to go through all of this again with Pat, Tony and me or not? Think about it!' I walked out and left them to make their minds up.

Colm O'Rourke and Joe Cassells were on to me the next day. Yes, of course they wanted to go through it all again and were prepared to do what had to be done. 'Okay,' I said. 'Let's do it right from here on in.'

There were other matters to be sorted out. Colm Coyle left the squad and flew out to Chicago. A number of the lads were very annoyed with him but he went because he thought they weren't taking the game seriously enough. On top of that, Marty O'Connell had quit too. He had not had a good game at full-forward against Kerry in 1986, although he had won his place on the strength of a brilliant display against Cavan in that position in a challenge match. The rumour was that he would be better at left half-back, but that we did not want him there because Pat Reynolds (who had won an All-Ireland medal in that position) would be jealous. It was such utter nonsense! There was never an ounce of jealousy in Pat Reynolds. Marty might have potential, but there were things he would have to bring to his game as a defender. He was a very clean player, as strong as an ox, but he was also a ballwatcher. As a half-back he would need to be a manwatcher. When he did not play well against Kerry, a certain person (who had nothing to do with the team) told Marty he would break his legs if he ever played for Meath again! So, not surprisingly, Marty pulled out of the panel.

When we got past Laois in the first round of the Leinster championship, I could see Marty's big curly head on the terrace. I spoke to him that evening. 'Look, Marty, if you want to be part of this, turn up for training on Tuesday evening. Forget this stuff that is being spoken about you and Pat Reynolds. You know it's nonsense. I know it's nonsense.' Marty duly turned up for training. I rang Colm Coyle in Chicago and cleared the air with him also. He had been so disgusted with that day in Charlestown but had not said anything to his colleagues. Coyler would ultimately return too, although the lads were more accepting of Marty's return than of Colm's.

The team was beginning to fall into place.

CHAPTER FIFTEEN

1987 and All That

Laois were our opponents in the first round of the Leinster championship. Of course this bought back memories of 1985 and the possibility of revenge! We started slowly but picked up in the second half and ran out winners: 1-11 to 2-5. Victory came at a price, however. Both Colm O'Rourke and Kevin Foley went off with shoulder injuries, joining Padraig Lyons on the injured list. On the positive side, Joe Cassells made his debut at centre-half forward and played well. Another piece of the jigsaw was in place. And Brian Stafford put over seven points. When we played Kildare in the Semi-Final we scored fifteen points – Brian Stafford scored ten. My instinct and Ollie Campbell's coaching were bearing fruit. On to the Leinster Final and once more the Dubs stood between us and glory.

Meath-Dublin matches are tough matches and this one would be no exception – but it was a terrific contest. Thankfully, O'Rourke and Foley were fit again. During the Semi-Final against Kildare, Colm was pacing the sideline hoping to play, but Marty O'Connell replaced him. And it was in the final that Marty finally got the left half-back position that he put his stamp on. Mattie McCabe replaced Joe Cassells (due to a hamstring injury), and duly supplied his customary goal against

Dublin with an extra couple of points for good measure. A successful manager needs fifteen great players as well as six or seven good substitutes, especially now when five subs are allowed. In 1987 there was serious competition for places and only three subs permitted, and there was an imposing list of subs all eager to play. Mattie was waiting in the wings. Terry Ferguson and Kevin Foley were being challenged by their respective brothers Barry and Frank. Finian Murtagh was fighting hard for his place and proved his worth in the Leinster Final by coming on for David Beggy and scoring two points.

Kevin Foley was the new kid on the block that year. He was working as a vet in Wexford and would not have been that well known inside Meath, let alone outside the county. He was as tough as nails, wiry and much taller than he appeared on the field. With his unruly mop of hair he looked like Mario Kempes of Argentina (where, ironically, Kevin's father had been born). Kevin was a fearless grafter who never sought the limelight, who let the ball do the work with great lay-offs to his midfielders. At right half-back he was the perfect complement to Bobby O'Malley behind him and Liam Harnan on his left. He got caught up in the white heat of that battle, resulting in himself and Charlie Redmond being sent to the line, but Kevin Foley had arrived. Another major part of the jigsaw was in place, and for the second year in a row we triumphed over the Dubs.

That year Derry were our opponents in the All-Ireland Semi-Final. Colm Coyle returned from Chicago to strengthen our squad. On the basis of his Leinster Final performance, Mattie McCabe would get the nod over Joe Cassells. It is said that Joe went very quiet for a couple of weeks, then put his head down and got on with life. Fate, however, intervened. On the Tuesday before the Derry match, Mattie looked a bit off the pace in training. A trip to the hospital revealed that he'd been playing with a broken leg. This meant that Big Joe was back in the team. Mattie admitted that he remembered getting a knock, but he so much wanted to play that he was prepared to go through the pain barrier.

In the event we had a comfortable win over Derry by 0-15 to 0-8. Dermot McNicholl was the Derry player to look out for, and he went on to become one of the best footballers of his time. Holding him in check was the key to our success – Kevin Foley did the job brilliantly. We were nearing the top of the mountain. After a gap of seventeen years in the wilderness, Meath were in an All-Ireland Final. It was a wonderful feeling. We were going to play against Cork, the new kings of Munster.

This was a totally new experience for us. The game had changed considerably since Meath's last All-Ireland Final experience. So too had the media's approach to the game. There was much more intense and in-depth coverage of the games. The national newspapers – together with RTÉ – each had their own Gaelic Games correspondents: Mick Dunne for RTÉ, Donal Carroll for the *Irish Independent*, Peadar O'Brien for the *Irish Press*, Paddy Downey for *The Irish Times* and Jim O'Sullivan for the *Examiner*. All of these correspondents along with the local press had to be accommodated for interviews and features. At the same time it was important to prevent the lads from getting caught up in the hype and from over-involvement with the supporters. Training went on in Dalgan Park where hundreds of supporters, especially children, would turn up nightly. I thought: let the supporters have their fun. It was important for us to concentrate on the training and then relax in Bellinter – our haven.

One of the most important aspects of our preparation was to go through Eamonn O'Farrell's videos of our games to date and then analyse and assess the Cork team. How would we cope with the likes of Larry Tompkins, their chief scoretaker, and with Shay Fahy and Teddy McCarthy, their strong midfielders? We talked about absorbing pressure and, while watching your opponent, not to lose sight of what you do yourself. We reflected on the lessons of Kerry in 1986 – the need to hold concentration and not to panic. We needed to be a seven-point better team.

The concept of a press night in Dalgan was much more sensible than the old haphazard approach. Our press night went well. We instilled in the players that they talk about football and nothing else. They were not diplomats or public relations officers or anything else. This had nothing to do with what you work at, where you live, or your family. You were a Meath footballer and that is what you would talk about. It was important for the players to be happy and at ease in dealing with the media. This would be a big help to them in their own lives afterwards, for example, in handling job interviews.

Outside of that there was a whole carnival going on and the players would have to remove themselves from that. Flags and bunting were displayed across the county. Everyone was delighted to be in the final. Special songs were composed and sung. An Post brought out a special postcard to wish Meath well. Seven and a half thousand cards were sent – it was an extraordinary outpouring of goodwill. But for the players, winning the Sam Maguire Cup was all that mattered.

The organisation and preparation for the All-Ireland Final is massive. It is the sum total of all the little things that is important. Nothing can be left to chance.

We were fortunate to be given complimentary playing gear. Through a contact of Bernard Flynn we managed to get wet-gear for training in bad weather. On one night when the rain was lashing down, Jinksy Beggy turned up in a vest and light togs. He had forgotten the wet-gear. Two days later I met him strolling down Grafton Street in brilliant sunshine – in the wet-gear! It was as if it was too good to wear in training, but it was a badge of identity that Jinksy was proud to wear in public.

At an early stage, Fintan Ginnity and Liam Creavin called to my home one night on their way home from Croke Park. It was approaching midnight. My mother made tea for us all and we sat down to plan our approach for the big day. We decided that we would sort out the players' tickets so that they wouldn't be distracted by trying to source them, as they had been the previous year.We discussed what outfits the players would wear and the timetable for the All-Ireland Final day. Playing the match was the all-important thing for the players – we had to sort out everything else for them. I spoke with Kevin Heffernan. 'Heffo' had been down this road so often with Dublin. It was my first time to experience this stage of the games and, while Pat Reynolds and Tony Brennan had been there, it was twenty years before and the world had changed greatly in that time. Heffo's advice was simple and direct: Take the pressure off the players. Croke Park will tell you what you can and cannot do on the day. Agree with everybody and then do what you think is right yourself.

The scene was set for our greatest day ...

CHAPTER SIXTEEN

Final Day

All-Ireland Final day is an exceptional day in the Irish calendar. It is unique. There is drama. There is history. There is pageantry. Everybody wants to be a part of it. Emigrants and Irish people working abroad have a special link with home that day. Phone calls, texts and emails come from all over the world. Everyone is united in the excitement and the importance of savouring this very special day.

As a manager, you wake on that Sunday morning wondering if the lads are okay. Have they slept well? Are they worrying too much about today? Are you worrying too much? You could worry a hole in a pot, so that by the time we all meet up you are partly shell-shocked, especially when this is your first experience of Final day.

The arrangements went literally like clockwork:

- Assemble at the Grand Hotel, Malahide, at 10.30 in the morning.
- Go for a walk along the beach before having a light lunch.
- Check into the rooms and change into the official outfits.
- Pose in the grounds for a team photograph.
- Then head off in the team coach with a garda motorcycle escort.

- Arrive at Croke Park at 1.30pm.
- A brief look at the minor match to gauge weather and pitch conditions.
- Change in the dressing room.

There is a popular conception that before releasing the players out onto the pitch, the manager is almost literally going through the roof in motivating his team, roaring and ranting, possibly breaking the leg off a chair to make a point! The reality is much different. I said a few words of encouragement and Mick Lyons, as captain, did the same. That was it. All the talking had been done in those nights in Dalgan and Bellinter. All I could do now was hope that the things we talked about had registered with the players and that when the pressure came on (as it inevitably would) they would react to it in the right way. Half of the training I had done with these lads was to help them absorb the tension of this day. They had planned their whole life about this day. They had trained with a fierce intensity. Some of the training matches were much tougher than the actual championship matches, with tempers occasionally flaring among colleagues. They had done it all. Now was the time to give their all. When the referee threw in the ball I would be living every single moment of those seventy minutes.

On the day of the All-Ireland, one of the most frustrating things from my point of view was the dug-out. In those days you spent most of your time in a cramped dug-out, seeing only a forest of legs in front of you, whereas almost everyone else in the stadium has a better view than you as manager. Our line-up was the same as for the Semi-Final. Mattie McCabe had lost out. Colm Coyle was on the substitutes bench. We got off to a slow start and found ourselves five points down after twenty minutes. It could have been worse, were it not for Mick Lyons's full-length block on Jimmy Kerrigan. We did not panic and slowly worked our way back into the game, aided by Colm

O'Rourke's fisted goal. By half-time we had moved into a one-point lead. I could not have been in a worse place to try and assess a game – in the dug-out. The supporters, of course, can see it all and won't be slow in giving you their assessment of the game. As far as they are concerned, they have paid the money and now they call the tune. They want only one result – their team to win – but of course they can't know that one player is shaking off a 'flu or another is troubled by a kick on the calf muscle. No, if only they could get down to that dug-out they would sort out all the problems in no time at all.

We had got a grip over Cork at centre-field and with Larry Tompkins off-form with his shooting and our 'ace' Brian Stafford very much on form (seven points, four from play) we moved into a commanding lead and won by six points: 1-14 to 0-11. The sight of Mick Lyons lifting the Sam Maguire Cup triggered unbridled joy for Meath people everywhere. It was the break-up of the old regime of Dublin, Offaly and Kerry (who would imagine that after their victory in 1986 it would take Kerry eleven years to reappear in an All-Ireland Final?). We were the new kids on the block, but it had been a long, hard road and we had beaten a powerful Cork team who would suffer a second All-Ireland defeat before coming back to win two titles in a row. I was so thrilled to see great players like Colm O'Rourke, Joe Cassells and Mick Lyons finally get their reward after years of toil and frustration and a fellow like Bobby O'Malley come back from serious injury and go on to become one of the great corner-backs of the game. Then there were the exciting new boys like Kevin, PJ and Jinksy for whom nothing could equal winning an All-Ireland medal.

For me personally, there was relief and satisfaction to an extraordinary degree. I had never for a moment doubted my ability to bring this bunch of lads to the top. I might not be able to do it by myself, but with the help of Pat Reynolds, Tony Brennan and the back-up team, I knew we could do it. And what a back-up team: Jack Finn, our doctor;

Anne Bourton, our physiotherapist; 'Mockie' Regan, our masseur; Mick McAuley, our gearman and 'Scubs' Whyte, our driver. Paul Byrne, son of the legendary Frankie, was our goalkeeping coach, and Kevin Hourihane, a PE teacher in St Patrick's College, Navan (and ironically a Cork man!) worked on the players' fitness levels. They had all played their parts in getting all the details right.

When that final whistle blew, the energy seemed to drain out of me. I could not speak. It was all nearly too much for me, as the reality set in. The reality was that the fans were going crazy – and rightly so. Twenty years was a long wait – so many of them had not even been born in 1967! It was great that the torch had been passed on and that we would no longer be living in the shadows of the 'good old days' and former 'greats' like Jack Quinn or Peter McDermott. A whole new generation would welcome Sam Maguire on his tour of town squares, village halls and schoolyards. Above all, I was thrilled for the lads – the entire panel plus the extra players who had come in for those intense training matches. I had never experienced the thrill of winning an All-Ireland medal, so I could only surmise at the joy they were feeling at 5.00pm on Sunday, 20 September 1987. It was a great, great reward for them, and a great, great day for Meath.

There were others who had contributed to that joyous day. I thought of Tommy Reilly, an old and valued friend, who had been associated with the great Walterstown teams of the seventies. His father had passed away only weeks previously. I had asked Tommy if he would help us out with fundraising for a holiday for the players. These were pre-sponsorship days. Neither the county board nor the players could be involved. Tommy formed a committee with people like Gerry Harrington, Tom Ryan and Jacksie Kiernan and they organised a huge Joe Dolan concert. While the board was not involved, it lent its name to the venture and it received the first ten thousand pounds earned. There is almost a book in that venture alone. The concert was a great success and the players' holiday was guaranteed. We also needed spending money for the players as these were difficult economic times and money was scarce. Denis Smyth of Toyota Ireland had been a great supporter of ours through thick and thin. He was able to provide cars to us at cost price, which were then raffled. The proceeds provided the lads with spending money on their holiday. They had earned it.

The whole sponsorship thing had always been a thorny issue. Even back in 1984, when we reached the Centenary Cup final, it raised its head. Puma (based in Ashbourne) offered us football boots. The grand old man of Meath football, Mattie Gilsenan, was sent to talk to me about the offer. 'Mattie,' I said, 'you have been involved with the game all your life and never sought anything out of it, apart from the satisfaction of winning. In my own tinpot way, I have been involved with hurling and football all my life and I don't want anything out of it either. But if someone is going to give us a present of a set of football boots I would be very grateful indeed!' 'Dammit,' said Mattie, 'I never thought of it like that!' That was the end of that little problem.

When sponsorship did become official, Kepak were a wonderful support to us for fourteen years, thanks to Noel Keating, but Tommy Reilly and his committee, and latterly Shane McEntee, continued to raise funds. The generosity of Meath people has never ceased to amaze me and it was something I hoped we would never abuse. This allowed and encouraged the players to be good ambassadors. In all our travels, on holiday trips and All-Star tours, they were always exemplary, never giving an ounce of trouble. People wrote and spoke to me about that. It was a fantastic tribute to the players, their families, their clubs and most of all their county. How proud I was to be part of all that, but I would still love to have played and won in an All-Ireland Final!

The Meath 'family' also extends far beyond the county boundary.

This was brought home to me forcibly the following year when I was the guest of honour at the Meath Association Dinner in New York – or rather, I was one of the guests of honour. The other – and probably more welcome one – was Sam Maguire. On the flight over, Sam travelled in style in first class, while I was down at the back of the plane. Coming through customs with Sam at JFK Airport, I was confronted by a little lady in a blue gaberdine, standing with hands on hips, eyeing me curiously.

She: Where are you goin' with *that*?

Me: To a dinner in New York.

She: You bringin' it in or out?

Me: In today, out tomorrow (we were playing Dublin in the National League first round two days later).

She: What's that thing worth?

Me: Thirty-three thousand pounds – sterling.

She: And you're carryin' it about like that?

She proceeded to give me a lecture on how stupid I was and attracted a crowd of about one hundred people who wanted to be photographed with a replica of the Ardagh Chalice, even though they hadn't a clue what it represented! I was almost late for the dinner but I got a tremendous welcome. I was overwhelmed by the reaction of the 'expats'. They had travelled from all over, just to meet Sam – and me. Fr Joe Foley, who said Grace, came from Chicago. I met six young lads from Dunboyne, none of whom had a US visa. They were looking over their shoulders all the time, but they were also looking for a *Meath Chronicle* or a *Meath Weekender* – any bit of contact with home. The occasion was hugely significant for all present and it was truly amazing and moving for me to experience it. Before I left New York I was asked to visit a man who was very ill with cancer. He had been a substitute on the 1943-44 Roscommon team, so naturally I brought Sam with me. I could almost see the energy pouring into that man. Putting his hand on Sam meant so much to him.Of course Gaelic Football is only a game, but it's a culture too, a way of life. It's what we are.

CHAPTER SEVENTEEN

Mister Kepak

When Noel Keating left his native Kilrush in County Clare at the age of sixteen with his butcher's knife on the back of his bike to ply his trade in Dublin, it was the beginning of a career that would ultimately make him one of the most successful meat-exporters in Ireland. It began with a butcher's shop in Francis Street in Dublin and culminated with Kepak Meats, with plants in counties Meath, Carlow and Roscommon. It was no overnight success story, however. Noel had big ideas and loved a challenge, but he struggled in the early years when he experienced huge difficulties in getting a meat-exporting licence. A large part of his success was due to his wife Marie, who had a great business brain. She was the perfect complement to Noel. He had the vision but it needed the two of them for things to happen. And they did happen when Noel and Marie bought a farm in the middle of the Kilbride-Ratoath-Dunboyne triangle in north-east Meath. Noel had bought his first cattle from the Quinn brothers, Martin, Gerry and Jack (of an earlier Meath footballing dynasty), and I got to know him through that connection from a long way back.

Noel was always passionate about sport and while he was ever a proud Clareman he would also be a regular supporter at Meath matches. When we made the big breakthrough in 1987 and reached the All-Ireland Final for the first time in seventeen years, I considered the situation. Win or lose, there would be a big reception for the team. This would be the scenario. There would be a banquet for the team in Dublin on the night of the match. Next day there would be a lunch for both winners and losers and then we would head for Navan via Clonee (the 'border' with Dublin), Dunboyne, Summerhill (home of our captain, Mick Lyons), and Trim, a journey that would take at least five hours. The lads would have played a tough match, would hardly have hit the bed at all that night (especially if we won) and would be physically exhausted and emotionally drained by the time they got on that bus. They would need a stop-off point to relax and get some 'soakage' into them. I went to see Noel Keating.

I knew Noel well enough to be able to approach him with an open heart. I put the question to him simply. On our way home, would there be any chance of stopping at the factory in Clonee in order to use their facilities and have a cup of tea or whatever? The response was equally simple and direct: 'No problem, Seán. Leave it to me!' The rest is history. We won the All-Ireland Final. The county went bananas and we certainly needed a stop-off in Clonee. When we arrived over the border in Clonee, there were thousands of delirious fans to greet us. When the bus pulled into the Kepak plant there was a band there to meet us – and a bull, painted in the Meath colours. There was a barbecue for five thousand people. The party was just beginning. Noel had organised a reception in the factory for the team. They were taken upstairs and wined and dined in style. Eventually we got back on the bus, refreshed for the Royal Tour, but Noel Keating had made his mark with Meath football. From that day on, he and the players were like peas in a pod and, on a personal level, his relationship with me had reached a new height.

Where Meath football was concerned, Noel hardly ever missed a

match, whether championship or challenge. He helped us out gener-
ously with whatever needed to be done to further the team's progress,
ultimately to the point of putting a helicopter at our disposal to collect
players like Kevin Foley, who was working in Cork. Team sponsorship came in officially in 1991, but long before that Noel Keating was
an unofficial sponsor to the players – not to the county board, as they
were bound by strict rules and regulations. If a player needed help
with raising a mortgage or getting an interview for a job, Noel was
there for him. The old adage was true of him: 'If you want to get something done, ask a busy man.' Even though he was a close friend and
confidant of mine, he would never ask me about the innermost details
of what was happening with the team. He would never cross that line
or expect me to cross it. That is the way he was and I loved that about
him.

When team sponsorship became officially accepted in 1991, I
approached the county board and said: 'If I ask Noel for sponsorship,
he would not say no! We should give him first option.' Unfortunately
that did not happen and controversy ensued. I was told on the Thursday night before our first-round match with Dublin that another
sponsor had been found. I was very unhappy, considering how generous Noel had been to us for years, but I said to our captain, Liam
Hayes: 'We have a match to win. Let's not get caught up in this.' The
match was drawn, with the replay fixed for the following week – it
was the beginning of an epic battle. The sponsorship still had not
come through. Then after the second match (another draw, after extra
time), I vented my displeasure with the sponsorship mess to the
county board. I knew Noel was terribly upset at having been passed
over and was being derided, in some quarters, as a result. There was a
two-week gap between the second and third matches with Dublin, so I
decided to go down south with Tina for a few days to get away from
all the hassle. (We had married the previous December and the

following months seemed to have been taken up morning, noon and night with training for that crucial first-round clash with Dublin. As a result, Tina saw little of her new husband.) Noel came into me on the Thursday and asked what I was up to. I told him we were heading for Bunratty in Clare and from there on to Kerry. 'I'll come with ye,' he said. And he did. We stayed in his mother's house in Kilrush, and had a great time there on the Saturday before travelling across to Kerry on the Killimer ferry, accompanied, of course, by Noel. The big news came through that the county board had sorted the sponsorship issue and Kepak were the official sponsors of Meath football. Noel was delighted as he was dealing with an awful lot of Meath farmers. Even more importantly, the players were now happy. They had wanted Noel on board all along. The sponsorship flourished from there. Noel became an integral part of our set-up and played a huge role in fund-raising. Noel was just a part of the team, he came on holidays with the team to Fort Lauderdale in Florida and became very close to the lads.

After that second match with Dublin in June 1991, the county board asked if I wanted to take the team away for a break. I declined, but when we drew for a third time the offer was repeated. I canvassed the lads for their opinions – and also their wives, as most of the team were married. The saga had gathered such momentum at this stage that everyone was going to the matches, so it was important to hear the partners' views also. All the partners were of one mind: whatever needs to be done, do it. Again, we had a two-week break before the fourth match. David Beggy had returned to his work in Scotland on the Sunday night. I followed him to scout around for a suitable location for the break. I needed Noel Keating's advice. He was in a meeting with Michael O'Kennedy, the Minister for Agriculture, when an urgent phone-call came through to say that Mr Keating was needed in Scotland on very urgent business. He joined me at Dublin airport and we flew to Glasgow. Jinksy picked us up in his GT Escort. I could see that Noel was nervous on the road. He was used to a larger executive car and, of course, whether on the playing-field or the road, Jinksy knew only one way to travel – VERY FAST. We survived the experience and looked at a few locations, before ending up near Loch Lomond at a place called Drymon, probably best-known for being Billy Connolly's birthplace. We visited the Buchanan Arms hotel and instantly knew that this was what we had been looking for – scenic location and good sporting facilities including nice small pitches. I returned and put the proposal to the county board. They approved it with the added bonus that partners could come too. This was only proper because those women had contributed hugely to the team's success so far. It was a major logistical problem getting them all out there and it cost a small fortune, but then we were lucky to have a generous sponsor, who also came with us to Drymon. We had dinner on Friday night and trained very hard on Saturday before enjoying a variety of activities: golf, touring, clay-pigeon-shooting, archery. That evening the priest in the tiny local church was almost overwhelmed by the size of his congregation at Mass. After dinner that night the team and mentors watched and analysed videos of the previous matches with Dublin, while Freddie Bourton, husband of our physiotherapist, Anne, entertained the women with a series of charades. Then on Sunday morning we went out on the training-pitch and practised solidly at that sweeping team-move that would ultimately cause Dublin's downfall six days later.

The weekend in Scotland was ground-breaking and absolutely vital for us. After three matches with two periods of extra-time both Meath and Dublin knew everything about each other. There was no escape from the mounting tension and hype at home, so it was crucial to get away. Even more crucial was Noel Keating's support; he agreed to match every pound that the county board raised. I never got involved in fundraising or sponsorship at all. It simply wasn't my job, but from day one I stipulated that for every fifty pence of fundraising that went to the county board, fifty pence would also go to the team fund to be used for what was needed at the discretion of the team management. Ironically, when the Beef Tribunal was set up to investigate beef-export practices, it moved in on the meat factories and one of the first things the Revenue Commissioners asked to see were the Meath Team accounts ... So it was just as well we were not doing anything underhand.

And then on Sunday, 18 April 1993, Noel Keating collapsed and died suddenly, at the age of fifty-three. It was quite simply a major explosion that turned all our lives upside down: my own personal life, that of our team and supporters, his loyal and devoted employees, his friends and his family. I think of men like Paddy Fennor and Brendan McDonagh who had been with him since the Francis Street days, his friends from County Clare – many of whom were in Croke Park that day supporting the Banner County – but most of all his wife, Marie, and their four young children. You would have taken a lease on his life – he was as fit a man as you could meet. But suddenly the big tree was down and its crashing fall echoed across the Royal County and beyond.

I remember that week so clearly. The previous Monday, Easter Monday, Noel had arrived in our house with his friend Joe. Noel was godfather to our eldest child Seán and to mark Seán's first birthday he planted a tree at the end of our garden – with a ceremonial tree-planting spade previously used by President Mary Robinson, which Noel had bought at an auction. He was that kind of man. He was in and out of our place all week, combining Fairyhouse races with a series of business meetings. One of those meetings was with a French sheep-importer, Jan Mackay. Noel and Jan travelled to Hackettstown by helicopter to finalise the deal, but were forced to land in a farmer's yard somewhere in Carlow, because of fog. They duly closed the deal in the farmer's yard. On Saturday Noel was due to go racing in England but decided not to, as he felt a touch of 'flu coming on.

I went to eight o'clock Mass on the Sunday morning and called in to his house afterwards, as I regularly did. On arriving there I discovered that Noel had had 'a turn'. We tried everything to revive him, to no avail. Noel was gone. I carried my friend down the stairs in my arms to the ambulance-men. Noel was one of the finest men it was my privilege to know, larger than life, a noble man, a soulmate. I recalled him taking me aside a few days before I married Tina. He put his arms around my shoulders and told me how delighted he was for me and spoke warmly of the importance of family. Noel's mother had died suddenly in his arms at the Galway races the previous autumn. It had a devastating effect on him and I don't think he had ever got over it.

Noel Keating's greatness is in the way he is remembered. Each year there is an anniversary Mass in Kepak for Noel and each year his friends and colleagues turn up to remember him. On the first day that it became official to put the name Kepak on the Meath jersey, our captain, Liam Hayes, stood up and said he was proud to wear the Meath jersey and honoured to have the Kepak name on it. He was speaking for the entire team. Noel was as proud as punch but he liked winners too. He loved the ethic in the Meath team, the willingness to give your all. He was also incredibly proud of his Clare roots and when John Maughan made the breakthrough for Clare football in 1992 by leading them to a Munster title, Noel did not see Clare wanting either. Once when Clare played Meath he wore a Clare jersey to the front and a Meath jersey at the back.

Noel was good for us and we were good for him. It was wonderful that Kepak directors Liam McGreal and John Horgan continued to support Meath football, as did Noel's family. I met them all a week after Noel's death and they assured me that they would continue the sponsorship. And so it happened – Kepak, the family firm supporting the Royal County through good times and bad. The amazing thing was that Kepak had absolutely nothing to gain from sponsorship as it was a totally export-oriented business.

Meath football owes a great deal to Noel Keating. So do the charities he so unobtrusively helped. And especially – on a career and personal level – so do I.

CHAPTER EIGHTEEN

1988

1988 was a fantastic year for us: National League glory, an All-Stars trip to the US and a long championship campaign culminating in All-Ireland glory – and, of course, controversy. Most of all it was a long footballing year that put huge demands on amateur players, but they rose to the challenge magnificently. We came through a tough winter league campaign, drawing with Dublin and Derry, and beating Armagh and Kerry. The Armagh match was notorious for Colm O'Rourke's sending-off, thereby depriving him of an All-Star award for 1987. The Meath supporters were incensed at the referee – the former Sligo 'great', Mickey Kearns – and would not let him leave the field. I had to persuade some of our players to go back onto the field and accompany Mickey off it. We did this with some difficulty. It was not a pleasant experience on a freezing December afternoon in Kells.

Despite all that, we had a good League campaign. In the spring of 1988 we beat Cork and Mayo, and lost to Monaghan. We had more or less the same squad that had won the All-Ireland in 1987. We introduced a young wing half-forward in the Dublin match – eighteen-year-old Brendan Reilly from Dunboyne. Brendan would go on to serve his county well as attacker and defender over the next ten years.

He was part of the continuity you need in a team. No team can become a private members' club. It is more like a family and will have squabbles like any family, but because it is family, you get on with life and surmount differences. If it was any other way you would never speak to one another!

We scraped past Down to reach the National League Final. Once again Dublin were our opponents. We seemed to have lost it to a Mick Galvin goal, then seemed to have won it with four successive points only to have it drawn by a last-minute point by Joe McNally. Another Meath-Dublin draw. The replay had to be postponed for five weeks to accommodate the All-Stars trip to the USA – two matches in Boston and an extra one in San Francisco. Unfortunately, we had three major defections for that trip. Trish O'Rourke was expecting a baby so Colm stayed at home. Gerry McEntee's work requirements ruled him out and Liam Hayes was getting married, although he would join us for the San Francisco match. It was a tragedy that three of our greatest players who had been so much part of our success in 1987 could not be part of this tour also. As it would transpire, they would not be rewarded for their brilliant 1988 campaign either; it has been one of my great regrets that this was so because that trio were the ones that largely made it happen.

Prior to the trip I spoke with our captain, Mick Lyons, about its importance and the dilemma we faced in having to replay the League Final within days of our return. Mick spoke to the team: 'We had our holidays in January, this is a football tour and we'll train everyday if Seánie says so. And we'll have a good time as well', and they agreed to my training schedule. I remember the late Mick Dunne, RTÉ's Gaelic Games correspondent, expressing disbelief in his reports from the tour – for the first time in the history of the All-Stars, players were actually training. My attitude was that if people were paying to bring us to the US, the least we could do was to show respect and train. As a result, Fr Seán Hegarty, the All-Stars manager, got his fellows training also. Some of the latter were saying that the Meath boys had gone mad. We hadn't, we were just a football team, and while of course there were banquets and receptions galore, there was football to be played.

The extra match in San Francisco gave everyone the chance to play, because even on those trips only three substitutes were allowed. We even gave our reserve goalkeeper Donal Smyth a run at full-forward in Boston. These were not just exhibition games. The All-Stars wanted to win just as much as we did, and with great players like Mick Kennedy and Ciaran Duff of Dublin, and Larry Tompkins of Cork facing us, you can be sure they were competitive matches. The All-Stars duly won the series, but they were great games and drew large crowds. We met a gang of Meath supporters including Tom Holton and John Horgan, who drove non-stop from Toronto to Boston for fourteen hours, just to shout on the lads. It meant so much to them, and equally it meant an awful lot to us. Tom Holton was on the same Meath minor team as myself. Tom kindly took the whole team out for a meal afterwards. Little did we realise that this was the start of an epic year for us.

The League Final replay against Dublin was a powerful game. It was probably our best display of that whole period. Despite having Kevin Foley sent off early after a fracas, we were in control throughout. Liam Hayes ran twenty yards through the Dublin defence and hit a wonder goal, one of the best I have seen in Croke Park. We won: 2-13 to 0-11. Brendan Reilly scored the second goal. Continuity! We were National League champions, but it was already late May and two weeks later we would begin our defence of the Leinster title against Louth. As All-Ireland and League champions we were up there to be knocked down. Suddenly we were becoming cheeky – beating Dublin most of the time.

We got past Louth in the opening match in Drogheda rather easily:

3-13 to 0-9. A good start – but in the next round against Offaly we took a while to get going. We were down by four points at half-time but outscored Offaly by fifteen points to two in the second half. The inside line were brilliant, racking up sixteen points between them. Once again it was a Meath-Dublin final, for the third year in a row. We had a major problem when Brian Stafford was ruled out through injury – it was a huge loss. PJ Gillic would be our free-taker. I spoke with PJ and Mattie McCabe beforehand. 'Goals win matches, lads. You had better get them early!' And that is exactly what happened. We scored two goals in the first quarter-hour, courtesy of the two lads. Colm Coyle took his chance well when he came in for Stafford. After such a brilliant start we nearly let it slip and were relieved when Charlie Redmond ballooned a penalty over the bar in the very last minute: Meath 2-5, Dublin 0-9. Another intense uncompromising battle, but given the strong personnel on both sides, you would expect nothing less.

'Staff' was back for the Semi-Final against Mayo and contributed nine of our sixteen points. For the first forty-five minutes we were coasting. Mayo only managed two points in that period but then, in the space of a few minutes, they scored two goals and had a third disallowed. We survived to win by five points. What caused the lapse is not clear, but there had been an upsetting incident when PJ Gillic's father, Aiden, was taken ill in the stand and removed to our dressing room. People were very upset at half-time which was then only a ten-minute break. Aidan Gillic was eventually moved to the minors' dressing room, but there is no doubt that our lads temporarily lost their focus in the second half. And so, for the second year in a row, it was a Meath-Cork showdown.

Cork got the perfect start, an early goal from Teddy McCarthy, and were generally on top. It is a mystery how they did not win but we stayed with them and actually led by a point at half-time. It was a dour struggle from there on and Cork seemed to have won it in the last minute with a Larry Tompkins point – his eighth point in a masterly display. But we had a master at the other end too. The ball was kicked out and from a sideline free, Jinksy grabbed the ball and went down in a tumble of arms and legs. A free in. The debate still rages over the merits of that free and as the years go by, the folklore grows. Jinksy had won the ball and the free, but it still had to be converted – a free in the last seconds of an All-Ireland Final to level the scores. It was serious pressure, but Brian Stafford took it in his stride and put the ball over the bar, his eighth point of the game. We had a lifeline and we were absolutely delighted to get a second chance, as we had not played at all well.

On the following morning we assembled in the Grand Hotel, Malahide. We intended to have a proper meeting to analyse our performance but the discussion was self-generating and a lot of people had their say, just to clear the air. The consensus was that we had been pushed around on the day – and that it would not happen again. We would condition ourselves for the replay, which would not take place for three weeks. Because of this long delay, Tommy Reilly suggested we take the players away for a break the weekend before the replay. We went to the Ballymascanlon Hotel outside Dundalk on the Friday night, had a meal and relaxed. On Saturday we trained and again had an evening meal. There was a nightclub in the hotel. I took the lads down to the adjoining lounge after the meal. People who recognised us were teasing us, saying we must have no intention of winning an All-Ireland, but we were just trying to ease tensions and break the sequence of events. And so to bed, but some of the group got 'sidetracked' and found their way into the nightclub, thinking I would know nothing about it ...

On the Sunday morning we had another training session in the Cooley Kickhams GAA ground. Some of the Louth county panel and some of the previous night's 'clubbers' observed us with some fascination. They watched as our lads almost literally took lumps out of one another. Because of the three-week delay, the feeling was that all places were up for grabs, so there was no holding back. The session was played with the same intensity as the replay would be played a week later. We came home and Pat, Tony and I picked the team. There were three changes: Terry Ferguson, Colm Coyle and Joe Cassells were in the starting line-up. The training sessions had shown us who was in form and we made our call as selectors. It was, and always is, a difficult call, but once you made it you could not stand in the middle of the road. In any event this was a terrific bunch of players and their loyalty to the cause of a Meath victory was extraordinary.

The 1988 All-Ireland Final replay will be remembered by some for Gerry McEntee's momentary aberration when after 'a bit of a schemozzle' (as Micheál O'Hehir would say) he gave a slap to Niall Cahalane and was sent off by Tommy Sugrue. In fairness to Gerry, it was very much a spur-of-the-moment thing. There was no premeditation, but he had to go. After the match Niall Cahalane came into the dressing room, put his arms around Gerry and said, 'Sorry, Gerry. I made a meal of it.' We were a man down after only seven minutes. This was going to be an uphill battle.

Joe Cassells was making his first full championship appearance of the year, having been injured when he played in Boston. He was captain of the team and an extraordinary man, who was leading his team in an All-Ireland Final on the eve of his thirty-fourth birthday. During the course of the match a few unusual things happened. Colm O'Rourke kicked a point with his right foot and Joe Cassells kicked one with his left. Bernie Flynn had a glorious League campaign and was 'man of the match' in the League Final replay with a tally of five points. He was so tightly marked during the championship that by his standards he had a poor championship, but everywhere he went he took two markers with him, thus making space for others. I was under pressure to drop him. People were saying Flynn has got too big-headed. I said no. His opponents were all watching him because he is the main man. The great thing about all these matches was that scores would always come from someone else. At one stage in the second half we moved Jinksy into corner-forward and told him to stand on the end-line. He drew the attention of two defenders. Meanwhile, Bernie moved out to half-forward and scored a great point.

Colm O'Rourke's performance showed the greatest display of determination and sheer never-say-die attitude that day. When Gerry McEntee was sent off, PJ Gillic looked at me. I gave him the nod and he moved outfield. Colm looked at me. I gave him the nod and he moved out – all over the field. He played corner-forward, half-forward, cen-trefield, half-back. Colm was doing everyone's job – he was even attempting to do Tommy Sugrue's job as referee. Jack Boothman, chairman of the Leinster council, said to me afterwards that he had never seen a man covering as much ground or playing in so many positions in one match. Colm O'Rourke is an incredibly strong man. He just threw people out of the way as if they were not there. He was like a man possessed. His pal, his buddy from college days, had been sent off and he was going to put things right. It was one of his most incredible displays ever, among his many great days in a Meath shirt.

It was a hard, tough match. We had resolved that we would not be pushed around as in the drawn match, and fourteen men had stuck with that resolve. In the end we survived by a point. The critics were out in force but it was a powerful day for us. In the space of twelve months we had won two All-Ireland titles and a National League. This was a truly mighty achievement by a team that would have been deemed 'no-hopers' just a few years earlier. Our achievement was not only the result of a hardworking team, but also: detailed preparation, the support of the background team (medics, physiotherapist, masseur and the driver), Tommy Reilly and his fundraising team and, of course, the selectors. Those twelve months were a wonderful time for all of us and most of all for the supporters, who were loyal and encouraging from the start.

The homecoming was fantastic. Slowly, what we had done was sinking in to me. When the bus reached Dunboyne it stopped at the bottom of the railway bridge outside my home. My mother was not well at the time and was sitting in the car across the road waiting for us. I went across to throw my arms around her. Right there and then I wanted to stay off the bus and not go an inch further. I never felt so totally drained. This was a new experience for me. The scale of the whole achievement had got to me. I just wanted to go into the house and put my feet up, but of course we had to move on to Dunshaughlin, Navan, Trim. I wanted to be there to share in the euphoria of the crowds who had been starved of success for so long, but I felt I had nothing left in me. My voice was gone but when duty called and I would have to address the crowd, the voice would come back. But at that moment outside my home in Dunboyne I never felt so drained in my entire life. That's what winning an All-Ireland does to you.

CHAPTER NINETEEN

Royals, Rebels and Rows

The repercussions of that Final Replay went on for quite a while. There was severe criticism of the over-physicality of the game and the bad-tempered spirit in which it was played. At the press conference on the day after the match, the President of the GAA, John Dowling, had some harsh words to say about the nature of the match, promising that he would 'deal with it at the appropriate time and place ... ' I had great respect for John Dowling. He was a great GAA man and a great referee who had officiated in both codes. I don't believe there was any malice intended in his words. He would not have wanted to see a player sent off in the showpiece game of the year, particularly during his presidency, but the way things were said and taken up got totally out of hand. Later, when the medals were being presented, some of the lads refused to receive them from him. If we all had our lives to live over again, things might be different to the way they turned out on that night.

There was nothing premeditated about the event. I was late, as I had to attend to someone who was very ill and I thought I would miss the actual presentation. It was a double presentation, as Meath had also won the All-Ireland Junior Football on the same day as the seniors. It was fantastic to see players like John McEnroe, Declan Mullen, Jody Devine and Robbie O'Connell getting recognition for their service to Meath junior football. We decided to hold the presentation in Warrenstown College – an accessible venue open to all our supporters at a reasonable price. The intention was right but it didn't work for some reason, as only a small crowd turned up. Fr Tully, who had coached the 1949 team, was celebrating his Golden Jubilee as a priest and I sought to have him co-present the medals with John Dowling. I felt the GAA President would not take umbrage at this.

I did fear reprisals towards John Dowling because a lot of people had been going on about what he had said about the Final at the post-match reception. Things went out of control and, in the event, Gerry McEntee and Liam Harnan refused to accept their medals from the President. It was unfortunate and unfair to John Dowling, his family and the office of President of the GAA. What happened was not right, but it happened, and there was a lot of remorse about it subsequently.

Maybe we paid the price afterwards. At the GAA annual congress the following Easter, held ironically on 1 April and even more ironically in the Grand Hotel, Malahide, our All-Ireland base, a lot of delegates raised an almighty stink about Meath football and the damage it was doing to the Association's image. On the same day, Mickey McQuillan, Bernie Flynn and myself were in Belfast helping out O'Donovan Rossa's Club which would later go on to win its first senior club title in thirty years. We were there because we were asked. We were there free of charge with no expenses sought or taken. Winning back-to-back All-Irelands had not gone to the lads' heads. They were still prepared to help out clubs like O'Donovan Rossa's. In Dublin the cry was how damaging we were for the Association and here we were in Belfast promoting the same Association. Despite having won the National League and All-Ireland titles in 1988 there were no official trips to reward the lads in 1989. We never got an explanation for this. I was very disappointed for the lads as on the previous All-Star tour they had been exemplary in training for the games and promoting the GAA. If, through a couple of fellows making a decision – be it right or wrong – the entire panel was going to be punished, that was a great pity. It should not have happened.

It would be an understatement to say that after the 1988 Final we were not 'flavour of the month' for many people, or flavour of the year for that matter. Newspaper articles and letters accused us of being cynical and over-physical in our approach to the game. We got little credit for the distance we had come. When we won the Leinster Final in 1986, it was a breakthrough and many people were delighted for us. When we won the All-Ireland in 1987 that was great, but naturally everyone wants to beat the champions. When we repeated the achievement in 1988, it compounded matters. The game is about competing, about winning (not 'at all costs', as some accused us), about how much you want success. A number of our players had been competing for a long time. They may have felt they should have won games – as far back as 1976/77 against Dublin – but they didn't. They had been deemed 'failures'. They had been beaten by four points in the Leinster Final of 1984 and by ten points in the Leinster Semi-Final in 1985. Then suddenly they cracked the code in 1986 and went on to win three Leinster titles in a row – and Leinster is a very competitive province. We went on to win the League and All-Ireland double in 1987/88, repeated the All-Ireland win in 1988 and came back to win the League in 1990. And yet, as one magazine notoriously put it, we were for some people 'the pariahs of Gaelic football.'

Certainly there was an edge between Meath and Cork at that time. In a sense, it was unfortunate that both teams peaked around the same time. Cork went on to prove what a good team they were, winning back-to-back titles in 1989 and 1990. We came back and just failed to win in 1991. You could be fanciful and surmise that either team could have won three, four, even five titles in a row if the other team had not been around. It is also often overlooked that there were great passages of football in those Meath-Cork games. There were powerful skills on display and, yes, at times it was very physical, but Gaelic football is a physical game and you deal with the situation as you meet it.

Meath were described by some people as a 'cynical team'. What do they mean by that? Were we a ruthless, win-at-all-costs outfit? No. Were we a committed and competitive team who yearned for All-Ireland glory? Yes. There are very, very few pretty All-Irelands. The Final is just that one step away from the ultimate reward. There is going to be tension, nervousness, mistakes. Rarely will you see a Final reported as a 'wonderful game'. Invariably there are unexpected heroes on Final Day. Big-name players are tightly marked or have an off-day and lesser players shine. We came into the 1988 Final as All-Ireland and League champions. Everything was known about us. We were up there to be knocked down. We had given a wonderful display in the League Final against Dublin – hardly the mark of a 'cynical' team. We had a panel of good footballers who certainly would not pull back from any challenge, but there was no one who played against them who was not able to get up and go to work the next day. Everybody likes to be liked and it is a hard fact of life that when you are champions, everyone wants to beat you and many want to take you down a peg. For all that, we did get credit in places where we would not have expected it. Again it was said that from 1986 on we never met Kerry (and were accordingly supposed to be a lesser team) but the fact is that Kerry were not around. Cork were Kings of Munster at that time.

Looking back, I wished then that people would realise what a good team Meath were. We had some marvellous footballers in that squad – some were gifted ball-players, others were more traditional and tenacious, all of them committed to the cause of Meath football. Most of them won All-Star awards. The game we played was a very simple one. We played to our strengths – always had players available to take the ball, pass it to get out of trouble and then put it into the forward line, because we had as good an inside forward line as ever played the game. Outside of that line you had another gifted line – PJ Gillic, a young man of great strength who could deliver a sixty-metre pass with deadly accuracy with either foot; Jinksy Beggy, always guaranteed to do the unexpected, and Joe Cassells, the wise and experienced general. We had two big and stylish midfielders in Gerry McEntee and Liam Hayes, and when Gerry dropped back in defence, Joe Cassells went centrefield. It was very simple football.

At wing half-back, Marty O'Connell had every skill you would want in the game. It took him a while to find his true role, but in his days as a forward he would have experienced some of the treatment our forwards were receiving from opposing defences. On the other wing Kevin Foley was as tenacious as they come and in the middle was Liam Harnan, a traditional 'stopper' centre-half, but a brilliant footballer and an incredible passer of the ball. He might not have had lightning pace, but he knew where the ball was going to be and there would be no easy passage around him. If you look at the half-back line of the great Kerry team of the seventies – Páidí Ó Sé, Tim Kennelly (RIP) and Jimmy Deenihan – there were no wilting flowers there! They were tough men who had steel in them. Our full-back, Mick Lyons, was in the same mould – traditional and resolute. Bobbie O'Malley was one of the great corner-backs and on the left flank few forwards had an easy game against the long-armed Terry Ferguson. Behind them all in the last line of defence, Mickey McQuillan was brave and consistent.

At that time every free and sideline ball was kicked from the ground so there was a lot of man-to-man marking. Our way of counteracting that was to create space through players taking up different positions. That became our strength and we played to it. For years I had seen Colm O'Rourke with markers in front of and behind him and then he was accused of 'inviting the foul'. Such nonsense. For such a big, strong man what Colm achieved was incredible, but he suffered a lot of defeats before he ever knew victory. And no one savoured the successes of 1987 and 1988 more, especially in 1988 when his long-time pal was sent off. It is also suggested that Meath were the original insti- gators of the 'blanket defence' that has become part of modern football. It was not blanket defence, it was just being available. You had worked hard enough to win the ball; there was no point in raffling it!

The intensity of those Meath-Dublin championship matches was ferocious. If Dublin won, that was fine. If Meath won, that was fine. Once it was over, it was over. It might not have been pretty for some people, but it was still admired by many others and it ultimately brought success. In the twenty years before 1987, only a handful of teams – Dublin, Kerry, Cork, Offaly, Down – had won All-Ireland titles. When we made the breakthrough, teams like Cork, Down, Donegal and Derry followed. Suddenly it became possible for a wider range of counties to win. It was not 'win at all costs'. The game was there. You had your chance. If you were beaten, your chance would come around again, if you were good enough and committed enough. Our lads had to create their own tradition. On the very first night I met with them I told them to forget 1949, '54 and '67. They had to blaze their own trail and when we won again in 1996, no one would have been more delighted than the 'oldtimers' of 1987-88. The torch had been passed on. You look forward, not back.

Cork should have won on the first day in 1988, but they didn't. The folklore will grow over the years about Jinksy winning that last- minute free, but it still had to be converted. In truth, both teams had lots of other chances. Then came the replay and all the controversy but there was also great respect between the teams. In 1990 when Cork had their revenge, there was not a bad word from our lads. After the reception on the following day, it was Beggy who started the sing-song: They are the champions, lads. Let's get on with life! In January 1989 both squads ended up in the Canaries for their holidays. Things were awkward for about an hour – until fellows began copping themselves on. Mick Kennedy and Ciaran Duff were there also. Duffer said to the Cork lads: 'If I was you I'd be sitting down with those Meath fellows, finding out what they did to win last year.' Of course, some players were a bit aggravated, but there was nothing to it. We were all glad to be there. There was still a lot of unemployment then. Most of the lads did not have cars. It was very different to now. Only for Tommy Reilly and his fundraisers, we would not have been there at all.

There was fierce rivalry between Meath and Cork but terrific respect also and over the years tragedies and social occasions mellowed us all. Many Meath players travelled to Cork to attend the funerals of Michael McCarthy, the brilliant young forward who had punished us in 1990 and John Kerins the goalkeeper who thwarted us so often over the years. After all – it's only a game ...

CHAPTER TWENTY

Back to Earth

Winning an All-Ireland title definitely changes the life of a player. When we won in 1987 I said to the lads: 'Your lives will never be the same again. You are no longer just footballers – you are medal winners. People know you, will recognise you in the street, and will demand a part of you, whether it be to open a new supermarket or promote a greyhound race ... That is all lovely, but there has to be a cut-off point, so that you can prepare to defend your Leinster and All-Ireland titles.'

Apart from that, winning an All-Ireland title is physically very demanding for amateur players. To remain the last men standing takes a heavy toll and is very draining. And then, when you win the ultimate prize two years in a row, plus winning a National League title in between, together with a demanding All-Stars trip – and both League and All-Ireland finals going to replays – the tank must inevitably be running low. I know our supporters would have been dreaming and talking of 'three in a row', but I would not have been thinking that way at all. At that time the National League began shortly after the All-Ireland Final. In our case, because the All-Ireland replay had taken place in October, we found ourselves facing into the first round of the league against Monaghan just two weeks later. Not surprisingly, we lost and proceeded to lose a whole string of league matches including the one against Dublin, whom we had become so accustomed to beating regularly over the previous two years. Our sole victory in that campaign was against Down. We still had basically the same panel though some of the older warriors opted out for the league. When Mick Lyons broke his leg in 1989, the omens were not good.

We had an easy victory over Louth in the opening round of the 1989 Leinster championship, but there were warning signals in our Semi-Final victory over Offaly. Some great saves by Mickey McQuillan and a vital goal by Colm O'Rourke got us through to the final – once more against Dublin. This time around Dublin manager Gerry McCaul had done his homework and prepared his team very well. Dublin's Tommy Carr, Keith Barr and Eamonn Heery were a tremendous half-back line. They were known for coming forward in attack but this time they stayed back and cut off the supply to our forward line. Liam Harnan replaced Mick Lyons at full-back and we moved Terry Ferguson to centre half-back. Very early in the game Terry went for a ball with Ciarán Duff who gave him the grandest little push in the back on the blind side of the referee. A gap opened up and there was no one better to exploit it than Ciarán. He went straight down the middle, taking seven or eight steps. I can still see Robbie O'Malley screaming at the referee to 'count the steps', but Ciarán kept going and practically tore the net apart with the 'goal of the year'. We got back into it with a by-now trademark Mattie McCabe goal, but our misery was compounded when a Vinny Murphy shot took a deflection off Marty O'Connell for Dublin's second goal. We lost by five points and while we might have considered the origin of Ciarán Duff's goal unfair, you have to see the two sides. Duff and the Dubs had experienced heartbreak in 1986 and 1987. This was their day.

People said I should have 'warmed up' Mick Lyons – run him up and down the line to unsettle the Dubs, but I would not insult Mick by doing that. He himself probably felt he should have played, but they are the choices you make as a selector and you live with them. It was the Dubs' day and hopes of a fourth successive Leinster title and a third All-Ireland in a row were gone. We were back down to earth with a bang!

I suppose most people thought that was the end of that squad, but we had a few surprises left yet. A new 'four quarters' game was introduced experimentally into the 1989-90 National League. We tore into the campaign with victories over Monaghan and Tyrone, racking up six goals and twenty-eight points, then surprisingly lost at home to Louth before beating Wexford and Mayo, racking up another nine goals and twenty-two points. We had a scoring average of three goals and twelve points over five games. And then we travelled to Kiltoom to play Roscommon. It was an absolutely atrocious day. Incessant rain had made a quagmire of both goal areas. Roscommon destroyed us, winning by 1-19 to 0-6. Junior McManus had a brilliant game for Roscommon and gave Marty O'Connell a torrid time. The Roscommon fans teased poor Marty, but the Meath supporters, huddled in the rain, were loyal to the core. 'Go on, Marty,' they yelled. 'Take out your medals and show him!' If that wasn't bad enough, three weeks later we travelled to Casement Park to face Antrim. They put four goals past us and beat us by ten points. The scoring averages were rapidly going in the other direction. We sat in the Casement Park dressing room contemplating our exit from the League, when a lifeline came in the form of news that Roscommon and Tyrone had drawn in their final match on the same day. It meant that we finished in joint second place in division two and the scoring averages had worked in our favour.

We were in a three-way play-off with Mayo and Tyrone, both of whom we beat to reach the quarter-final against Donegal. We had moved the versatile Colm Coyle to centre-half-forward and Colm Brady, an exciting young player from Simonstown, was fitting in well as Liam Hayes's new midfield partner. Donegal got a run at us in Clones and led by six points, entering the final quarter. However, two goals by Jinksy got us back into the game and we ran out winners by five points. We scraped past our great rivals, Cork, in the Semi-Final, thanks largely to Brian Stafford's eight points. We had played eleven matches to reach the League Final and in those eleven matches 'Staff' had scored an incredible six goals and forty-one points. At the other end of the field we replaced Mickey McQuillan in goals with Donal Smyth. We had conceded twelve goals in our League campaign – not all of them were Mickey's fault, but we felt Donal deserved his turn. Down were our opponents in the final. They were a rising team with stars like James McCartan and Micky Linden. It was a terrific contest but we held out to win by: 2-7 to 0-11. Colm Brady won the Man of the Match Award. That Down team would have their revenge in the All-Ireland Final a year later, but for now we were National League champions. Despite rumours to the contrary, we were not over the hill yet.

We had a comfortable passage through the Leinster championship with comprehensive wins over Longford and Laois. In the final, for the fifth year in a row, we faced Dublin. Liam Harnan and Colm Coyle were out with injury, but we had an eager and tenacious new player in the half-forward line – Tommy Dowd, who had a brilliant game. Colm O'Rourke scored a goal in the first minute and we built up an eight-point lead, but in the second half the wind played havoc with Donal Smyth's kickouts. Dublin came back at us and got to within a point but we held to win by three points, thanks to a spectacular catch at midfield by Gerry McEntee who had come on late as a substitute. Again it was great to see Colm O'Rourke lift the Leinster trophy as Meath captain.

In the All-Ireland Semi-Final we faced Donegal whom we had

beaten earlier in the League quarter-final. It was a terribly tough match – hard knocks were given and taken. I remember having to take PJ Gillic to Beaumont Hospital after the game. He had taken a heavy blow to the ribs, but he had been our best player. Goals win matches and we got three that day – two from Bernie Flynn and one from 'Staff' – and together with a phenomenal performance from Liam Hayes, we ran out winners by 3-9 to 1-7. One very eminent GAA journalist predicted in his match report that 'no Ulster team will win the All-Ireland title in the next ten years ... ' How wrong could he be: 1991 – Down, 1992 – Donegal, 1993 – Derry and 1994 – Down! That is the wonderful thing about the game – there is always another chance. In that 1990 Semi-Final the much-vaunted Donegal half-forward line of Martin and James McHugh and Joyce McMullan were all replaced and yet, two years later they were the stars in Donegal's great win over Dublin for their first-ever senior title. There is always a chance and it was wonderful to see great footballers like Anthony Molloy and Martin McHugh take that chance in 1992.

So, for the third time in four years, it was a Meath-Cork final. We had won the previous two encounters, but this time Cork had the momentum of going for two titles in a row plus the hurling-football double. We were still without the injured Liam Harnan. Gerry McEntee was back at centrefield, so we moved Colm Brady to left half-forward, causing Tommy Dowd to lose out. It was another of those difficult calls for selectors, but six years later Tommy would captain another title-winning Meath team. There's always another chance.

On 16 September1990 a strange, strange grey autumn day and it seemed to mirror our performance. Even with the supposed advantage of an extra man, when Cork's Colm O'Neill was dismissed, we never got going, never sparked. Michael McCarthy (RIP) put over two points from play, Paul McGrath hit one point from play, Shay Fahy scored four points from play at midfield and Larry Tompkins converted four frees. And that was it. Eleven points was enough to win the title, as we only managed nine points, six of them coming from Brian Stafford. The Cork manager, Billy Morgan, had chosen his team well to do the job. They totally smothered us and we just could not break them down.

So Cork had their 'double double' and good luck to them. Teddy McCarthy joined that elite band of players with medals from both codes. Gerry McEntee had come back from the US to play. He took an almighty wallop and had to go off. A lot of people thought that was the end of Gerry in a Meath jersey but it wasn't. In 1991 Gerry watched the first two games of the four-match saga with Dublin, but he was back in the fray for the third match and went on to win an All-Star award. Some player!

This, of course, was a new experience for us. We had lost our first All-Ireland Final and there would inevitably be 'inquests'. At a press conference before the match, a journalist heard someone say: 'Cork have no bottle' – and he printed it. Naturally, Billy Morgan used that to motivate his men. We had beaten Cork in the League. When Billy announced his team for the final, two of our senior players said it was the worst Cork team ever picked. Nothing I could say after that could undo those words. We were over-confident, but in fact Billy had chosen his team very well and on the day things went well for them. Gerry McEntee half-blocked a Shay Fahy kick and it went straight over the bar. If Gerry hadn't touched the ball, it might well have hit the corner-flag. You get days like that.

Some critics said we were wrong to start Gerry and should have played Tommy Dowd after his Leinster Final performance. As a selector, you just have to make the call. Colm Brady was still a very young player and did not cope as well as he had done in the League, particularly with high overhead catches, but it is very difficult for new young players to keep their form in the white heat of championship. Again, it was said that the Cork half-forward line of Dave Barry, Larry Tompkins and Teddy McCarthy would take our improvised half-back line of Brendan Reilly, Kevin Foley and Marty O'Connell to pieces, but in the event they got no scores from play. We still had one of the greatest inside-forward lines of all time, but they never got going that day. Again, you get days like that.

People said our use of Mick Lyons as the extra man was terrible, but it wasn't deliberately terrible. You try things and inevitably some work and some don't. We were five points down in '87, but we did not panic and went on to win. We were a man short in '88 and still won. This time it did not work for us, but there were no real excuses. Cork was a better team on the day and, as winning captain, Larry Tompkins was very gracious.

For a Gaelic footballer, losing an All-Ireland Final is the worst possible experience. It comes at the end of a long year (we had played twelve matches to win the League title in 1989-90) and a tough championship campaign. You have put in so much training and made so many sacrifices. You have one hand on the Sam Maguire Cup and it is snatched from your grasp. It is a shattering experience. For a manager, the experience is just as bad. You feel you are responsible. You think and hope you have everything right – all the little things that in total will add up to success. You always naturally feel your geese are swans and, even though you are facing some fantastic footballers, you feel your lads as a group will pull through. When it doesn't happen you put on a brave face, but it hurts.

The fact that there will be another chance (hopefully) helps to ease the pain somewhat. There are also lessons to be learned in defeat and you hope that next time you will implement them. Overall, having taken teams through almost one hundred championship games and having lost about a quarter of them, I have to say that every defeat takes so much out of you – it is unbelievable.

CHAPTER TWENTY-ONE

The Story of Tina

The Yeates family has been established in Dunboyne for a very long time and has been closely connected to the Boylans throughout that time. My grandmother was very good friends with Tina's grandmother. The Yeates family were not afraid to mix with a republican family like the Boylans, especially after the arrest of my father and his three brothers. Tina's grandfather, George, was a Protestant and his wife was a Catholic. Sadly, his young wife died leaving him to bring up three sons, George Jr, David and Freddy. The boys were reared as Catholics and were educated in Brunswick Street CBS. George Jr married Mary Boland and the union produced nine children: four boys and five girls. Tina is the second daughter.

At home I grew a lot of fruit on our farm, we had thirteen acres of raspberries alone. The children from the village would come in their hundreds to the farm to pick fruit, as did their parents in many cases. They were paid by the pound picked and the money earned paid for school books, clothes or a holiday. Also a hierarchy would develop. Good pickers became packers and they moved up the line as the years went by. There was one particular group of eight girls who came to our house regularly, at Christmas and Easter as well as in summer, and they became particularly friendly with my mother. They became known as 'the choir' and they are still close friends today. Tina Yeates was one of the choir.

When Tina finished school she studied nursing for people with mental disabilities. This is where Tina encountered the religious order 'The Daughters of Charity'. Their work was mainly with the poorest of the poor, the disabled and the marginalised in society. Their ethos was to care for and respect these people. This ethos attracted Tina to enter the order. Some people might have been surprised by her decision, but I wasn't. Tina stayed in contact with my mother by writing regularly and visiting when she could, especially at Christmas, when she would be allowed home for the day. At that time we were good friends, but no more. Her work took her to Dublin, Limerick, England and West Belfast.

My mother died on 15 October 1989. There was a card from Tina at her bedside when she died. Tina asked permission to go to the funeral but her request was frowned upon because at the time in religious orders the community directive was – you have left your previous life behind and it was not recommended that you revisit that life again, especially at the stage that Tina was at in the community. At the time Tina was based in St Vincent's Hospital, Richmond Road in Dublin. She was very upset by the sisters' reaction, but it was only one of a number of aspects of community life that never made sense to her.

When you worked with homeless people sleeping in a London doorway or in bombed-out Belfast houses, you didn't have time to worry about small things. It was the now that concerned Tina. Even on the night she graduated as a nurse, she and another nurse put an entire ward of people with severe mental disabilities to bed before she went to her graduation dinner. She was that kind of person. She broke the order's rule and came to my mother's funeral. It was the beginning of her disengagement from the Daughters of Charity. She left the order in the spring of 1990. In the end the parting was amicable and she remains great friends with the order to this day. The sisters attended our wedding and are still very much part of our lives. Seán Óg's second name is Vincent after Vincent de Paul.

She called in to see her friends, me included, and told us she hoped to go to Australia as a nurse. At the time she would have had little awareness of my football involvement. She was in London when we won the All-Ireland title in 1987 and when she saw myself and Mockie Regan and others from Dunboyne on television, she could not believe it. Her family had always been involved in motor-racing and would not have been GAA people. Tina probably did not even realise Meath had a half-decent football team. Hard to believe, but true.

In the summer of 1990 Tina got her emigration papers for Australia. She called in one evening as I was going to a silver wedding celebration for Willie and Deirdre McEntee. I asked her if she would accompany me, and as she also knew the McEntees, and she came along. I was supposed to go from there to a twenty-first birthday party for a friend's daughter but instead we went home and started chatting … that's how it all started. We would 'go places' and visit friends, but we were not 'going out' in the accepted sense. When her uncle David had to go abroad on a business trip, Tina ran the garage business for him and of course I would be in and out for petrol, but it was all very casual and simple. One night she came down to a football training session and Mick Lyons asked: 'Who's that lassie? She's a grand-looking girl!' And she was a lovely person and a lovely neighbour. She would occasionally work with the herbs or help out in the clinic – just because she was interested. We had always been great pals. In 1979 when Pope John Paul II was in Galway, 'the choir' came with me to Galway.

Christmas 1989 was an emotional time for me. After my mother's death it was the first Christmas I was free to do my own thing. I turned down offers from my sisters to go to them but I insisted on staying at home saying whoever wanted to come would be welcome. I bought the turkey, but of course I hadn't a clue about cooking it. When I asked chef Fran O'Neill (a brother-in-law of my friend Brush Shiels) he insisted on cooking it for me. After Christmas Mass, Noel Keating came around, as did my neighbours, Eamonn and Betty O'Farrell. I visited my mother's grave and when I came back Noel gave me a cassette of Pavarotti singing *Panis Angelicus*. As I listened to it, I cried like a child. It was pure emotional release. Later Fran cooked a lovely dinner and my sister Pauline and her family came from Birr. That night Brush Shiels and his family joined us for music and *craic* but there was no Tina present that night ...

She came home a few days later to visit her parents and called in, as usual. I left her home that night, as usual. I was 'going out' with someone else at the time, but on reflection something happened that night, something weird and extraordinary. I couldn't explain it but I could not go out with the other woman again. In August 1990 it seemed the die was cast. Tina was ready to go to Australia and she called around shortly before she was due to set off. We talked into the small hours and I suddenly found myself saying to her: 'Would you not think of staying here and hanging around with me?' Talk about a casual proposal! Tina never got a chance to answer because at that moment the doorbell rang (at 2.00am!). It was a friend, Owen Lynch, who was upset over the death of a neighbour. Tina made tea for us, stood up and said: 'Well, I'm going home.'

For some reason we did not get to talk again for two weeks, when Tina reminded me of my casual question and asked had I been serious. 'Of course I was,' was my reply. 'Okay,' she said. And that was it! We were married in December of that year 1990. I suppose it would have been a surprise locally. When the engagement was announced the team organised a party and never have I been so embarrassed. It never dawned on us initially about booking a hotel for the reception and, being December, every place was booked up so we put up a marquee at home and invited neighbours and friends. The ceremony itself was very quiet, just for the immediate families, and it took place in Our Lady of Sion Church in Bellinter. Even though the weather was atrocious a huge crowd turned up at the marquee and we had a mighty celebration. From there Tina and I went to Fitzpatrick's Hotel in Killiney in Dublin, where Seán Barrett TD, who had learned of our marriage, left a bottle of champagne for us. The hotel management did not seem to know we were newly-weds and asked us if we would mind moving to another room as there was a honeymoon couple arriving! We agreed as we were going home the next day anyway. Christmas 1990 was Tina's first Christmas at home for eleven years so we joined the Yeates family for the festive season and had a great time.

After Christmas we flew to Florida and from there to the Bahamas, to discover that the hotel we had booked into had been sold and closed. We ended up staying in another hotel that cost $239 a night, and didn't even serve decent tea. Two weeks there and back to Florida, and we eventually met up with the team in Clearwater where the lads were enjoying their winter holiday.

I was forty-seven years old when I got married and there was a fair difference in years between myself and Tina. On our wedding day I went through scenes of sorrow. I could foresee all the problems and pitfalls that Tina might face. My father had been much older than my mother and I was conscious of how mother had to look after him in his old age. We discussed this and Tina had no problem with the age-gap, but my parents' experience still troubled me. It had nothing to do with the possibility of Tina being a 'football widow' – I talk very little about football at home. Even when I go out, unless someone else brings up football as a topic, I would not bring it up. I was and am mad into things other than football – motorsport, flying little planes, music.

Every Saturday night I would go to the Clontarf branch of Comhaltas Ceoltóirí Éireann or to the *Píobairí Uileann* for a traditional music session. I worked very hard, spending long hours at the herb business, but I maintained a good work-life balance. No, it was the senior years that troubled me ...

Tina is very organised, very practical and has a terrific sense of humour. Our happiness was complete when our firstborn, Seán, arrived in the Coombe hospital on Palm Sunday, April 1992. The hospital staff were brilliant, as this was a miracle for both of us. Their quick action saved his life. It was an amazing feeling to suddenly have a son. I was so excited I was about to ring my mother, before remembering that she was no longer with us ... It was a great blessing and a great joy to share with our families. Luckily Meath were not playing that day (some people were saying I organised that) but they were due to play Derry on the following Sunday in the quarter-final of the League. On the Tuesday the excited new dad called into training, just for a minute, to discover that my fellow-selectors could not make it and we had eleven players on the injured list ... I was back in at the deep end and had to pick a team to play Derry. We lost the match but we had unearthed two future stars: Enda McManus and Graham Geraghty. Seven years later, as we watched Seán Jr make his First Communion, I said to Tina: 'Isn't this hard to believe? It won't be long 'til we are at his twenty-first birthday party.' 'I know,' Tina laughed, 'and I'll be telling him to wheel in your daddy!'

And then in February 1994 came Ciarán in a hurry. Tina had sent me home from the hospital and I was only in the door at home when the word came that Ciarán had arrived. I remember when I went to see him, the ever-practical Tina pointed out to the under-pressure student nurses that they had put on the monitor upside down. Dáire arrived in September 1996, on the Monday before the Meath-Mayo All-Ireland Final. When the word got out the media wanted to photograph me in the hospital and make a story out of it. I refused. We were just blessed and fortunate parents and this was personal and private. There were other babies in the hospital who were sick and possibly dying. The Matron smuggled me in through the back door to avoid a media scrum. Tina was well enough to attend the Final which, of course, ended in a draw.

Doireann Boylan entered this world in December 1999, our first girl, which was a source of great joy for Tina. She was so thrilled that she asked the nurse: 'Are you sure it's a girl?' Aoife Boylan arrived in May 2001. When we reached the All-Ireland Final that year, some people had noticed a pattern. Boylan baby in 1996 – Meath win the All-Ireland. Boylan baby in 1999 – Meath win the All-Ireland. Boylan baby in 2001 – Meath are sure to win the All-Ireland. As we all know, Galway had other ideas. When Tina was pregnant with Aoife she watched the aftermath of the horrific Omagh bomb and was moved by the story of one little victim, a boy called Óran Doherty from Donegal. She vowed if she had a boy she would call him Óran. When she gave birth to our sixth child, a boy, in September 2003, he was duly christened Óran. End of the line! We were truly blessed with six beautiful children in the space of eleven years. They are our heart, our lifeblood.

All six of them are healthy, thank God. And thank God, not one of them is perfect. I remember when Seán was being christened, I just wanted him to be his own man. And, boy!, is he his own man at fourteen. They are, after all, only on loan to us. They are all as different as night and day. Some of them are mad into sport, others music, others neither of those things. I am sure that will change over the years as they grow and develop.

It was never going to be easy having a family of that size and managing a football team. When Des Cahill of RTÉ Radio interviewed me on my retirement from football management, he made the point that I had been a manager for all of his broadcasting career. It has been a time of astonishing change in Ireland, particularly over the past decade – more change than I would have seen in two generations previously. Yet despite the riches of the Celtic Tiger economy, we have the poverty of loneliness. So to have a healthy and loving family and be able to get on with your life is a great blessing. There were times when I got things wrong in football and times when I got them right. You can make mistakes but with the support and comfort of family, you can get over them.

I never won an All-Ireland medal, but I knew what it took to achieve excellence in sport. When success comes, everyone involved feels they have done it. That is how it should be, but ultimately it is the lads on the field who make it happen with a little help now and then from Lady Luck! All I can do is create the environment for that to happen. Similarly, in my professional work I encounter a lot of illness and pain. I try to help insofar as I can, but some twenty per cent of patients who come to me are not for me at all. All I can do is refer them elsewhere and reassure them. Where would I be if I did not have a life-partner supporting me in all of these things? Tina had her own career, which is possibly 'on hold' for now, but I could not think of anyone better to rear our children. She chose the names for all of them and rightly so, since she carried each of them for nine months. She also lost a baby, between Ciarán and Dáire, a baby that is just as precious to us as the six we have.

Tina is a very straightforward and uncomplicated person. If I got into the car and went off for five or six hours, she would never have to question me about what I was doing – and the same holds with me in her case, but all I know is that I would miss her. At times she has had to go to the US for family occasions and the place is very different without her. Obviously there are plenty of times when I annoyed the hell out of her and I would be difficult, not intentionally, but she would still make me laugh. There is an unwritten bond between us

and we are so lucky to have it. Being married to a herbalist and football manager can't have been easy for her. The clinic is attached to our
house. People are in and out, all of the time, people who are sick and
need help and time. Many a time I would be set to go someplace, but
someone calls in need of help. It may be all right when there are just
the two of us, but when you have children expecting you to go someplace, you just cannot let them down. Now, at least, I don't have the
football to blame.

I still don't know what Tina saw in me, but whatever it was, I am
glad she saw it! When she got her emigration papers for Australia, her
mother observed that she did not seem too excited about it. Maybe she
felt something was happening – who knows? She has her own life
with 'the choir'. They still meet regularly for dinner in each other's
houses and a couple of years ago they all went off together for a week
to celebrate a Big Birthday.

Tina is a major player in my life but she would never ask me about
the problems or controversies I might have with the football team. Similarly, in meeting people, she is just herself and not the manager's wife.
During the football season, I might be at a selection meeting on Monday
night, have training on Tuesday, Thursday and Saturday, and then a
match on Sunday. Not easy for Tina, but we worked around it. Life is
all about compromise. You meet it as you see it. If circumstances
changed and I was needed at home, I would have no problem in
adapting, because I am so fortunate in having Tina. When I made the
decision to retire from management, we had not discussed it in detail.
Ultimately it had to be my decision. Tina might have seen the strain I
was under at times and would not have liked to see that happening,
but that is as far as it went. We never discussed my falling out with
players and I think that was right. It was only sport, after all. Over the
years many sportspeople came to the house and Tina always made
them welcome. That's home. When I made my retirement decision I

rang her. She was in her father's car at the time. She just said: 'That's okay, if that's how you feel.' That's Tina.

CHAPTER TWENTY-TWO

Managing

Away back in 1982 when I was chatting with a few players in the Imperial Hotel, Dundalk, I came up with what is in retrospect a prophetic statement – 'I might never play in an All-Ireland Final, but I think I know what it would take for a team to get there.' To this day I cannot explain why that thought came into my mind. At the time, I was only helping out with injured players – but later that year I was appointed manager of the Meath senior football team – or more correctly, 'coach/trainer' – a temporary appointment that lasted twenty–three years ...

There is no magic formula in managing a team. It is largely a matter of being in the right place at the right time and creating the right environment for success. At the outset, you are looking for certain levels of skill, confidence and vision in a player. Character is paramount also. You're looking for a Colm O'Rourke, a Liam Hayes, a Trevor Giles, a Tommy Dowd – a player who has natural talent but is also working at that talent. A player who has the ability to do something that stands out and something he has worked on. You bring in young players with a view to two years ahead (even if you are not going to be around then yourself) – especially lads from junior clubs who are playing at a level where they have more time to dwell on the ball. You try to ensure that they don't develop bad playing habits.

During the selection process, people speculated that I had my own favourite clubs and players. But it's just not true; the opportunity was there for everyone. We held loads of trials, and I believe that very few good players slipped through the net. You can have hundreds of good players at club level but not hundreds can play at inter-county level.

My father would always *ask* me to do something rather than *tell* me. He was very encouraging. A manager should work in a similar vein. You are a leader but leadership is all about responsibility. The fact that you have authority, that you can blow the whistle on the training ground, doesn't entitle you to walk over people. You are not involved in a put-down syndrome. Rather, you are trying to get lads to confront the issues that might cause defeat. It is a two-way process, having leaders on the field who are confident in themselves and in you on the sideline observing them; so it is a teamwork thing, a partnership. Often you could be missing key players in a crucial match, but suddenly players who might have been considered 'lesser lights' come of age. All they need is your encouragement. It's lovely to see that happen – players taking on responsibility and leadership and showing confidence.

Talking of confidence reminds me of the 1996 All-Ireland football final when we played Mayo. I suppose thirty-one counties would have wanted Mayo to win. And to cap it all – the teams would have to be introduced beforehand to President Mary Robinson, who came from Mayo. For us, it was a question of not giving the high ground and we spoke to the players about that. When you run out on the pitch on All-Ireland day, there is a whole ritual to be gone through. You have seventeen minutes to the throw-in – three or four minutes of kickabout, then the photographs, meeting the president, the parade and the national anthem. That whole pageant can soak lads' energy.

Half the training you have done would be to absorb the pressure on that day.

We were very conscious of the Mary Robinson factor. We had a number of players whose families came originally from the west of Ireland. But it was significant that the team were united in their Meath roots. So when Tommy Dowd, the team captain, introduced our goalkeeper Conor Martin, it was very important that President Mary Robinson knew that Conor was from Ballivor, even though his mother was from Mayo. Mark O'Reilly may have been a grand-nephew of the great Paddy Kennedy from Kerry, but he was Mark O'Reilly from Summerhill who wanted to play and win for Meath. Darren Fay, was the son of Jimmy and nephew of Mickey – both of whom had given great service to Meath – but today he was the Meath full-back from Trim wanted to bring back another All-Ireland to Trim. Next was Martin O'Connell – a legend in our game – who had taken a lot of pressure after a controversial Semi-Final – he was nephew of another legend, Mick Higgins of Cavan, but he was from Carlanstown and that's where his roots and his pride were embedded. And then we came to Colm Coyle, the independent man on the team, a free spirit. His father and uncles had played for Donegal, but again he made it clear that he was from Seneschalstown and he wanted to win for Seneschalstown and Meath. The president duly shook his hand, but he held on to her hand and said to her: 'How are things at home?' That was just Colm's way, but of course the lads got a laugh out of it and it eased the tension for them.

A sense of humour is essential in competitive sport. I remember during the Leinster final against Dublin in 1996 Tommy Dowd clashed with Keith Barr and got a cut on the head. Later on Keith's brother Johnny came on as a substitute. He ran into Tommy, result-ing in a second cut for the Meath captain. After the match – which we won – Tommy was coming up out of the dressing room to do media interviews when he hit his head against an iron bar and had to have four stitches inserted. On seeing this, some of the Dublin supporters chanted: 'Tommy – Keith Barr! Johnny Barr! Iron bar!' It's all part of the *craic* and the humour that goes on and it would be an awful shame if that were lost out of the game.

Patience and taking the time to nurture players are also an important part of management. Sometimes this can be interpreted as – 'Boylan is too set in his ways, too slow to change'. If you work through training sessions, the O'Byrne Cup and the National League, you come up with a championship fifteen. I would not like to think I am as fickle as the wind at that stage ... Of course, players will make mistakes, hopefully less so than the opposition. It was said that there were certain players that I would never take off and that was true. Those were players who had that flash of brilliance that could turn a game around, even if they had been playing poorly up to then. No team I know is blessed with that many quality players that it is only a matter of taking off three or four players and putting on three or four substitutes. When you have spent a lot of time getting a player onto the team, you need patience to let things happen for him. Having said that, we made changes very quickly on many occasions – and we often got caught out too. Sometimes players 'went off the boil' and were dropped. I had to do what was right for the team. That was my job. But I believe that a lot of the time, hopefully, I got it right ...

Focus and concentration on the matter in hand are crucial for both the manager and the players. All through my career I would not go out on the night before a match and I would have butterflies in my stomach on match-morning. I had to find my focus and get 'inside the head' of my players. I would rarely be distracted on the sideline, no matter what was going on elsewhere. The image of me sitting on the football on the sideline is a good one, because I was literally 'on the ball', trying to keep a continuity of thought on what was unfolding on the pitch. On the morning of the 1996 Final, one of the players had sixty people call to his house to wish him well – how could he perform at his best with such distraction? You try your best to insulate players but it is difficult. Nowadays so much texting goes on – another distraction. Players are also hounded for tickets in the run-up to a big match. I always said to the players – deal with your official allocation and that is it. Walk away. I have many friends who play for Ireland at different codes. I would always respect them on big match days and keep my distance.

There is an old saying: 'Victory has a hundred fathers while defeat is an orphan.' The line between victory and defeat is very fine indeed. Winning trophies and medals is wonderful, but the great thing about success is what it does for your people – lifting them up on a great wave of goodwill, humour, friendship and solidarity. It's just wonderful to see people throw their arms around each other in the joy of victory – it makes me feel I am in a very privileged position. Fortune is fickle of course. You can be top of the pile today but through injury, illness or sheer bad luck, the whole thing can be swept away from you overnight. It is important to be as gracious in defeat as in victory. I was so fortunate to have crossed swords with great players and managers and to have pitted my wits against them. There can be only one winner. If you have done your best and lost, there is no shame. Shake hands, wish your opponent the best of luck, knowing that if you meet him again, you'll do your best to win the title back.

I had a great friend years ago – James Nolan from Monaghan. He was a great footballer but he contracted polio and spent twenty-seven years in a hospital bed in Cherry Orchard Hospital, unit 7. There was a pressure-chamber beside his bed which opened and closed the muscles of his throat. By forcing his voice against that chamber he learned to speak again. One night while a group of friends were visiting James, we played 'spin-the-bottle'. Whoever the bottle pointed to had to sing – and of course it stopped at me, who couldn't sing a note. I borrowed a mouth organ and tried to play 'Kevin Barry'. I was bad enough playing it but James tried to sing it – or croak it – from his bed. It taught me the lesson that you might not be able to do something as well as somebody else, but give it your best shot and nobody can blame you.

Perspective and balance are as important in sport as they are in life. The former Clare hurling manager, Ger Loughnane, tells a great story about the American swimmer, Matt Biondi, who had won five gold medals at the Olympic Games. When you win there is terrific pressure to keep winning. The fans demand it. In Biondi's case, he came second in his sixth event – which was a tremendous achievement – but he was approached afterwards by an American reporter who suggested that Biondi must be devastated at failing to win a sixth gold medal. 'Yeah, I'm a bit disappointed,' Biondi replied, 'but when all is said and done, when I go home from the Olympic Games, my dog will still lick my face.' Sport is a serious business. You prepare very hard. You sacrifice an awful lot, but when you go home your dog will still greet you, irrespective of the result.

There is, however, a whole other world in managing a team that the general public would never know – a whole range of minutiae that have to be addressed. I remember in the run-up to what turned out to be my last match – against Cavan – I spent the entire day on the phone, which wasn't unusual. I was dealing with the county board regarding club matches; consulting with our physiotherapist on the fitness of players; trying to arrange for four individual injured players to get them away to the sun for a few days; negotiating with the travel agent about this and liaising with my co-selectors; trying to iron out a fixture crux in the Cavan match, because one of their key players was getting married ... it just went on and on. You might say why not walk away from it or delegate it to others, but there are certain things I would want to keep a handle on. I knew the players' injuries. I knew what they needed. I had the contacts. Further, if I had to go the county board with every 'little' problem, I would not get up in the morning. It is a matter of mutual trust between the board and myself.

The accusation has been made that Meath were often a cynical and dirty team, prepared to win at all costs. I reject that totally. I would never send out a team with instructions to be cynical or dirty. Meath footballers are wholehearted and resolute. They always wanted to win and fought very hard to win. Remember, they got plenty of abuse too, but they were very forceful in the way they got on with the game. I would never for a moment apologise for their character and their never-say-die attitude. There were times when we were not flavour of the month and people wrote harsh things about us and spoke out in public – at GAA congress and elsewhere. At the same time myself and the players were often at the far end of the country giving our time and our help *gratis*, just for the love of the game we were supposed to have demeaned ... Whether it was up in Ballymena or down in Cúil Aodha, presenting medals to the winners of Division Four of the Junior championship, we were so privileged that people thought so much of us to invite us there.

Liam Harnan used to say, 'Players win matches, but managers lose them!' And there is the belief that every year your team is beaten, you have 'stayed too long ... ' My career got off to a fantastic start – winning an O'Byrne Cup and a Centenary Cup, reaching a League Semi-Final and narrowly losing a Leinster Final – but in 1985 Laois hammered us in the Leinster championship by ten points and we barely survived in Division One of the League. It was a case of 'Boylan must go'. I was opposed by Paul Kenny for the manager's job and survived. It would have been easy to walk away, but I reckoned I knew more about the players than anyone else and I knew there was more to come from them. I was vindicated in 1986 when we made the breakthrough in Leinster and went on to greater things in subsequent years. It was important for me to show the players that I had not lost faith in them. The core members of the team wanted me to stay. Others didn't and said as much. I had no problem with that. When I was given back the job I just got on with it. No team is going to win a title every year. Again in 1992 and 2002 there were those who said I had 'stayed too long'. I was never a man to walk away from a job. It was not a matter of ego. As long as I still got a buzz from the job, I had faith in Meath and I had faith in me.

Finally I must dispel the notion that 'Boylan must have made a fortune out of managing Meath.' I was never in it for money and, if anything, being manager over the years cost me a fortune rather than making me one. I dug into my own pockets regularly to ensure players had what they needed. Maybe it was my own fault but I reckoned that the county board often had enough expense to deal with, so I supplemented whenever I could. I am not talking about treating the players' injuries here in the clinic at no cost. I am simply talking about helping out players financially, for example when we went away on trips. I was in the game for love, not money. End of story.

No manager will survive without balance in his life. When I was with the players I gave it my all. I put them first and they did the same for me. You can be passionate about something but if you become fanatical about it you lose sight of all the simple things around you. You are not seeing the wood for the trees. Even though our home life had to be planned around club and inter-county championships, we still had a home life. There had to be time to experience the joy of going to a show or a movie, playing with the children, holding birthday or First Communion parties, going for a meal with Tina or even just walking down the street in Dunboyne or Dublin. There is so much goodness out there. I would hate to miss all of that. Sport is a huge part of my life, but I love music and reading and people, and I have other passions like motor-racing and flying. That is what gives me balance. And of course I am lucky to be involved with the soil also – its richness and life-giving properties mean so much to me.

CHAPTER TWENTY-THREE

The Game

Gaelic football is essentially a very simple game, a game with wonderful skills like high fielding and the solo run, and a game of physical contact, with the 'fair' shoulder and the blockdown adding to its excitement. It has, of course, changed dramatically over the last thirty years with the introduction of new rules and with increasingly professional approaches to coaching and training. The modern running game bears very little resemblance to the more static game of the sixties when backs stayed back and forwards stayed forward and tall midfielders battled for dominance in the centre of the field.

In the seventies Dublin and Kerry brought the game to a new level, particularly with the introduction of the hand-pass when the ball was almost literally thrown around the park. Some people compared the game to basketball. Certainly the foot-pass went into decline. At our peak in 1987-88 we tried to combine both hand- and foot-passing. We pulled Gerry McEntee back from centrefield as an extra defender. Terry Ferguson, Bobby O'Malley and Kevin Foley were brilliant hand-passers and could deliver it quickly to Gerry, while Joe Cassells would come from the 'Forty' to midfield – his natural habitat. At the same time Liam Harnan and PJ Gillic could deliver brilliant ball by foot with power and precision right down to the inside forward line.

The most significant change has probably been allowing frees and sideline balls to be taken from the hand. Prior to that, taking frees from the ground allowed the opposing team crucial seconds to regroup in defence, as the ball was inevitably driven forward. Now, from the hand, you could deliver it anywhere – backwards, cross-field, forwards. This had huge implications for a team's style of play, but with all rule changes it is a matter of how well you adapt to them. From 1987 to 1991 Meath were a big, strong, physical team. Some people would still see those attributes as making up the typical Meath footballer, but the game changed and so did we. I remember after the 1999 All-Ireland, Brian Cody, the Kilkenny hurling manager, said to me: 'I thought Meath footballers were big, muscular giants – sure these are only little fellows!' And they were, but they would not step back from a challenge! I love that in a player. Okay, so they didn't have the physique of former players. So what. We would play the game in a different way. We adapted. The way we played in 1996 and 1999 was so different to our game in 1987-88. The common denominator was that they would not shirk from the battle – I really love that in a Gaelic footballer!

The National League used to be a fantastic competition but it was often bedevilled by the constant introduction of new rules. Good and bad came out of those changes. Years ago a goalkeeper was not allowed to 'solo' the ball within the square. He could only hop it but in winter the goalmouth was invariably churned up in muck and there was no way you could hop the ball! Thankfully that has changed. Then we had the game of four quarters and the goalkeeper kicking the ball out of the hand (thus diminishing the art of high fielding). Thankfully those changes died the death! In 2005 we had the yellow cards/red cards/sinbin debacle. The intention to reduce pulling and dragging was good, but the execution became impossible. It all became too confusing for referees. Any good referee will know when there is malicious intent in a foul. What actually happened was that the game was almost being refereed by people on the sideline: 'That's a yellow, ref., he has to go!' Also the referee knows that he is being assessed by monitors, thus reducing his autonomy. There are quite simply too many rules and the interpretation of those rules has been inconsistent and has led to confusion. If you had twenty youngsters playing rugby or soccer and then switched them to Gaelic football, they would be lost because of the number of rules. Over the years Joe Lennon and his associates have tried hard to simplify the rules, but there are still too many rules about what you can and cannot do in Gaelic football.

One positive step forward would be the introduction of two referees as has been done successfully in the International Rules games. The pace of the modern game demands this. Players put in a phenomenal amount of training. In 1996 when Meath drew with Mayo in the All-Ireland Final, I was under pressure to bring back some 'oldtimers' for the replay, as had been done in 1949 when Jim Kearney was brought out of retirement. But that was then, when play-ers only had three weeks' 'collective training' before a final. This is now, when there is continuous training and continuous playing: for club, college, under-21 and senior county teams. The stakes in the game have gone so high and yet these are still amateur players. They still have to get up in the morning and go to work. There is very little time for rest and consequently inter-county careers are much shorter now. Unemployment is virtually gone. Now players must put the same application into work as they do with sport. Sport may win them introductions for jobs but it won't keep the jobs for them. There is a fierce intensity in the game – county managers are requiring players to give their all, but so too are club managers, college managers and under-21 managers. There is a huge need for greater co-ordination between club and county. Failing that you will have player burnout.

So is going professional the answer? I have serious reservations about this. On a personal level, if I had been offered payment, I would not have managed Meath. I would have felt I was letting people down if I wasn't doing my job right. As it was, I gave nearly every waking moment to the job, and even when I was working at the 'day job', I was still thinking of my managerial job. In our set-up, I always liked the fact that the major stars were anxious that the 'lesser lights' should have the same 'perks' as them. The rewards should be the same for everyone. I don't like the current trend in sponsorship when a dozen or so 'stars' from different counties, in both codes, are used to promote a product. That can only promote division. I totally agree with administrators being looked after – assuming they are the best people for the job. Outside of that I would have a lot of reservations. If there are to be rewards, let them be the same for everyone. Our sponsors, Kepak, ensured from the start that whatever the county board got in sponsorship, the players' fund got the same.

To come back to the playing rules, we need to simplify and clarify them much more to avoid confusion. At inter-county level I would suggest having two referees and doing away with yellow and red cards. I would have no problem with a referee putting a player off for a period, or entirely, at his discretion. If an action is seen as deliberately intending to hurt, the perpetrator should be sent off. In the 2005 All-Ireland Final, referee Mick Monahan did an excellent job but in the opening minute he was writing in his little black book, thus breaking the pattern of the game and causing players to lose concentration. It would be better to give the player a quick warning and let the game settle down. Should we have video consultation, as in rugby? I would have no problem with it but Gaelic football is a very different game, played on a bigger pitch. Certainly, we could do with the assistance of technology in deciding on controversial 'point or wide?' issues, by using some sort of bleep.

There has been a lot of debate about the International Rules Series following controversial incidents in 2005. The problem of dangerous tackles has to be firmly addressed but the game has many good aspects. It is a great reward to play in your sport at international level. The late Micheál O Hehir had the vision twenty-five years ago. He wanted to promote hurling in Australia and invited me to coach an Australian hurling team. I wasn't involved in coaching then and could not give it the time required – but it was nice to be asked. The Compromise Rules game, as it was initially known, had its origins in Meath's trip to Australia in 1967 as All-Ireland champions. When it was properly established in 1984, it evolved after a rocky start and improved as a game with terrific skills on display, but the great problem with it has been the timing of the series. The games are played at the end of the season, both here and in Australia. They come very soon after the All-Ireland championships and for the players who feature in those games there is a serious risk of burnout. For all that, it is a tremendous honour for players to be selected at international level. I don't like to see Gaelic skills such as the pick-up taken out of the game, but a player can still 'chip' the ball up, if he has the skill. The quick release of the ball is a good idea. I love to see high fielding – one of our traditional skills – rewarded with the 'mark'. I would be in favour of adopting the mark in Gaelic football, but the player should be restricted to four steps, not six as in the International Rules. Generally these games have been enthralling and added to by the notion of amateurs taking on professionals – and there have been some great contests of skill, strength and endurance. I would love to see the international dimension broadened. It might seem farfetched and it would take time, but it would be wonderful to have a few more teams involved.

When the 'back-door' system was introduced into the championships some years back, opinions were divided. There are many who would argue that you should not get a second chance in a knock-out competition, but against that, both Galway and Tyrone would say the system has been an unqualified success, having been champions through this system in 2001 (to Meath's cost) and 2005 respectively. For the back-door system to be an absolute success, there would have to be an open draw from the start. No provincial championships. As the provinces are constituted, the larger ones like Leinster and Ulster are at a disadvantage because they have to play more games. More games offer more to the spectator but they can also prove quite expensive to the fan if your team gets a prolonged run in the championship. As long as the provincial structure remains, I cannot see an open draw happening, because the provincial councils would object. Yet there has to be an open draw for the back-door system to work properly. For me personally, this would create a dilemma, because I absolutely love the cut and thrust of the Leinster championship.

It is often argued that ultimately the championship belongs to an elite group of counties. It will always be a struggle for counties with small populations but I don't accept that there should be an elite group. Look at the examples of Wexford and Fermanagh in recent years. They experienced big days in Croke Park and, while it may have taken a lot out of them, they now know what that experience is like and what they must aspire to, if they want to savour it again. The way Limerick have progressed is also encouraging, but it takes an awful lot of dedication and sacrifice. If you based success on population alone, Dublin would be winning the All-Ireland every year, yet they have only won one title in the past twenty-odd years. Growth takes time – it is only in latter decades that Gaelic football has become popular in Dublin's southside.

Success is cyclical too. Kerry had that barren spell from 1986 to 1997. Out of nowhere Ulster counties dominated from 1991 to 1994. Currently Tyrone and Armagh are very strong so we could be in for another period of Ulster domination. It is not by chance, however, that Ulster teams seem so far ahead. If you put in the work, you will reap the rewards. I remember going to Sligo in 1996 to present 150 coaching certificates. It was no great surprise to me that Sligo had a surge in fortune five or six years later. Tyrone were kings in 2005, but the amount of work they are putting into their game is huge. Some people have decried their style – in one notorious instance it was described as 'puke football' – but equally the hand-passing game of the seventies was decried by many as handball or basketball, rather than football. It depends on how you adapt to the rules. When Down's exciting brand of football won the day over Kerry in 1968, the pessimists said Kerry would not win an All-Ireland for another ten years. Guess who won the title in 1969. 'Possession' football demands huge work and commitment and Tyrone have had that commitment to an extraordinary degree. No matter what skill you have, if you are not industrious and willing to sacrifice for your fellow-players, you will only partially succeed. Some other team will find a way of breaking down possession football but they will need particular personnel to do it. Kerry never stopped trying in 2005 but just could not seem to get that vital break. In 1996 our squad in Meath would not compare in stature to the 1987-91 squad, so we had to play a different type of game and play to the strengths we had.

Gaelic football is an evolving game. We hear talk of 'strategic aggression' – There is a whole new language being used. There are different mindsets. Psychologists and image consultants now feature in the backroom. Evolution is nothing new. In days gone by, if you produced a deodorant in the dressing room, you were a 'sissy'. It's an evolving game and it is a question of how you adapt.

CHAPTER TWENTY-FOUR

A Walk on the Wild Side

Come and take a walk with me around our Dunboyne 'estate' – not so much an estate as a tidy little farm of sixty acres. In my father's time it was a real farm, stocked with cattle and crops, but now it is different. In fact, to the untrained eye it probably looks more of a wilderness. People probably saying: 'In the name of God, the place is a mess. Wouldn't you think Boylan would do something and get rid of those weeds?' Let's take a closer look.

We are crossing the middle field. It is a bright, warm afternoon in May 2006, and we need more days like this because we had a very wet spring and planting is behind schedule. There are acres and acres of *linseed* here. We use linseed in poultices, especially for ligament problems, but I actually sowed the linseed a couple of years ago to bring up the fertility of the soil. We had major flooding in the area a few years ago and when the Office of Public Works (OPW) came in to improve the drainage, this land suffered a lot with spoilage problems. The linseed helped to restore its fertility.

If you look closely you will see other plants growing here too. There's the *ox-eye daisy*. We use about an acre of that every year. We use the whole plant, leaf, stem and flower. Dr Donal Cregan, who was a former president of Castleknock College and St Patrick's Training College, he had good reason to be grateful to this little plant. In 1941, one of the Vincentian priests contacted my father to tell him that Dr Cregan was very ill. He had been operated on for a kidney stone but the stone had moved to a position where the surgeon could not touch it. As a result, Dr Cregan was gravely ill. My father came home, went out to the garden for some ox-eye daisy, made up a mixture and sent it in to the Mater hospital. Dr Cregan was so weak that he could only sip the mixture from a teaspoon. Ten days later, he walked out of the Mater and continued taking the herbal mixture for six months. He went on to live a long life, working in St Patrick's Teacher Training College and in Africa.

We had five acres of ox-eye daisy planted here at one time. They still come up wild and we save the seed from the plants. It is virgin seed, pure and uncontaminated. Next year we will sow about two and a half acres of it in another field. Just beside the ox-eye daisy is a *milk thistle* plant, an incredible herb for liver conditions. The Dublin School of Pharmacy was looking for a large quantity of milk thistle some years ago and we had loads of it growing wild. To make sure it would look well when the School arrived, we pulled all the weeds and grasses around it. To our horror, the next day the milk thistle was all covered in powdery mildew! The surrounding grasses had been giving off a chloroform that kept the mildew off the milk thistle. It was a case of nature looking after its own! We often get visits from pharmacists. In 1994, twenty-seven Italian pharmacists were amazed to find *marguerite* growing wild here. As far as they were concerned, that plant only grew in the Alps!

Here also in this small area, a metre square, is another useful plant. It is the *wild turnip*, whose root, with its very distinctive smell, is used in the treatment of certain nerve problems. And here is probably my favourite plant – *parsley-piert*. You have to look hard for it as it grows along the ground as a creeper, unlike the parsley you grow in your garden. Our workmen will pick a lot of parsley-piert and save the seed from it, as they do with the other plants like the ox-eye daisy. It is very labour-intensive work, but the lads are very skilled and know what they are looking for. We are short of parsley-piert seed this year, so Warrenstown College has propagated a lot of it for us. I have a special affinity for this plant. When my father was given a year to live in 1923, he took parsley-piert to get rid of inflammation in the infection he had. It worked for him, so naturally I have great belief in its curative powers. Anyway, I hope you understand now that this field is anything but a wilderness! It is full of interesting and very valuable plants. Tomorrow, please God, we'll start pulling up the parsley-piert. If we had tried to pull it before now in the wet ground, we would have made a mess of it.

Before we leave the middle field, here's another short story. I broke this field some years ago to plant fruit. Prior to that the field had been untouched for generations, probably back to my grandfather's time. When I ploughed it, I was amazed to see it covered, three weeks later, in *fumitory*. Fumitory, or 'earthsmoke', is so called because its rapid growth resembles smoke dispersing. It was originally used in the treatment of leprosy. There were two leper colonies in this country years ago – one in Ringsend, Dublin and one down the road from here at Loughsallagh near Clonee. This is evidence that traditional herbalists of old would use plants native to their area. Fumitory had obviously been growing wild around here and lay dormant until I broke ground that had not been disturbed for a very long time. The local Horticultural Adviser thought I had planted it because of its rapid growth. It was an amazing sight.

Walking along the headland now in the shade of the hedgerow, God's bounty is all about us in the weeds and grasses. Plenty of *dandelion* or, as the Dublin people call them, 'jinny-joes'. It may be the scourge of the modern suburban lawn but the dandelion is a great herb. Its roots will remove the effects of excess caffeine in the bloodstream. You can actually buy dandelion coffee nowadays. Its leaf is used to get rid of tannic acid – important for a nation of tea-drinkers like the Irish. The dandelion is a very kind herb and good for the liver. There is *robin-run-the-hedge*. You will know it by its cleavers, little hooks that enable it to stick to everything. I use it today in the treatment of a modern ailment like ME, but in wartime it was used in the treatment of haemorrhoids, when the lesser celandine was unavailable. And, of course, there is no scarcity of *nettles*. I use them a lot. They are the best antihistamine in the world. So many nuisance 'weeds' are in fact very useful to the herbalist.

Now we are in the hurling field – a field of history and herbs. Away back, between 1908 and 1912, when Dunboyne won a string of county senior hurling titles, this is where the hurlers trained. It is even more famous as the site of a historic rally in 1917 when Michael Collins and Arthur Griffith addressed the Irish Volunteers. They came from all the neighbouring counties: Louth, Wicklow, Offaly, Kildare and Dublin. Three special trains ran from Dublin. The Saint James Brass Band played for the rally. What a sight that must have been. Right now it is being prepared for the sowing of parsley-piert. A machine will lay down the plastic covering but the plants will be put in by hand. It is a very kind herb, used to treat the inflammation of muscles and joints. Down in the corner we have eleven beehives. We use honey and sage to treat throat ailments. Sage is also good for the memory. It aids circulation through the capillaries. Over there is our reservoir of spring water. We use it to irrigate the plants. Despite all the rain we still need to irrigate, because this is typical Meath soil. In a dry period it will go as hard as a board. Further down is the little river from which all the flooding came. It is called the Castle Stream and it feeds into the river Tolka. It looks innocent now but the OPW have done a lot of work on it.

We are now in the Wood Field. It is covered in *oilseed rape*, six or seven acres of it. Oilseed rape gives off a beautiful scent. We did not plant it – the seeds were obviously carried here by birds or on the wind and it spread all over the field. We will harvest it and offer it to the neighbours to use as silage. We will then rotovate it into the ground as organic matter. Needless to say, we never use pesticides or herbicides. Over there where the trees are is the site of the original farmhouse, the priest's house which was burned by the yeomen in 1798. Nothing remains of it now.

Now we have entered the old railway line that ran from Dublin to Clonsilla and on to Navan and Kingscourt. Of course the track is long gone and it is now like a leafy avenue. I own this part of the line. I bought it in 1968. It is very useful to us for access to the fields. There is talk now of restoring the line, so I suppose a compulsory purchase order will arrive some day in the post.

Again here in this lovely leafy 'railway walk' there is an abundance of God's bounty. There are lots of *cowslips* growing wild. We cultivate them and use them in the treatment of inflammation of the bowel. The cowslip is also wonderful for rejuvenation of the body. People talk about how good oil of evening primrose is for rejuvenation but we find the cowslip is the best. Here's the *wild strawberry*. In the cultivated strawberry the fruit grows under the leaf but in the wild strawberry the fruit is above the leaf. It is used in the cleaning of teeth and also helps to reduce fever, for example in the case of sunstroke. There's another nuisance on your lawn, *plantain*, but it is very useful in the treatment of constipation. The *lesser celandine* is quite like the buttercup. If you pull up the root you will see a signature of its use. The little tubers on it are like piles! We use it in the treatment of piles, not the root but the part above ground. You have to be careful in harvesting it because the plant gives off a vapour that is harmful to the eyes. We don't need to cultivate the lesser celandine as it is plentiful in the wild.

Overhead, the *hawthorn* is coming into bloom. We will make use of the haws later on. The haw is great for the tired heart. The haw extract mixed with marguerite is a great tonic.

Of course, to harvest plants like these you need a knowledgeable staff and I am fortunate in that respect: men like Peter Hynes, Laurence O'Neill and Jack Dowdall work outside for me all year round and they know their plants. Marty Reilly, who makes up a lot of the brews in the laboratory, comes from a great horticultural background. These men collectively have great wisdom. They probably don't realise how much they know. Over the years I grew up with all this wisdom, absorbing it from my father and other men and then studying it at an academic level.

At last, here is the *garlic mustard*. Take a leaf, crumble it in your hand and smell it. It is an absolutely beautiful herb. We use it in poultices for inflammation, but it is also wonderful in a summer salad, it's a bit like the wood sorrel. People long ago used plants like these. They weren't crazy or ignorant, they were wise, knowing what to pick and what not to pick. My sister Frances will come down here to pick garlic mustard, take it home and mix it with lettuce, which can be very bland, to make an exciting salad. The garlic mustard is growing all along the railway walk here – you can imagine the scent in high summer.

Here also you have lemonbalms, horsetails, yarrow and comfrey all growing wild. The *lemonbalm* is well named. Again, crumble it and rub it in your palm and inhale that lovely lemon scent. It is a wonderful relaxant. The Germans love to use it in their tea to help them unwind and 'de-stress'. The *horsetail* is used to combat hardening of the arteries. There is nothing to compare with it, but the problem is to stabilise it. When you make up a mixture from it in summer it will be green in colour, but in winter it changes to a rosé colour. The *yarrow* plant has a lovely white flower, although it can also be mauve in

colour. It is used in the treatment of kidney complaints and of rheumatism also.

And here is the broadleaf *comfrey*. It can be purple or cream in
colour. We use it as a poultice in the treatment of broken bones. In fact,
its name in Irish is *lus na gcnámha briste* – the plant of the broken bones.
It helps speed up recovery from fractures. In 1988 on the Saturday
week before the All-Ireland Final Replay against Cork, our centre-
halfback Liam Harnan broke a bone in his shoulder and it looked as
if he would miss the game. We applied a comfrey poultice to the
shoulder and gave him physiotherapy every day. Eight days later he
played against Cork. He had the shoulder strapped but had no injec-
tions. He had no problems with the shoulder then or since. Finally,
there is the *mullein* plant, with its woolly leaves, like a mouse's ears. It
was used years ago to treat tuberculosis of the lung. It was simply
boiled in milk and given to the patient. So no matter where you go, in
hedgerows and wild places, these useful plants are all about you.

We have completed our walk and are now crossing the lawn
behind the Herb Clinic. I hope you enjoyed it. On the way are some
interesting trees and plants. There's a lovely *eucalyptus* tree, whose oil
eases aches and pains. Beyond the eucalyptus is a bank of *yellow furze*
or 'whinnies' as my mother called them. No particular medicinal
use, but when the wind comes from the right direction it will waft
their beautiful aroma into the clinic. Here is some *rosemary*. We use
quite a lot of it. Up to the sixteenth century, it was used as a painkiller
– chewing its leaves was said to ease headaches. And finally, there is
the *gingko* tree with its lovely opaque fanlike leaves, not unlike the
maidenhair fern that is found growing among the rocks of the
Burren. Indeed it belongs to the same family. The leaves are used in
the treatment of artery problems. There are thirty acres of gingko
growing down in Kerry, specifically for medicinal use. The Chinese
adore this plant and it is considered sacred in Japan. Nowadays you

must have a licence to make medicines from the gingko, yet it grows naturally here and in Kerry. Maybe that is one of the heresies of progress.

We are home again. Here in the yard is a tray of a very famous plant – *lovage levisticum*. It looks a bit like celery. If you take a few leaves and chew them it will remind you of a strong Indian curry. Levisticum has a dramatically strong pungent taste. The Egyptians used it long, long ago as a breath freshener. We press the juices from the complete plant and use them together with the marguerite to help oxygenate the blood. It was brought here from the Himalayas by a missioner in 1943. It took my father twenty-three years to grow it properly. Levisticum is a much-prized plant. Ten years ago the extract from its root was fetching £3,000 a kilo on the world market.

We have two large stores where we dry the herbs and save the seeds. To get one bag of dried herbs you would need twenty bags of wet herbs. We have a big drying machine that uses a heat-exchange system, by taking hot air from the coldroom in the laboratory, piping it into the drying store and circulating it through the herbs. We work a year ahead in case – God forbid – of a crop failure, so there are two years' harvests in the store. It takes four or five days to dry a consignment. If we were to dry it in the sunshine, we would lose too much of the natural oils. The plants are all labelled by their Latin and 'local' names. When levisticum came here first, it was known as 'the stuff up the garden'. It is still labelled SUTG!

Finally, there are two laboratories. In the first one, the water-based remedies are prepared here – washed, brewed, strained and filtered into the coldroom under the guidance of our physicist, Ron Adams. We use spring water from our own wells and we have to be very hygienic with elbow-taps and constant washing of filters, but it is basically a very simple operation. In the other laboratory, Colm Redmond and Owen Lynch prepare all the concentrates based on industrial alcohol.

These have a much longer shelf-life than the water-based preparations and they facilitate people who come to us from long distances. It means they can take away a large supply in a big container which will last them a long time. The whole process is at the one time sophisticated and straightforward.

In the distance I see our daughter Doireann following the workmen about, just as I used to do as a child, absorbing all that wisdom without realising it. I cannot imagine a more wonderful place in which to grow up.

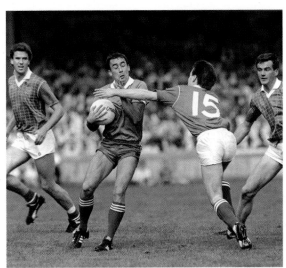

Above: Meath, All-Ireland Champions 1987-88. *Front:* PJ Gillic, Terry Ferguson, Bernard Flynn, Robbie O'Malley, Liam Harnan, Kevin Foley, Liam Hayes. *Back:* Colm O'Rourke, Mick Lyons, Mick McQuillan, Gerry McEntee, Brian Stafford, Martin O'Connell, David Beggy, Joe Cassells.

Left: Liam Hayes, Bernard Flynn (15) and Colm O'Rourke close in on Kerry opponent Ogie Moran, All-Ireland Semi-Final, 1986.

Left: Colm O'Rourke evades a Niall Cahalane tackle, All-Ireland Final vs. Cork, 1987.

Below: Tina, me and Seán Jr watch as 'Mr Kepak' – my good friend and sponsor of the Meath team – Noel Keating plants a tree to mark Seán's first birthday, April 1993. Noel died six days later.

Training session in Dalgan Park. Trevor Giles leads the way, followed by Graham Geraghty.

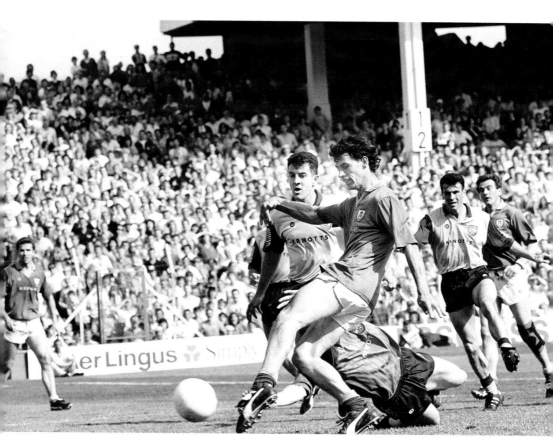

Kevin Foley rounds off a fantastic Meath movement by scoring the goal that silenced the Hill and saw Meath defeat Dublin in the fourth match of their first-round marathon tie, 1991.

Above: Guarding the Lyons Den! Mick Lyons dispossesses Vinnie Murphy of Dublin, Croke Park, Leinster Championship 1991.
Below: The New Heroes. Meath, All-Ireland Champions 1996. *Front:* Paddy Reynolds, Mark O'Reilly, Colm Coyle, Conor Martin, Darren Fay, Enda McManus. *Back:* Trevor Giles, Graham Geraghty, John McDermott, Jimmy McGuinness, Barry Callaghan, Martin O'Connell, Colm Brady, Tommy Dowd, Brendan Reilly.

Victory Jig! Trevor Giles, Paddy Reynolds and John McDermott celebrate Meath's All-Ireland victory over Cork, Croke Park, September 1999.

O'Byrne Cup tie. Miserable January day Meath vs. Kildare in Newbridge. 'We have a bit of work to do, lads ... ' Selectors: David Beggy, Colm Coyle and me.

Above: Happiness and sheer relief. Celebrating Meath's All-Ireland victory over Cork with Evan Kelly, Croke Park, September 1999.
Below: My last day out as manager in Croke Park. Dublin manager Paul Caffrey offers commiseration after Meath lose to Dublin, Leinster Championship, June 2005.

CHAPTER TWENTY-FIVE

1991

We had reached three All-Ireland Finals in four years, winning two of them. The players had put in a great effort but many people now saw them as an ageing team who had their best years behind them. Not surprisingly, I did not see it that way. After all, we had won the Leinster Final and the National League title in 1990 and had lost the All-Ireland Final by two points. It was hardly the sign of a team that was 'finished .There was a great work ethic in that team. They liked to work hard but I was concerned about the mileage on some of the clocks. I remember walking down the 'centre aisle' between the two old pitches in Dalgan Park one November evening and voicing that concern to Dr Jack Finn. I felt I could not risk the type of stamina work we needed to do on the pitch – but we could do it in water, following the example of the American athlete Joan Benoit. Jack agreed and we put the idea in motion. Gerry O'Reilly and Sonia O'Sullivan sourced the buoyancy aids for us in Atlanta. The county board were very supportive, as those aids were very expensive. Eoin McEvoy arranged the availability of the swimming pool in Gormanston College. We tried hard to keep everything fairly confidential. Imagine being beaten in the first round of the championship and then revealing that you had been training in water. We could never face the people of Meath.

The reaction of the players varied. Most of them could not swim. Getting into the water that first night was a strange experience. Even our sponsor, Noel Keating, got in on the act and joined the lads. Our physiotherapist, Anne Bourton – who is a powerful swimmer – got in also to reassure the lads who were fearful in the water. Later, Gerry McEntee called in on a visit home to Ireland, surveyed the scene and said, 'That's it! Boylan has finally gone over the edge!' We persisted and only did our first work on the pitch three weeks before our first match.

That first match would pit us against our arch-rivals in Leinster – Dublin. For years 'seeding' had kept us apart in the early stages of the Leinster championship, but now there was an open draw and the first two teams out of the hat were Meath and Dublin – and not even in the first round, but in a 'preliminary round.' Talk about the laws of chance. The implications were obvious – to be ready for the Dubs in a preliminary round we would need a level of fitness that we would normally need for a Leinster Final. We had had an undistinguished League campaign, managing to survive in Division One. We had some changes in personnel, but not many. Gerry McEntee and Joe Cassells had retired. Our new midfielder, Colm Brady, had a fantastic season in 1990 but then got injured and was a huge loss. Tommy Dowd and John McDermott had come on the panel and Brendan Reilly was coming back from injury. Some promising ex-minors, Hugh Carolan and Terry Connor, were drafted in but essentially we had almost the same team from the 1987-88 days. Another young man, Graham Geraghty, was deemed too young for the senior team as he still had another year in the minor ranks. I had to build up the lads mentally for one more assault on the title as they had put in a huge effort in 1990 to try to win the title for Colm O'Rourke as captain. Now there was concern that Colm and Mick Lyons were just going through the motions in training. I took the two lads aside and spoke to them – not an easy thing to do!

'Well,' said Colm, 'does my reputation not speak for itself?'

'I'm not talking about your reputation,' I replied. 'I'm talking about the other lads looking on now and seeing you just going through the motions.'

It was just as difficult saying this to Mick, a man who had never let us down either and had come back from having a broken leg, but it had the required effect. When the pair of them got really involved in a training session in Walterstown, everyone realised this was serious business and things started to come together.

Around this time also, the Media began to use Colm as a match analyst. There was talk about this among the squad, but I had no problem with it. My concern was that people would have their say but everything would be kept 'within house'. It was inevitable for a player like Colm, who had been at the top for so long, that his opinions on matches would be sought. Liam Hayes was a successful sports journalist with the *Sunday Press*. I remember asking his editor, Michael Carwood, to ask Liam to write about anything but Meath, but Liam had great strength of character and, in writing about Meath, he was true to his colleagues. When the 1988 All-Ireland Final ended in a draw, Liam was caught in a dilemma. He was due to go to Seoul the next day to report on the Olympic Games, but he decided not to go, thus putting his work and possibly his career in jeopardy. Having Colm work as an analyst was unusual, but he had more than earned the right to do so. I thought, when is the right time to start? We would have faith in Colm's integrity, and I knew he would not let us down.

Dublin under manager Paddy Cullen had won the National League and were flying high when they took the field against us on 2 June. We were ring-rusty, not having had a competitive game for some time. Over 60,000 spectators piled into Croke Park for a preliminary round of the Leinster championship. Little did we think what would follow ... We came back from five points down at half-time to squeeze out a draw: 1-12 to 1-12. We were relieved to survive. Dublin should have won that day and on the subsequent days, but these were typical Dublin-Meath games – packed with fierce intensity and passion. Anything could happen and in this instance, it did. A week later we were back again to do battle. This time we led by three points at the interval but Dublin caught up with us in the rain-soaked second half and we held on grimly for another draw. Disaster struck a few minutes from the end of normal time when Mick Lyons was sent off for a foul on Vinny Murphy. Technically we were able to bring a new man, Liam Harnan, on for extra time because it was a 'new game', but another thirty minutes still could not separate the teams: Dublin 1-11, Meath 1-11.

Suddenly this contest caught the imagination of a nation that had just come through the euphoria of the World Cup adventure in Italia '90. In the wake of all that, Gaelic games were perceived to be almost dead – and then these amazing games came along. They were very physical games – powerful football played with unrelenting intensity. At that time all frees and sideline kicks were taken off the ground, so there was very little space to move. They were a mix of all that was great and all that was stupid in Gaelic football. We knew each game would bring us along, although I suppose our opponents felt likewise. Paddy Cullen and his backroom team had been winners as players in the seventies, so the 'Blue Army' would expect them to win. On the other hand, we had beaten Dublin in four of the last five years. As the contest progressed it might have seemed that we as selectors were not always on top of things, but you can't be roaring and shouting all the time ...

These players were lads who had given everything to the game. They all wanted to be out there, but it was difficult for them to accept this as an opening round – if you did not win here, your season was over in June. In some ways they were weary of the chore that faced them, but at least I was convinced that we had been right not to have done the hard training on the pitch as the players would not have been able for it. Maybe we as selectors had too much faith in what they could achieve under pressure (and that was a compliment to them). Subsequently we were proved correct, but it was frustrating at times. We used thirty-one players in the four matches, among them Gerry McEntee, who came back on the panel from 'retirement' after the second match. Gerry and Joe Cassells had been our 'eye in the sky' for the first two matches, telling it as they saw it from the stand. In fact they went beyond that, berating Colm O'Rourke and Bernie Flynn for not giving the ball to new boy Sean Kelly, who had come back from serious injury in a League match against Donegal. It was understand-able – players like Colm and Bernie had been together for so long that they automatically looked for each other, making it difficult for the new man. Apart from his analysis, Gerry still felt he had something to offer, so he was back on the panel once more.

It was a difficult time also for Liam Hayes as captain, when it seemed as though things were not happening as in the earlier success-ful years. Every captain wants to see everyone putting in the effort in every session. The choice and role of captain are important. He is not just a figurehead. For a long time the captaincy had been an honorary posi-tion, given to a representative from the club champions. That system had served Meath well, going back to the days of Brian Smith and Peter McDermott, but sometimes players are not comfortable with the role of captain. A classic example was JJ McCormack from Walterstown, who was made captain for a Leinster championship first-round match, but gave the captaincy to Joe Cassells. Good for JJ! At a certain stage I decided that myself and the selectors would choose the captain. You could have great players whose club would never win a senior title, but who would make great captains. Marty O'Connell is a case in point. The captaincy is a crucial role and we as selectors felt it important to take the risk in choosing our captain.

After a break of two weeks, Meath and Dublin resumed battle on 23 June. During that break the chairman of the county board asked me if I wanted to take the lads away for a few days. I declined as I felt that we were all right for the time being. It was another tough match – tough but not dirty. Again Dublin should have won but a goal by Bernie Flynn and two late points by 'Staff' got us level. We went through to thirty minutes of extra time and it was unbelievable. Gerry McEntee came on as a substitute and showed he still had the flair for the big occasion. A goal for each side in extra time and we finished level for the third time: Meath 2-11, Dublin 1-14. Even referee Tommy Howard, a wonderful clubman from Kilcullen in County Kildare who made a great contribution to this saga, was coming down with cramp. Where and when would it end? The saga had now made the front pages as well as the back pages of the newspapers. The hype was becoming as intense as the matches themselves. Now was the time to take the lads away from all of this and so we took them and their partners away for a weekend in Scotland.

Saturday, 6 July 1991, a crowd of 60,000 plus packed Croke Park for a preliminary round of the Leinster championship. It was truly a watershed in the history of the GAA. Gaelic football was alive and thriving and if it was drama you wanted, this final act had it all.

Terry Ferguson – probably the fittest and most supple man on the team – put his back out while togging out in the dressing room. We gave Sean Kelly until the very last minute to prove his fitness, but he too had to pull out. Padraig Lyons came in for Terry, but fifteen minutes into the game his hamstring went. Early in the match Colm O'Rourke became the meat in a Keith Barr–Eamonn Heery 'sandwich' and was carried off concussed. Dr Jack Finn cleared all the substitutes off the bench to lay Colm flat and we were all relieved to hear him eventually say: 'He's coming round! He's coming round!' And true to form, the iron man came back on to the field. I gave Colm Coyle the nod to come out to centre-half forward to take the pressure off Rourkey. To compound all our troubles Bernie Flynn went off with an injured calf muscle in the second half. What else could go wrong?

Once again Dublin led at half-time and stretched their lead to six points in the second half. All was not lost. If these lads in green and gold had anything, they had heart. Stafford scored a great goal from a pass by the recovered Colm O'Rourke. Even when Keith Barr soloed up the field and put the ball over the bar, I wasn't fazed. I turned to Pat Reynolds and said: 'We're grand now. Once a half-back scores, he will want to score more and will lose focus!' Dublin were awarded a penalty but, fortunately for us, their penalty-taker, Charlie Redmond, had been taken off. Mick Lyons 'accompanied' Keith Barr in his run to take the penalty (or, as we like to say, Keith beat Mick in the run to the ball) and the ball went wide. I still had not lost hope. I remember being over on the Hogan Stand side, saying to Liam Hayes: 'Even if they score the penalty, you can still win. Throw the ball around like we did in Scotland ... ' There was only a minute or two left and we were still down by three points. Then it happened: Marty O'Connell retrieved the ball on his own end line and gave it to Mick Lyons. On to Mattie McCabe. A slick lay-off to Liam Harnan. He to Rourkey who is fouled and takes a quick free to Jinksy. He gives it to Foley who passes to Gillic and keeps running. Gillic to Dowd who passes to Rourkey and runs on to take the return pass and give it to Kevin ('I'm deadly from two yards') Foley. Goal! Eleven passes and not one Dublin player had touched the ball. To me, it was quite simply the greatest goal of all time for its team involvement and execution under pressure. I know I am biased, but the great Mick O'Dwyer told me afterwards it had to be one of the all-time great Gaelic goals and that is good enough for me.

And it came from an endlessly-practised move on a little soccer pitch in Scotland. But it wasn't over yet. We won possession from the kick-out and another passing move fed the ball to Jinksy who lashed it over the bar from forty yards. Game over. Delight for us. Devastation for Dublin. After five hours and forty minutes of hard-hitting, high-powered football, we had won by a point. The nation had been enthralled by a spectacle that we are unlikely to see happen ever again. It was right to play it out to the end, rather than have a penalty shoot-out – any player who took part in the marathon will tell you this. The Lord Mayor of Dublin gave a reception for both teams. It was a novel and generous gesture even if, from his perspective, the wrong bride turned up. Keith Barr and Eamonn Heery apologised to Colm O'Rourke for the 'sandwich'.

'Let's face it, Colm. You would have done the same yourself!'

'Yeah, but with one difference.'

'What's that?'

'You wouldn't have got up!'

The Dublin players and management were naturally shell-shocked but were gracious as ever in defeat. They had come up against a team whose unity and teamwork had developed over the years, a team who had huge self-belief and terrific honesty with each other – honesty without malice. Only once in a generation does a group like that come along. But nobody was blowing trumpets. After all, we had only qualified for the first round of the Leinster championship ...

My own reaction might have seemed 'unflappable' but I had to restrain myself. The general public would never understand all the things that go through a manager's mind: the worries, the doubts, the problems on and off the field. In the middle of that marathon I sat into the early hours talking one of the players through the serious financial worries that beset him. The support of my fellow-selectors Pat Reynolds and Tony Brennan was crucial. Everybody felt they knew how to pick the team but we knew things the public would never know. We spent hours analysing performance and choosing a balanced team. Our water-training had been vindicated and great credit was due to Fintan Ginnity and the county board for supporting that and our trip to Scotland. We got over the preliminary round.

Round one proper versus Wicklow. Anything that could be known about Meath was well-known at this stage. The lads were exposed like modern premiership players. On top of that, Wicklow was coached by a Meathman, Niall Rennick from Dunderry – so surprise, surprise – the game ends in a draw. We were so lucky to survive, but human nature dictates that you cannot peak all the time. We got through at the second attempt. Hugh Kenny of Wicklow was sent off for a harmless foul and our own Liam Hayes also walked after a fracas with his opponent. We consequently lost him for the Semi-Final against Offaly but in the event we had a comfortable win. The Leinster Final against Laois was played on a Saturday because of the backlog in fixtures. We won easily enough by six points despite losing Bobby O'Malley with a broken leg and Gerry McEntee's unhappiness at not being chosen to start the game. We were Leinster champions again, tired and somewhat depleted, but champions.

We faced Roscommon in the All-Ireland Semi-Final. It was a very physical match. Derek Duggan caused Meath, and especially Terry Ferguson, a lot of problems and with fifteen minutes to go we were five points down to a team who were playing 'out of their skins.' Roscommon came into the game fresh, whereas we had been playing all summer with no time to celebrate or recuperate. We were performing like professionals but we were amateurs. And then once more, Brian Stafford stepped up and hit six points in the last ten minutes. We had reached the All-Ireland Final by a solitary point. I did feel sorry for Roscommon. I think they may have lost focus when – with five minutes to go – the stewards came out and walked around the pitch.

Our Final opponents would be Down, whom we had beaten in the 1990 League Final. Bobby O'Malley was a big enough loss but the real bombshell came in the week before the match when Colm O'Rourke came down with pneumonia. On the Thursday Dr Joe McGrath (RIP) told us that Colm was not to travel, never mind play. But Colm had other ideas. The pneumonia cleared on the Friday. On Saturday and Sunday morning Colm did twenty minutes' work on the pitch. The medical advice was now: 'You'll get twenty minutes out of him in the Final – and no more.' The rest is history. After a quarter of an hour Down were leading by eleven points. Mick Lyons hobbled off with a knee injury before half-time and was a huge loss. Colm was mad keen to have a go but we stuck to the medical advice and brought him on with twenty minutes to go. He gave it his all and almost turned the game but we lost by two points. We got a lot of stick for not bringing Colm on earlier but we just could not take the risk. In retrospect, the three-week gap before the Final did not suit us. We had been playing almost every week in our nine-match summer but now after three weeks we had 'come down' and could not sustain the effort. I could not take from Down's excellence on the day. They caught us flatfooted and without Bobby and Colm – and ultimately Mick – it was a huge mountain to climb, but it was close. The final whistle blew as a sideline ball from Alan Brown landed in the Down square ...

Of course, we were shattered, physically and mentally. The Sam Maguire Cup would have been a fitting reward for the efforts of this amazing bunch of lads, but it was not to be. It was an amazing year in the annals of the GAA. We were proud to have been a part of it, but the 'bridge too far' was hard for the lads to take. For some of them, it would be the end of the road. Their hearts were broken but they got an incredible reception in defeat and ultimately handled that defeat with great dignity.

CHAPTER TWENTY-SIX

Valley and Peak

After the heroics of 1991 we might still have been seen as title contenders the following year, but instead Laois dumped us out of the first round of the Leinster championship. Such are the fickle fortunes of football. I took some flak over the team selection for that match, as there were All-Ireland medal-holders sitting on the bench that day – but again, that's football. You try things and a lot of the time they work, but sometimes they don't and you're considered the worst in the world. So it was back to normal living for the summer of '92. I love the story of the two Meath farmers trudging out of Navan after the Laois-Meath game. After a long silence one says to the other with a philosophical sigh: 'Well, one thing's for sure, Jemmy. There'll be no mastitis this year!' – a reference to the unmilked cows in the crazy summer of '91.

We entered a valley period again, beaten in the Leinster Semi-Final of 1993 by the old nemesis, Dublin, and again by the Dubs in the Leinster Final of 1994, thanks to a mighty last-minute point by Jack Sheedy. Again, fortune was fickle to Jack a year later when he wrecked his knee playing against us in a challenge match in Moynalvey. Although I celebrated my tenth anniversary as manager in 1992 I had no thoughts of standing down. I was still getting a buzz out of the job, seeking out new players and engaging in serious team-building with my new selectors Joe Cassells and Mick Lyons. We actually won the National League in 1994, beating a strong Armagh team, so there were signs of potential there. A rising star emerged that day when Trevor Giles scored six points. When I look now at a photograph of the victorious panel assembled at a reception in the Kepak plant, I see a lot of young rising stars greatly outnumbering 'old-timers', like Bob O'Malley (now captain), 'Staff', Marty O'Connell (now full-back), Bernie Flynn and Colm Coyle. There are many new faces: Trevor Giles, Graham Geraghty, Neville Dunne, John McDermott, Jimmy McGuinness, Willie Donnelly, Declan Lynch, Vincent Ryan, Donal Smith, Enda McManus and Conor Martin. Unfortunately, two other young stars, Hugh Carolan and Sean Kelly, had been plagued by injury.

Rebuilding a team is a slow process and demands patience while you strive to get a balanced outfit. We did all right in the 1994-95 League campaign, but we were by no means wonderful. Two weeks before the 1995 Leinster Final Mick and Joe told me that, win or lose, they were standing down for personal reasons. We then hit another trough in that Leinster Final, when Dublin beat us by ten points. We actually led by a point with a quarter of an hour to go but Paul Clarke got in for a Dublin goal and the floodgates opened. Naturally, the cry: 'Boylan Must Go' went up in some quarters. On the night of that Leinster Final, one of the 1987-88 team came down to the county club in Dunshaughlin specifically to advise me to walk away from management, but he talked to the younger members of the squad first and ended up saying to me: 'You can't go. They want you!' I thought long and hard about my position and I was opposed by Shane McEntee for the position of manager. The delegates went for me and that was it.

The rebuilding process continued. Frank Foley and Eamonn O'Brien came on board as my new co-selectors. Conor Martin was now first choice in goals. And a tigerish young corner-back, Mark O'Reilly, had won his spurs with Tralee Institute of Technology. In front of him another young dynamo, Paddy Reynolds, had come back from college in England. Darren Fay had come in the previous year and got injured in the Leinster Final, but was now back for the League. So too was the injured Colm Brady. John McDermott had now established himself at centre-field and we had options with Cormac Sullivan who was equally at home in goals or outfield. Up front we found three very strong and gifted attackers in Evan Kelly, Ollie Murphy and Barry Callaghan. Overall, we had a very young squad. The only 'veterans' remaining from the previous glory days were Marty O'Connell, Colm Coyle and Brennie Reilly.

I have a kind of instinct which has served me well in creating new positions for players. We converted Darren Fay into a full-back and moved Brennie Reilly and Graham Geraghty from defence into attack. Tommy Dowd had been full-forward in the 1994-95 campaign, but because he was such a whole-hearted player he took a lot of abuse in that position so we moved him out to centre-half-forward. Graham, Tommy and Trevor became quite a formidable half-forward line. We faced Carlow in the first round of the 1996 Leinster championship. After the heavy defeat by Dublin in '95 and with a young and largely unproven team, Meath would not have been fancied to do much, even by many of their own supporters. I could see a serious intent in them, however. I remember saying to Denis Murtagh on the way home from training in Gormanston in January 1996: 'If we get a bit of luck at all this year, we could surprise everybody ... '

Carlow were tipped to win because of *Éire Óg's* impressive performance in the club championship. In the opening minute Paddy

Reynolds went for a ball with an opponent who was at least a foot taller than him and won it. That set the scene. We ran out easy winners: 0-24 to 0-6. Our next opponents were Laois, who had promised a lot but who were under a cloud of tragedy following the horrific deaths of the Maher family in a house-fire in Portarlington, one of the family killed was Colm, a gifted half-forward. Even though the team wanted to play, their spirit was subdued and how they played at all is hard to know. We got through on the score: 2-14 to 1-9, and once again faced Dublin in the Leinster Final. It was nip and tuck all the way on a mucky, wet day. We switched Evan Kelly with Graham Geraghty and it worked for us. I can still see Evan brushing past Dublin's Paul Curran, a very resolute defender, as if he wasn't there. Meath 0-10 Dublin 0-8. We had avenged the '95 defeat.

We restricted our squad to twenty-four to keep it manageable and in fact we only used nineteen of them in the 1996 campaign, whereas in the 1991 marathon with Dublin we had used a total of thirty-one players. We played a very different type of game now, because we had very different players – not big and muscular but more athletic and pacy. It was then that Trevor Giles came into his own. He excelled in picking up a breaking ball, and in its distribution, and there was nobody better to dispossess a man without fouling. Graham Geraghty proved a revelation in attack. With each of them flanking Tommy Dowd, what a dimension those young men gave to our game. Today we talk about packed defences, but ten years ago Trevor and Graham excelled at funnelling back into defence and winning ball. They were powerful athletes who could carry or kick with incredible accuracy. And they both oozed confidence and self-belief.

We faced Tyrone in the All-Ireland Semi-Final – a strong team who had lost narrowly to Dublin in the previous year's final and would consequently be the choice of neutral supporters. On the Thursday before the match I said to the lads: 'You have won back the Leinster title. Why stop here? Go for it!' It became a sort of mantra that Conor Martin subsequently kept repeating to his colleagues. For such young players they had amazing belief in themselves. Nineteen-year-old boys like Mark O'Reilly and Darren Fay suddenly became men. I told Mark that Peter Canavan would probably move into his corner. 'That's okay,' Mark replied, 'I can deal with it.' Self-belief! The match itself became controversial for the injuries sustained by a couple of Tyrone players. Marty O'Connell was alleged to have stamped on a Tyrone player. It was entirely accidental. Marty is not that kind of player. Tyrone had a new team doctor and a couple of their players came out for the second half with heads bandaged like World War Two veterans ... Tyrone played terrific football at the start of the second half but our young lads withstood the pressure very well. Graham Geraghty had a phenomenal game and deservedly won the Man of the Match award. In the end we won comfortably: Meath 2-15, Tyrone 0-12.

Sometimes the bit of luck goes with you. Sometimes it doesn't, but you certainly need it to win a championship. In the Leinster Final of 1996 Colm Coyle had a brilliant first half against Dublin but something happened to his knee. It turned out to be a piece of metal from a previous operation that had been disturbed. Should we risk another operation and thus rule him out of the Tyrone match? We chose to let it settle. Colm did no training before the Tyrone match. Because he had been so influential against Dublin, Tyrone kept the ball away from him and this suited Colm. We had taken a chance and it worked. Against Tyrone, Mark O'Reilly took a heavy blow on the ribs and was not able to train until the Thursday before the All-Ireland Final. We took the chance of playing him against Mayo and again it paid off. Mark had a brilliant game on the first day against Mayo.

Enda McManus had joined us in 1992 and had a lot of injury problems, but he ended up one of the unsung heroes of the '96 team as a phenomenal centre-half-back and was a great reader of the game. He was immensely strong and yet unfussy. He had the ability to absorb pressure and do the simple things well. He would have played initially as a full- or corner-back but he blossomed as a centre-half-back. In 1995 Dessie Farrell of Dublin had destroyed us at centre-forward but now, in Enda, we had the man to plug the gap. During the 1995-96 League campaign we played John McDermott at centre-half-back, partly because Enda was injured, but also because we wanted to strengthen him as a defensive mid-fielder for the championship. John understood this and again a chance we took worked. On the downside, we lost Cormac Murphy with a cruciate ligament injury. The preparation for the championship was intense. At one time we played five challenge matches in eleven days! Frank, Eamonn and I felt the team was gradually sorting itself out. They were a very tightly-knit bunch of lads who had a terrific hunger for success. The veterans like Coyler and Marty couldn't believe it. They were driven by the younger players and felt they had to smarten themselves up or else they would be left behind. There was something extraordinarily serious about these young men. We decided to keep a tight panel of twenty-four it worked for us in 1996 but unfortunately would derail us a year later. The bit of luck ...

I was very impressed by Mayo's performance in the other All-Ireland Semi-Final. They had run Kerry off the field and shown strength and spirit that I had not seen in a Mayo team for years. We were facing a monumental task and I was worried. In the Final, we started favourites on the strength of our dismissal of Tyrone, but Mayo ran through us and built up a commanding lead. We looked dead and buried but the lads never lost heart. They fought back and got a draw from Colm Coyle's famous long-range punt (I am sure the folklore has it over one hundred yards by now), which eventually hopped over the bar. Ironically, the night before the match Colm had said to the squad: 'Look lads, don't believe what you read in the papers. There will only be a hop of the ball in it!' How prophetic was that. We were so relieved to get a second chance.

The replay will, I suppose, be remembered for twenty-seven seconds of madness or simply 'the row'. Darren Fay caught a ball in our goalmouth and got clouted – mayhem followed. Fellows who were not getting a kick of the ball ran half the length of the field to get involved. Others were trying to break it up. It was sheer madness and something I don't like to see happening, but it happened and once it was settled the game went on from there with very few frees awarded and quite an amount of really good football played. There were serious repercussions, of course. Liam McHale and Colm Coyle were sent off and while Mayo fans bemoaned the loss of their star, our loss was huge also. Colm Coyle had played championship football for Meath since 1982, had a couple of All-Ireland medals in his back pocket and was a hugely influential player on this young team. Subsequently Mayo had six players suspended while we had eight players punished for those twenty-seven seconds. When I look at incidents of a lot more serious nature that happened before or since that day, I wonder ... The media of course went to town on the incident. How often have we seen photographs or film rolled out again and again to highlight 'violence' on the pitch? Of course it should not have happened but it dominated a great achievement by a young team who had come from nowhere. Thirty-one counties would have wanted Mayo to win – and so would we if we had not been playing them. They had not won an All-Ireland since 1951 when, ironically, they had beaten Meath!

As in the first match, Mayo opened us up again and built up a lead with the aid of a strong wind but just before half-time Tommy Dowd won a penalty that Trevor Giles converted, reducing the lead to four points. Trevor's ability to read a game was crucial. Our winning score came from a shoulder tackle by Trevor, which enabled him to win the ball. He put a fantastic ball into the corner to Brennie Reilly. Then Brennie picks the ball up with one foot, sells a dummy, solos with the other foot and puts the ball over the bar. Meath have won their sixth All-Ireland and no better or prouder man than Tommy Dowd to accept the Sam Maguire Cup as captain. He too had played a crucial part in the victory. Early in the match we switched him with Brennie Reilly and it paid off ten minutes from time when Tommy won a free which the quick-thinking Graham Geraghty slipped to Tommy. Although falling off balance, Tommy slid the ball past John Madden in the Mayo goal to give us the lead for the first time. Between them, Trevor and Tommy had scored two goals and seven points. It was particularly gratifying for a player like Tommy to captain his team to All-Ireland glory. He was an inspirational leader, the new hero in a new age of Meath football. Every youngster in the county wanted to be Tommy Dowd. He was the people's man, with a terrific work-rate (despite having asthma), born for the big occasion.

To come from losing a Leinster Final by ten points in 1995 to winning an All-Ireland Final a year later was a huge turnaround. It is quite difficult for young players, even with natural talent, to achieve something like that. They cannot take that talent for granted but must work at it – and those lads worked very hard. They were a different breed to the 1987-88 teams, playing a different brand of football and their victory was the perfect tribute to those 'old-timers' now watching from the stands. The mantle had been handed on and Meath was back at the top again, with a victory that would give a confidence and a swagger to younger players coming up.

The victory was equally a great credit to all those who were involved at under-age level, men like Paul Kenny, Johnny Sullivan, Mattie Kerrigan, Patsy Duff, Ultan Fitzpatrick, Jim Cooney, Pat O'Neill and Tommy Mahon. I was delighted that our physiotherapist, Anne Bourton, who had been quite ill after the All-Ireland Semi-Final, was now well enough to be part of our big day. All through our bad times from 1992 to 1995 our sponsors Kepak stood four-square behind us, despite the untimely death of Noel Keating in 1993. Nothing was questioned. Whatever needed to be done was done. At times it was suggested that we only 'used' Kepak. What nonsense. I never 'used' anyone in my life. Whatever Kepak did for us was nothing to do with sponsorship *per se*. It was to do with friendship, pride of place, having people around you that inspired you. On the day after the Final, Kepak, under Liam McGreal, John Horgan and Brendan McDonough, held an amazing reception for us. Suddenly it was all too much for me. I was totally overcome with emotion and I burst into tears. We had had great times and sad times, but to be back at Kepak again with Sam Maguire was just so fantastic for all the people who were prepared to help us out at all levels – none more so than Fintan Ginnity, Liam Creavin and the Meath county board. The spectacular times were back again.

CHAPTER TWENTY-SEVEN

The New Heroes

When I described Tommy Dowd as a new hero in a new age of Meath football, he was, of course, only one of a group of heroes. Once in a generation, a player comes along with all the talents. Trevor Giles was such a player. Winner of All-Ireland medals at minor and under-21 levels, Trevor came on the senior team for the 1993-94 League. He scored six points in the National League Final victory over Armagh, yet failed to get even a nomination for an All-Star award. Winner of an All-Ireland senior medal and Player of the Year in both 1996 and 1999, he also starred in the International Rules series in Australia. He was unfortunate to damage his cruciate ligament in 1998, but being both a physiotherapist and a perfectionist, he practised what he preached in his rehabilitation and resumed playing seven months later, ahead of schedule.

Trevor was gifted with great balance and was equally good off both feet – and indeed could deliver the perfect pass with either hand. He was not a big man but he had a fantastic ability to dispossess an opponent without fouling. He knew when to tackle and when to stand off and had an extraordinarily wise head for a young man. Trevor just loved playing and where others would shy away from pressure, he revelled in it. He gloried in responsibility – the bigger the occasion the better he rose to it. It was unfortunate that we lost the All-Ireland Final in 2001 when Trevor was captain. It would have been the crowning point in a great career. His remarkable vision enabled him to split a defence with a pin-pointed pass. Trevor was a natural leader, who was a great help and inspiration to younger players and yet he was a most unassuming fellow. He would have graced any team in any generation in almost any position on the field.

A lot of Meath players had the ability to play in many positions, which has good and bad points Graham Geraghty was one such player. Graham was one of the most amazing athletes I have come across; he had an extraordinary natural ability with a great range of skills. Like Trevor he was of slight build, but taller than the Skryne man and equally adept with both feet. Off the field he seemed to have a devil-may-care attitude, but on the pitch he was a serious player with incredible mental strength. He was also a serious man for fair play. Some people may raise a wry smile at this, but it is true. He will be remembered for getting into trouble for passing racist remarks at an opponent in Australia. I am not condoning that, but what Irish journalists did not choose to report was that the first two times Graham went for the ball, his opponent tried to take him out of the game. Graham did not react, but when the same player went for Dessie Dolan, then a young player on his first Rules trip, Graham was in like a flash to protect his team-mate.

At times he might seem to drift in and out of games, but as with all naturally-gifted players, everyone wants to beat them and they don't always get the protection they deserve. Graham might not seem to be doing well, but then he could turn a game with a flash of brilliance. He was incredibly creative in defence – winning an All-Star award in 1994 – but when we moved him to the attack, what a threat that line of Graham, Trevor and Tommy Dowd posed to any defence! The 1996

Semi-Final against Tyrone was undoubtedly Graham's greatest day and again because he did not have an outstanding game in the final, he didn't get an All-Star award that year. He did get an invitation to a trial with Arsenal FC and probably could have plied his trade there, but Graham was very much a home bird and he loved Gaelic Football.

The great Kerry forward Eoin 'Bomber' Liston was once asked to name his 'greatest Meath team' and he came up with the following: McQuillan, O'Malley, Lyons, Fay; Geraghty, Harnan, O'Connell; McEntee, McDermott; Murphy, Dowd, Giles; O'Rourke, Stafford, Flynn. (Incidentally, on the subject of all-time greatest teams, it is said that to shorten a long journey back from West Cork, the Jimmy Magee All-Stars tried to pick the Dirtiest Team of All Time! All I am saying here is that Meath managed to get one player on that team ...)

Other young men stood out in 1996. Darren Fay was a schoolboy when he joined us a year earlier. People were telling us to put him in as corner-back and keep Marty O'Connell as full-back, but we saw greater potential in Darren in the middle, and how he vindicated our decision! In front of Darren, Enda McManus had returned to the team after opting out previously when things were not going well for him. He became an absolute rock, uncomplicated and unfussy, just what you want at centre-half-back. We had groomed John McDermott (Big Mac) in that position during the League campaign to improve his defensive qualities. Big Mac was the greatest mid-fielder I ever saw. Now at centre-field, aided by Jimmy McGuinness, he was a tremendous influence. He got and he gave and was a great support to Trevor and the boys in front of him.

Colm Brady had had a nightmare few years with injuries, but fought his way back to win a place in the final line-up. Up front were Evan Kelly, an immensely strong young player who had come from a junior club, Drumree, and Barry Callaghan, another nineteen-year-old but with the head of a thirty-year-old. Barry was a very smart player who never wasted a ball. He later played centre-half-back for us but suffered a lot of setbacks through injury.

A number of the 1996 team had experienced final defeat at minor level, but on the senior stage they had something different. They weren't afraid of losing. They weren't afraid of anything. They were quite an extraordinary bunch of lads. It is a tribute to their application and consistency that we started the same fifteen players in every round of the championship. We were working from a tight panel of twenty-four which served us well, but the same strategy caught us out in 1997.

Our opening match in defence of our title against Dublin was yet another typical Meath-Dublin battle – powerful, intense football. We raced into a ten-point lead but Dublin came back to within a point. We managed to get three points up and then last-minute drama. It wouldn't be a Meath-Dublin clash without it. Dublin were awarded a penalty, but to our relief Paul Bealin's shot came back off the crossbar. On to the Semi-Final against Kildare with Nigel Nestor now in the team after a brilliant League campaign. Another saga, almost equalling 1991. Three cracking matches. Our half-forward trio, Graham, Trevor and Tommy, kept us in the first match with eight of our twelve points, Trevor kicking a tremendous point to equalise in the dying minutes. The second match was a classic – terrific open play with forty-two scores. This, of course, was Jody Devine's Day. A great servant to Meath over the years, Jody proved the point that big games are often won by unlikely and unsung players. The match went to extra time. Trevor Giles had scored one penalty and had another one saved and fisted to the net to equalise in the last minute of normal time. Trevor's overall tally was an unbelievable 2-8 in an incredible match. In extra time, we went six points down but cometh the hour, cometh Jody. Four amazing points from distance helped to put us one point up, before Kildare snatched an equaliser: Meath 2-20, Kildare 3-17. Days like that live in the memory.

Perhaps not surprisingly, the third match was completely different. A lot of tension crept into the game, not helped by a slippery surface. Four players were sent off. We lost Mark O'Reilly and Darren Fay, but a new star was born when Ollie Murphy scored 1-4, enabling us to finally end the saga with a 1-12 to 1-10 victory. It was victory but at a cost. We faced Offaly in the Leinster Final and to compound our problems Martin O'Connell injured his back on the eve of the match. Our entire full-back line was now absent and we were also without Graham Geraghty who had been sent off in the second Kildare match. Even at full strength we would have been up against it. Under Tommy Lyons Offaly were on a roll and would be National League champions in 1998. They had a brilliant opening half against us and hit three spectacular goals before running out winners by 3-17 to 1-15. For us, it was the end of an amazing season. Offaly sadly seemed to leave their best efforts on the field against us and went out tamely to Mayo in the All-Ireland Semi-Final. We had our revenge in 1998 when in the First Round of the Leinster championship we beat Offaly 3-10 to 0-7. Our newly-converted centre-half-back, Barry Callaghan, and new corner-back, Donal Curtis, helped to ensure that there would be no spectacular goals this time and two more newcomers, Ray Magee and Stephen Dillon, grabbed a goal each.

We got one hell of a scare from Louth in the Leinster Semi-Final and only a masterly display by Tommy Dowd, who scored five points from play, helped us squeeze through by the narrowest of margins. Kildare, under Mick O'Dwyer, were our Leinster Final opponents and this time it was their turn for revenge for '97. To add to our woes, our captain, Brendan Reilly, was sent off in the second half and five minutes later Trevor Giles joined him on the sideline with a severely-damaged cruciate ligament. We were out of the championship and the muttering began, despite us winning an All-Ireland title and reaching two

Leinster Finals in three years. We had come from winning nothing to winning regularly, but for some people it was not enough. They could not handle not being top dog all the time. It takes a monumental effort to get to the top and an even bigger effort to stay there. You need that bit of luck and it deserted us in 1997-98. If we hadn't lost four players (from a restricted panel) in 1997 maybe ... if we had not lost Brennie and Trevor (and earlier Paddy Reynolds and Jimmy McGuinness) in 1998 maybe ...

But I would not for a moment deny Offaly or Kildare their victories. That is the great thing about Gaelic Football – there is always a chance to come back. Critics would say we picked the wrong players or ignored other 'better' players. When Mark O'Reilly came in, I was told he had a brother at home who was twice as good. The players we had were the players we had and generally they were the ones that performed. After Jody Devine's wonderful display in the second match against Kildare, he still was not picked to start in the third match. That's selectors for you! They have to make a call. And look at the half-forward line Jody was trying to break into.

In any event, I was opposed in 1998 as manager by Shane McEntee. I had no problem with that and, as it transpired, the delegates gave me a vote of confidence. Another season – another chance.

CHAPTER TWENTY-EIGHT

Other Passions ...

Between 1958 and 1967 Dunboyne was a mecca for motorsport enthusiasts each summer when the Leinster Motor Club staged their annual car and motorbike races. A four-mile circuit took the racers through the village, over two railway bridges and around two challenging corners at Sheaf o' Wheat and Loughsallagh. It was spectacular stuff that attracted all the big names of the time. Mike Hawthorn (after whom the circuit was named), John Watson, Paddy Hopkirk and Rosemary Smith were among those who competed for the Leinster Trophy, while among the motorcyclists featured in the 'Leinster 200' Race were legendary names like Ralph Rensen, Stanley Woods, Bob McIntyre and Tommy Robb who held the lap record at 95 mph. In the car event Timmy Reid scorched around the four miles in two minutes, twenty-two seconds – a speed of 101 mph – in 1965.

These were huge events in the life of the village. Crowds thronged the viewing stands at various vantage points. The races became community events. The ladies committee would organise catering for the motor fans and the money raised helped fund the local church and schools. Sadly, racing on the Dunboyne circuit came to an end in 1967 following the deaths of four drivers in the space of a few years. With the introduction of fibreglass car bodies, the cars became lighter and faster, and often disintegrated in a crash. The deaths brought a wonderful sporting spectacle to an end amid great sadness, and the races were moved to a purpose-built circuit in Mondello Park. For me, as a young fellow in my late teens and early twenties, motor-racing had a great buzz about it and I quickly caught the bug.

I could not afford a racing car, however, so I went for the next best thing: a go-kart. In 1963 I travelled up to Dublin with my friends, Ollie Pollard and Eddie Kenny, and invested in my first go-kart – a Villiers three-gear machine that cost me forty-two pounds and ten shillings. I was in my seventh heaven. This was a fantastic machine that could hit a top speed of 95 mph. It might seem dangerous, but the go-kart's centre of gravity was so low that you were unlikely to fall off. Men like Gerry King in Dublin and Dougie Hughes in Drogheda were very involved in promoting go-kart racing. Gerry was a nephew of Sister Eithne, the woman who had been Michael Collins's secretary. Initially the racing was on street circuits in places like Trim, Kilkenny and Dún Laoghaire, but eventually proper racing-tracks were built at Monasterboice in County Louth and Askeaton in County Limerick. I entered for my first race in Monasterboice in March 1964 but I burned out the clutch in practice. Eddie Kenny worked through the night to fix it and two days later I came third in a street race in Athy, despite having spun around three times! I was on my way ...

A few months later I moved up to a four-gear machine with a maximum speed of 115 mph. Go-karting is a terrific sport. Many of our top racing drivers like Derek Daly, Ken Fildes and Vivian Daly came up through the ranks of go-karting. For a number of years I raced all over the country with my friends. The demands of hurling and football prevented me from racing every weekend but almost every night I would be tearing up and down the avenue at home. Certainly every Easter weekend I would head for the go-kart meeting in Askeaton rather than go down the road to the horse-racing at Fairyhouse. I eventually competed at international level but I always drove for the sheer fun of the sport. I learned so much about cars and engines and how to respect other users of the road. I am a fast driver but a careful one. Go-kart racing also added to the wide cross-section of friends I had acquired through my work and other sports. And just like riding a bike, you never forget how to do it. When we took the Meath footballers to Lanzarote after our All-Ireland victory of 1996, the lads were mad into go-karting there. When I eventually got over my shyness at competing with young fellows, I showed them a few tricks. Mind you, I learned a thing or two also!

Another great passion of mine is flying. It's a sport which has always fascinated me. Around 1970 I had to go down to Ballyferriter in County Kerry to look at some herbs with the horticultural adviser, George Rennick. I was in a hurry to get back home for a hurling match, so we hired a Cessna four-seater plane from Iona Airways, piloted by the late Arthur Wagnall. I noticed that Arthur did not seem to be correcting the plane's movements and I mentioned it. 'It's not the plane's attitude we mind, it's the altitude,' was his reply. From that day I understood the principles of flying – move like a bird in the wind. I took lessons at Iona and later at Weston Aerodrome. One of the most honourable people I ever knew was a man called Padraig Ryan. Godfather to my son, Dáire, Padraig reintroduced me to flying at Weston. When I got into football management, my flying time was limited – except when we made an early exit from the championship. At Weston, men like Kieran O'Connor, Sean Bennett and Niall O'Connell, gave me great encouragement. One evening Liam Costello, the President of the Flying Club, took me up for a few circuits. When we landed, he got out and said to me: 'Now off you go. Do a circuit on your own.' It was my first solo flight. It was an amazing experience, one of the most exciting days of my life. When I landed successfully, I realised the whole club had been watching and a big celebration ensued.

Keeping the number of flying hours up in order to retain a pilot's licence was always a problem, but on the football team's trips to Florida I managed a number of flights, including a night flight that was quite spectacular. On one flight I was accompanied by our kitman, Mick McAuley. Mick is a great man to spin a yarn and he regaled the lads later with tales of the flight, as, for example, how the crocodiles were snapping at us when we flew over the Everglades. 'Not only that,' said Mick, 'but we heard on the radio that there was a space-shuttle launch that day [two hundred and fifty miles away] so Seanie had to pull over immediately to let the shuttle up.' Flying is something I just love doing. The sense of freedom is breathtaking. A few years ago when our son Seán was at Irish college on Inis Meán, it was such a thrill to visit him by flying down from Weston.

I suppose I like the whiff of danger in these pursuits. On a trip to Argentina I went rafting down a mountain river for twenty kilometres. It was an incredible experience. It's always nice to be close to the edge, just like on the day of a championship match. It keeps you sharp. It is the 'boy in the man' syndrome and, luckily for me, neither my parents nor subsequently Tina ever tried to stop me engaging in these adventure pursuits. I remember going into Terry Brady's shop in Fairyhouse some years ago to buy some of his delicious buns. I came out with a motorised buggy. On another occasion I went in for an ice cream and came out with a chainsaw. More recently it was a quad-bike. So, long live the child in the man!

CHAPTER TWENTY-NINE

1999 – Encore!

We faced into the last year of the millennium with several changes in personnel from our title-winning team of 1996. Cormac Sullivan had replaced the injured Conor Martin in goal. Marty had retired and Cormac Murphy fitted in as a dependable corner-back. Hank Traynor came in at wing half-back and Nigel Crawford now partnered John McDermott at centre-field. On the plus side, Trevor Giles was back, fully recovered from his cruciate injury, but we lost Tommy Dowd after a brilliant performance in the opening round. Above all else, 1999 was Ollie Murphy's year. The Carnaross man had been with us since 1995 but the veteran Colm O'Rourke and later, Ray Magee with some terrific performances in 1997, had kept Ollie off the team. That is the way it goes. These were very versatile players who could be moved around to give the team balance. When Ollie got his chance in 1999, however, he set Croke Park alight with a number of blistering performances, especially in the Leinster Final.

Early on in that season, I was uneasy about the way things were shaping up. We had not done well in the League. There seemed to be a malaise running through the team – it was like they were just going through the motions. After their exertions in '97 and '98, a mental weariness had set in. The ability was there but it seemed as though they were taking so much for granted. There was an added burden on the survivors of the 1996 team. They had never really got the credit they deserved for their enormous achievement as a young squad. It seemed that those 'twenty-seven seconds of madness' had tarnished their victory unduly. In training they now seemed to be practising rather than correcting their mistakes. I knew that they needed to be retuned mentally. I called Graham Geraghty, now full-forward and captain, aside and discussed the malaise with him. In order to crack that lethargy I told the lads that I wanted to see them every day for the following fortnight; between night and day sessions I was with them for eleven days. They would have to make another big sacrifice. In the process the team worked out their frustrations, displaying the brutal honesty that is needed among players, as long as all of that stays within the squad. In fairness to Graham, he played his part in getting them going.

A few days before facing Armagh in the All-Ireland Semi-Final, one of the lads was approached about joining the newly-formed Gaelic Players Association (GPA). He was unsure of what to do and went to Graham. The captain's answer was direct: 'Tell them to f*&k off! How many players rang us when we were suspended for a row we didn't start in 1996?' Now this had nothing to do with the GPA and its importance. We simply had to learn to stand on our own and earn things for ourselves. People might say you should have this or that, but in football you earn what you earn on the field of play.

We went through the 1999 championship without ever looking in danger of losing. I could not see those lads being beaten. That may seem big-headed or easy to say in hindsight, but the way those boys were shaping gave me a good feeling. We had comfortable victories over Wicklow and Offaly before facing Dublin one more time in the Leinster Final. This was Ollie's big day. He destroyed his marker,

Peadar Andrews, scoring 1-5 from play in a 1-14 to 0-12 victory. Armagh had emerged as a strong force in Ulster that year and were our Semi-Final opponents. A number of our lads would have remembered some of the Armagh boys from the All-Ireland Minor Final of 1992. One of those 'boys', Diarmuid Marsden, hit a cracking goal in the first half and we went in at half-time two points down. We also went in without Ollie who had been injured and carried off in a stretcher. Fortunately, we had an able substitute in Ray Magee. We made some switches and restricted Armagh to a single point in the second half and – with their cause not being helped by the sending-off of their full-back, Gerard Reid – we eased into another All-Ireland Final on a 0-15 to 2-5 scoreline.

All-Ireland Final day is a huge day in a footballer's life. Great things are expected from him, especially if he is a 'star' player, but how often does it happen that a 'lesser light' steals the show? Richie Kealy had been around for a while, but things had not always gone his way. In the final, he got his chance when he came on as a substitute for Nigel Nestor. He changed the course of the game against Cork when he went for a ball he shouldn't have gone for, won it, was fouled and won a crucial free. Suddenly it had happened for Richie on the biggest stage.

And then there was Enda McManus, who had had quite an extraordinary year. In April he had developed 'shin splints' which usually result from repetitive strain due to training on hard ground. This had been a very wet spring so Enda's complaint wasn't making sense. We decided to get him away to the Canaries for a week of sunshine and sea-water. His colleagues slagged him, but they understood the need to get him right for the championship. Enda came home and went straight to Blanchardstown hospital, feeling most unwell. The doctor treating him jokingly suggested he must have had about twenty pints of beer to be in the state he was in, but Enda wasn't drunk ... He doesn't drink alcohol. It transpired he had a viral infection in his pancreas, which controls sugar and sediment levels. Enda had been doing skipping to improve his quickness off the mark. This had resulted in a high amount of sediment being deposited on his shins. Once we had got to the root of the problem, Enda recovered, came on as a substitute against Offaly and playing through the rest of the campaign. He had an amazing first half against Cork when we played into the wind and rain. He and John McDermott were awesome. They simply stood between Cork, and dominated the game. This is how it went: Trevor, Evan and Graham scored the points; Ollie got his trademark goal; Mark O'Reilly won the Man of the Match award, but Enda was the man who came back and stood in the breach. Officialdom had the crazy notion that year of presenting the Sam Maguire Cup on a podium in the middle of the field. Each player took his turn to hold Sam aloft – except Enda. His shins were playing up again and he could not step up on the podium. The man who had done so much to win back Sam never got the chance to hold him up, centre-stage. A fantastic player and the most unassuming and laid back fellow you could meet. Enda almost missed that final, when he lay down for a rest in the team hotel, fell asleep and missed the team bus to Croke Park. A taxi got him there eventually with the help of a Garda squad-car!

Another bonus from that final was that two 'veterans' were fit enough to come on as substitutes. Barry Callaghan overcame his injury problems sufficiently to be able to replace Hank Traynor, and the great Tommy Dowd came on for Evan Kelly – both players winning their second All-Ireland medals.

We won seven All-Star awards in 1999. There had been no rows, no 'twenty-seven seconds of madness'. We had, I suppose, a better image and I was pleased that the '96 lads were belatedly getting credit for their achievements. In the autumn of that year Meath and Cork football teams and the Cork and All-Star hurling teams were invited to

Boston to mark the opening of the Irish Cultural Centre. It was a wonderful occasion – so different from the US trip in 1987 when the fans were looking over their shoulders, mindful of their illegal status. Now, times were different and the fans turned out in style. In fact a busload of Meath lads who had travelled down from New York ahead of us were allowed in as 'the Meath team'. Subsequently an over-enthusiastic security man would not let us into the stadium. There was uproar until the problem was ironed out. Our lads bonded very well with their old rivals, Larry Tompkins's Cork team, on that occasion. It was a nostalgic day, tinged with sorrow at the recent death of singer Charlie McGettigan's son in a building-site accident. This was also the day when Brian Cody, the All-Star Hurling manager, expressed surprise at the mere 'slips of fellows' that were representing Meath. 'Brian,' I assured him, 'they may look slips of fellows to you, but I guarantee you these lads will hold back from NOTHING ... '

Yes, 1999 was a good year.

CHAPTER THIRTY

Summers – Long and Short

After the heights of 1999 we came back down to earth with a bump in 2000 when Offaly knocked us out of the Leinster championship. We had earlier lost the National League Final to Derry after a replay. In that final Graham Geraghty was sent off for allegedly striking an opponent, although it was subsequently shown that he did not strike him. He was very unfortunate and so were we as we had to do without him for the Offaly match. In reality we had no excuses for the defeat by the faithful county. They were managed by Padraig Nolan, a teacher in St Patrick's Classical School, Navan, who knew our lads and prepared his team very well. Unfortunately, we just never got going. We were out of the championship at the beginning of June. It was a very long summer that year!

After the intensity of the previous four years – winning two All-Irelands, reaching four Leinster Finals and winning two – I felt for the players. It would do them no harm to have a break and explore other aspects of life. For me, it was certainly unusual. A few weeks after the Offaly match Tina and I were driving past Dalgan Park. 'Do you want to go in and drive around, for old time's sake?' she teased. 'You know, you can get help for an addiction like yours!' Of course, for once I could do other things, go on holidays, indulge my other passions like flying, but when you are away from football for a while, you can't wait to get back to it!

In 2001 we saw an awful lot of our close neighbours, Westmeath, almost too much of them. We came from six points down to squeeze past them in the opening round by a single point, but that wasn't the last we would see of them. Then a comfortable victory over Kildare brought us face to face with our old rivals Dublin in another Leinster final. The old saying held true: 'goals win finals', and we managed two: one from Richie Kealy, and a controversial one from Graham Geraghty who capitalised on an error by Dublin goalkeeper, Davy Byrne. Byrne was possibly blinded by the sun and dropped the ball. Graham was never one to spurn a gift like that and fisted the ball into the net.

We had won a Leinster title for the eighth time in my tenure, but instead of going straight into an All-Ireland Semi-Final a new system obtained. The GAA introduced a 'qualifier' system which gave beaten teams one more chance and thus offered fans more games. The 'back-door' system was born and it threw up some unusual pairings and some cracking games: the victories of Kildare, Sligo and Westmeath over Donegal, Kildare and Mayo respectively (each by a single point) come to mind. Little did we know the back-door system would be our ultimate downfall but more immediately the new quarter-final stage pitted us against – surprise, surprise – Westmeath. They were a formidable outfit, many of whom had enjoyed success at under-14, minor and under-21 levels, and Luke Dempsey had moulded them into an exciting team that had created a great buzz for their followers that year. This was their seventh game in the championship. When they cut us apart with three goals to lead by nine points at half-time, it seemed their long-sought championship victory over their neighbours was at hand and, boy, did their supporters let us know that as we went to the dressing room. However, our lads had been around the block a few times and the 'old hands' saved the day. The 'Graham and Ollie Show' got goals out of nothing, while behind them Trevor was always prompting and making things happen. We managed a draw and six days later we finally shook off Westmeath, winning the replay by five points. So it was on to meet Kerry in the Semi-Final ...

The Semi-Final, 2 September 2001, was surely one of the most bizarre and surreal games we were ever involved in. Who could imagine Kerry suffering a fifteen-point defeat? Certainly not me. They were unfortunate to lose a couple of half-backs in the course of the match and possibly lost their balance, but still something was not right. Here was a team that averaged a score of eighteen points in their previous four games, including two great tussles with Dublin. Now they could only muster five points, only one point in sixty minutes of play. I had this fear that they would wake up out of their slumber and come at us like a tornado, but it never happened and we cantered home by 2-14 to 0-5. It was a huge victory and a terrific performance by our lads, but nobody really likes to see a one-sided show like that. People will say Kerry demolished other teams in their day but Kerrymen would be the first to say that a win like that does no good to anybody. In the closing stages our fellows began 'showboating', slinging passes around for fun to the accompaniment of *Olés* from their supporters. This really upset me. It was one of the few days that I ever got very annoyed on the sideline. If I have learned one thing over the years, it is that you never lose respect for your opponents. That said, we were in another All-Ireland Final – our seventh in fourteen years – and it was good to be back, particularly after the disaster of 2000. As All-Ireland champions you always want to get a good long run at defending your title. We came off the rails quite suddenly in 2000 but now, a year later, we were back on track – or so it seemed ...

Nine days after that Kerry match the world was devastated by the destruction of the World Trade Centre in New York. I remember I was chatting with Tom Humphries of *The Irish Times* at home when Tina came in with the news. She had every right to be upset and worried, as she had aunts and uncles with families over there, some of whom worked in the police and fire services. The All-Ireland Final was a mere twelve days away but right now it did not seem all that important. Perspectives had changed.

They say Meath don't handle confidence well. If that is so, we had a major problem. How do you 'talk down' a team that has just demolished the previous year's champions by fifteen points? It is very difficult to bring players down to earth and insulate them from media and supporters. Most of them were All-Ireland medal-holders and very accessible to the media. As for the supporters, too many of them could not see their heroes beaten. It seemed like a case of: 'Ye only have to turn up, lads!' – it was shades of 1991 all over again. Our opponents were Galway, who had lost to Roscommon in the Connacht Semi-Final and then came a circuitous and difficult road, beating Armagh, Cork, Roscommon (easily) and Derry. Galway would be no mean opponents.

Every final is a fifty-fifty situation. The outcome will depend on who is ready and who performs, and on all the little things going right. On this occasion too many little things went wrong for us and Galway capitalised on them. We were level at 0-6 each at half-time. Galway's main threat, Padraic Joyce, had been very quiet. Who could foretell that he would cut loose in the second half with nine points? He could do no wrong, yet I felt for a long time we could snatch it. The little things mounted up, however. Nigel Nestor was sent off, unfairly, I thought, as he should have got a free himself beforehand. Ollie broke a bone in his hand and his final was over. Trevor missed a penalty. Some days the luck goes with you and some days it doesn't, but there is no doubt that Galway were fantastic and John O'Mahony had them well-prepared. I felt sorry that we had gone so close after another great campaign. I was particularly sorry for Trevor. To see him lift the Sam Maguire Cup would have been just reward for all he had done for Meath, but it was not to be. I was proud of the lads – they brought as much dignity to defeat as they had to victory – and that is very important.

For the next four years we would, unfortunately, see a lot of the back-door. In 2002 we got past Westmeath (again) only to fall to Dublin in the Leinster Semi-Final. We were unfortunate to lose John Cullinane at midfield through injury in the first minute, but again goals win matches and this time Ray Cosgrove helped himself to a pair. We were off to 'the back-door' for the first time and in an amazing qualifier in a jammed Páirc Tailteann we were four points down to Louth with two minutes to go. Enter Graham (by helicopter – he flew up to the match from a friend's wedding in Wexford) with an injury-time goal following another minutes earlier by Richie Kealy and we survived, again. Typical Meath, the pundits said. They never give up. I would like to think it was 'typical Meath'. That's what I always emphasised. There's always a chance … We followed with an easy win over Laois, another Graham and Ollie Show, but came unstuck in an unsatisfactory match against Donegal.

Poor Westmeath. They had to face us yet again in 2003. They drew with us, only to lose the replay by nine points. Kildare knocked us out of the Leinster championship by a single point and our 'back-door' route was closed off by Fermanagh, who were to repeat the dose the following year, beating us by a point after extra time. There was a time when to be beaten by a county like Fermanagh might have seemed a humiliation but there was a whole new order in place now. When Kerry won in 1986 who could have foreseen that it would be another eleven years before they would be back at the top? I would like to think that Meath's victories in 1987/88 opened up new vistas for other counties. Prior to 1987 Meath had been in the wilderness for twenty years. I am sure other counties were thinking: If those fellows can do it, why can't we? So much helped previously 'weaker' counties make the breakthrough: increased competition among third level colleges, the use of video for match analysis, heightened media coverage, a new breed of manager and more sophisticated training programmes. And, of course, they now had at least a second chance through the back-door system. Counties like Sligo, Limerick, Westmeath (at last Leinster Champions in 2004) and Fermanagh were now on the big stage in earnest. After beating us, Fermanagh went on to beat Donegal and Armagh before losing narrowly to Mayo in the All-Ireland Semi-Final. So it turned out that it was no shame to lose to a team of that quality.

After yet another intense tussle, Dublin knocked us out of the 2005 Leinster championship by two points. After a bright start on the back-door route, hitting a total of 5-12, all from play, against Antrim, we scraped past Leitrim after extra time before making our exit to old rivals Cavan in a scrappy game. The date was 17 July 2005 – after twenty-three amazing years, it was to be my last match in charge of the Meath Senior Football team ...

Even though we played some good games in the qualifier system, it never seemed to suit us. Maybe we were so used to having to win prior to the introduction of that system, we never seemed comfortable with the notion of losing and not being out of the running. That may sound naive but I could never experience the same buzz in the players' mindset in training for a qualifier – no matter how hard I tried. They had been so used to going the direct knockout route. The supporters seemed similarly affected. I could be wrong, but that's how I felt in latter years.

It was not down to a lack of commitment but other factors intervened. It was not a question of scarcity of natural talent. I have always maintained that there are oceans of talent around. It was said that we had very little success latterly at underage level and while I agree that there can never be enough done at underage level, the people in charge did the best they could with what they had. It was more a question of dissipation of that talent, leading to burnout. Nor was it a question of being left behind by changing football styles. We had to change and adapt ourselves between 1988 and 1996. I had no doubt that Meath could cope with any new style. It was a matter of looking at what you have and formulating your game plan around that. It did not mean we had to try to copy the styles of other teams – that style may work for them, but not necessarily for us. No, the problem was a lot closer to home than all of that.

CHAPTER THIRTY-ONE

A Word on Water

I am holding a book in my hand. It is quite an old book, published in 1892. It is the only authorised English translation of: *My Water-Cure, as tested through more than thirty years and described for the healing of diseases and the preservation of health.* This little book, translated from German, is the record of a system of water cure practised for over sixteen years by Sebastian Kneipp, the parish priest of Worishofen in Bavaria. In 1892 it had already gone through thirty-six editions. Over forty years ago when I joined my father in the production of herbal remedies he handed this book to me and said: 'Read it and understand it.' I did and I do!

It is a basic and practical book. Nowadays Kneipp would be called a hydro therapist. *My Water-Cure* details a system that Kneipp used to cure his patients. His fame spread quickly across Europe. The book is divided into three sections: cold-water applications; the pharmacy of medications to be used in water cures; and diseases which can be treated by Kneipp's water cure (including actual case notes). It is a basic and practical book. My father was a great man for the 'basics' – understanding the value of water, the riches of the soil and the importance of fruit (as evidenced by his planting a little orchard as his gift for newly-weds).

I think we will see the day when water will be the new oil, considering its value and importance in our lives and the fact that the shortage of pure water is a global concern. Kneipp wrote about the value of compresses and affusions on swollen limbs. In olden days, elderly people could not avail of physiotherapy but they used hot and cold compresses to good effect. On the playing field what was often referred to as 'the magic bottle' was often no more than a bottle of water. If you did get a knock and applied a compress quickly, it certainly helped. Before the introduction of ultrasound treatment a cold compress helped relieve aching limbs and internal bleeding. Even today I would be reluctant to give young players ultrasound because it could weaken the blood vessels. But a hot bath which opens pores and takes the tension out of veins, followed by a cold shower to stimulate circulation, will often do wonders for a player's recovery. Again, in days gone by, people went to holy wells for their curative powers. If you put a sprained ankle into really cold well-water, it will certainly reduce the swelling. Plain pure water has a real value that we often take for granted.

Who would have thought forty years ago that we would be buying water in the shop? We know its value now in clearing toxins out of the system. People who drink a lot of alcohol on a night out and then drink a couple of pints of water will have a much greater recovery rate the next day. In 1988 the Meath team went to the US to play the All-Stars and then faced Dublin in a National League Final on their return. I told the lads if they abstained from alcohol on the way home and drank plenty of water they would have no jetlag problems. It is a common practice today for players to keep hydrated but then it was not so common. We played Dublin eleven days later and beat them, turning in quite a brilliant performance in the process.

If you add genuine herbal extracts to pure water you will have remedies for a variety of ailments. Kneipp has a whole section on this in his book – ranging from the nettle ('the most despised of all plants') which, made into a tea, will 'loosen conglutination in chest and lungs and cleanse the stomach of superfluous matter ... ' to strawberry leaves which, again made into tea, will be 'one of the cheapest, most wholesome and nourishing beverages ... ' for a sickly child. The quality of the water to which the herbs are added is all-important. I know with certainty that the herbal remedies we make up in our clinic with our own spring water are infinitely better than those made with tap water.

Kneipp's book was written over a hundred years ago and looks dated now, but many of his principles remain. He lived in unsophisticated times when there were many respiratory ailments. Above all he recognised the value of water, a gift given freely to us and that we largely take for granted. He was no genius but a simple man of the people, whose study of nature's gifts and shrewd insight into human nature made his work a bestseller of the time. When my father gave me *My Water-Cure* over forty years ago he was simply underlining the value and importance of pure water in our everyday lives. Forty years on, as water sources dry up or are threatened with pollution, I feel that value and that importance more acutely than ever.

My Water-Cure carries the inscription, *Aquae omnes laudent nomen Domini,* may all waters praise the name of the Lord.

CHAPTER THIRTY-TWO

Reflections

What I love about Gaelic football is its particular skills – especially high fielding and being able to kick with both feet – its strength, its physicality and its intensity. I love to see 'lesser' players pitting their skills against the big players, bringing on the quality of the game in both. I love the intensity and physicality that drives players on, refusing to shirk a challenge. Of course bad things happen. There are nasty fouls, late tackles, but when the tackles are honest it's rare that players get hurt. Gaelic football is so much part of our culture. Everybody gets involved. It is parochial. It is pride in your colours – it is tribalism at its best! It is one of the true remaining amateur games and should be on a world stage. I would love to have it on show at the Olympic Games ...

What I like least about the game is pettishness – the refusal to accept that someone else is better than you on the day, the notion that you have to win all the time. Failure, it seems, is not an option nowadays. Yet, in my experience, we often learned more from our defeats which helped us to win at a later stage. There is such fierce pressure to win now on players and on managers. I was appalled to see Kerry manager Jack O'Connor being interviewed minutes after his team had lost the 2005 All-Ireland Final by a very narrow margin. Almost the first question he was asked was: 'Where now for Jack O'Connor? Is it the end of the road for him as manager?' The same happened to Kilkenny hurling manager, Brian Cody, just after his team had lost a fantastic hurling Semi-Final to Galway. It is very hard to understand how journalists can be so greedy and so insensitive in their search for information, when all a manager wants to do is get in among his players. He is polite enough to grant an interview and then he is asked these questions. I had the same experience myself. It is highly insensitive and just unacceptable. We are playing a game therefore only one side can win.

The general public has a better understanding than the media of what it is like to be beaten. Wasn't it wonderful to see supporters from Mayo, Down, Kerry and Tyrone together on Hill 16 on All-Ireland Final Day 2005, sharing the *craic* and the banter, probably going for a drink afterwards and not a bad word out of them? Everyone loves to win. Everyone would love to be Brian Dooher raising the Sam Maguire Cup (and no more deserving man to do it) but there can only be one winner. Defeat nowadays is too often deemed to be failure. To me failure is the day you cannot do it anymore. As long as you are able and can aspire to winning, that is all that matters. There must still be honour in participating.

I was fortunate to play for Meath hurlers for twenty years. It was the greatest honour to put on that green and gold jersey, to have the opportunity to train and try to win with my team-mates. Of course it mattered if we lost, but we had the chance of going out again and trying to improve and win. I could have played other sports but I loved hurling – pitting our wits against our opponents and at the end of it all, shaking their hands. I just loved that. I would hate to see the day when fans have to be segregated, or cannot walk down the street without fear of attack, or you can't walk into your opponents' dressing room and say a few words.

The game has developed phenomenally. We now have psychologists, dietitians and specialists of all sorts among the backroom staff. Personally I would take any help I can get to help me attain success – within legal limits – but it is the players who perform on the day and every time the ball is kicked, it is to a large extent a lottery. Things go in and out of fashion. Once upon a time, pasta was the buzzword in the players' diet. Now the humble spud is seen as the greatest source of fibre and top athletes are turning to it. The important thing is not to get too carried away with any particular fad. One particular 'fashion' that worked for us was training in the swimming pool in 1991.

One of the prime reasons for the great growth in Gaelic Games has been the extraordinary amount of time and dedication that volunteers have given to underage teams. This is wonderful but I worry about it when it becomes competitive. The notion of giving medals to under-six players is wrong. Once you introduce the element of competition to very young players, the game takes on a different mantle. Just let the kids play for the fun of it. It gets worse when unscrupulous adults play overage children at underage level. Once you introduce an 'acceptable' level of dishonesty to children, you are starting to chip away at the fundamental rules of society.

Sir Alf Ramsey would have been a great hero of mine as a manager. His leading England to World Cup victory in 1966 was an amazing achievement. He had some wonderfully skilled players in his team but he needed men like Jack Charlton and Nobby Stiles to complement those skilful players. A combination of silk and steel! I suppose the reader will draw inferences about the make-up of the Meath team – be that as it may. I also remember Liverpool gaining promotion from the old Division Two under the captaincy of Tommy Smith – another man of steel. Even on days when he was not playing well, he was still a leader on the field. He had that never-say-die attitude – just like Roy Keane. The ability to do the simple things well and to keep doing them is, for me, phenomenal. I always admired the managers like Ramsey or Shankly for the belief they had in their players and what they could achieve with them. Loyalty to the club was a big thing then. You knew that a player like Billy Wright, who won 105 England 'caps', would never leave his club, Wolves. But then real professionalism took hold and players could be bought and sold more readily. I found it hard to accept that within days of Liverpool winning the European Cup in 2005, five or six of their players were on the transfer list.

If the GAA ever goes professional they will have to face up to the problem of a transfer system and I would worry about that. If a player were dropped by his county and then sought to play for another county, it would be difficult to deny that to him. What I would favour is to have retired 'greats' going on loan to weaker counties, especially in hurling. It would give the whole scene such a lift. I remember a few years back seeing the great Johnny Dooley come on as a substitute for Offaly against Meath in Navan. Meath hurlers were actually doing well at the time, but Johnny (who was almost literally playing on one leg) did half a dozen things that were pure magic. The Meath fans applauded him, they just felt privileged to be there, watching a master craftsman at work. Johnny was in the twilight of his career, but he had the skills and the simplicity to come on and do his stuff. There was no bigheadedness about him. Most Gaelic players are unassuming like Johnny Dooley, they just want to play – and long may it be that way.

There are so many Gaelic footballers I have admired over the years – it is invidious to select a few. Matt Connor of Offaly had such silky skills and his scoring rate was amazing. Going back further, Sean O'Neill of Down was an exciting player to watch. He was so clever in his movement and when he moved from wing-half-forward to full-forward he brought a new dimension to that position. Jimmy Barry-Murphy of Cork was a great goalpoacher. At centrefield, big Brian Mullins of Dublin never wasted a ball in setting up an attack. And then there was the great Kerry team of all the talents: John O'Keeffe was mighty at full-back; Jack O'Shea was regal at centrefield; John Egan was such an incisive forward and the 'Bomber' Liston could turn on the proverbial sixpence – amazing for such a big man. For me, however, the unsung hero of that Kerry team was 'Ogie' Moran at centre-half-forward. He was so pivotal to the team, totally unselfish in winning the ball and moving it on. To win eight All-Ireland medals from the one position is absolutely incredible. And still he wasn't nominated for the 'Team of the Century' – even more incredible. I was fortunate as a teenager to sit in the old corner stand with my father at the All-Ireland Final in 1956 and watch Galway's 'terrible twins', Sean Purcell (RIP) and Frank Stockwell, tear Cork apart. They were a joy to behold. There were so many great players over the past fifty years – it really isn't fair to try and isolate a few of them ...

The greatest moment in my career would have to be winning our first All-Ireland title in 1987. Suddenly, the mantle of twenty years was lifted and it was such a thrill to see great players achieve their dream, knowing what they had been prepared to do when they were given the opportunity. It was very humbling for me to be a part of it and so close to it, while never having had the honour of playing in an All-Ireland Final. In 1970, Meath won the All-Ireland Junior Hurling title. I was on the senior team at the time but it was still a great thrill to follow the lads and see them pull it off. I would just love to have been playing. In 1987 things were not going well for us early on against Cork, but we had the composure to keep going. Mick Lyons's great block on Jimmy Kerrigan stands out and then Colm O'Rourke setting up the goal with a pass to Bernie Flynn, before finishing it himself. It was so fitting that it was 'Rourkey' who clinched the match for us. He had been there so long and had gone through so much pain. Back then we didn't have the modern sophisticated methods of rehabilitation after injury, so Colm did it the hard way. His wife Trish was such an important support to him. Rourkey deserved his moment of glory. We could all polish his boots, but none of us were fit to wear them. 20 September 1987 was a truly glorious day, but there were many other great days too!

Conversely, losing a Final or any big match is a low and painful moment, and we have had our share of them too, but as a manager, the lowest moments for me were whenever I had to tell a player that he had not made the team or the panel. There is no easy way of doing it and no manager likes doing it. No matter what a manager will say, no player will ever understand why he hasn't made the team. He will always feel that he was good enough or that at the very least he deserved a chance. He has put a lot of effort in and he is devastated. I hated being the messenger. For me it was worse than losing a final. I have made mistakes, I know, but if I believe something I would be very hard to shift. You need steel in a manager just as much as in the players. I was always fiercely protective of my players and I would not tolerate anyone doing or saying anything harmful about them. We had a terrific bond. I just loved the fact that they would go out on that pitch, give their all and never shirk from battle. I really loved that!

CHAPTER THIRTY-THREE

Decisions

The introduction of the qualifier system into the All-Ireland championship was not the only change that would influence the fortunes of the Meath team. At club level the Meath county board revamped the county championship. The old system had four divisions with four teams playing each other on a league basis. It meant that a club could only afford to lose maybe one match if they wanted to progress, and so the competition was quite intense. The new format had two divisions of eight teams. This meant that a club would now play seven matches and could lose two and possibly draw another one – and still qualify for the Semi-Finals. I fully understood the intention behind this change, to give players more matches at club level, but to me it seemed that for the first time it was almost being bred into Meath players that it was all right to be beaten.

From a county team point of view, in the old system you timed all your preparation towards the first round of the Leinster championship and had possibly one round of the club championship before that date. Now we would have three rounds of the club championship interrupting our inter-county preparation. There was a greater danger of losing players through injury. I spoke with the county executive about this but they felt the new format was the right way to go. I told them that unless we got an extraordinary run of good fortune, it could be ten years before Meath would win a Leinster title again. I naturally hoped I would be proved wrong, but I was being practical, not defeatist.

That was only the tip of the iceberg. Most young fellows go to third level colleges now and inter-college competitions like the Sigerson Cup are quite intense. The Sigerson Cup was once the preserve of a handful of universities, but is much wider in scope now and is taken very seriously. There have been instances where students trained for their college at 6.30am and were expected to train for the county under-21 team that evening. If you were on the county senior team you now had seven National League matches in a row during February-March. Where was the time for rest or recovery or, dare one ask, the time for study in the case of students? The situation was farcical.

Every club team now has a manager and he naturally demands his players to be present for training at that level also. For inter-county players this was a crazy set-up. These are amateur players but a professional standard was being demanded of them. In fact I doubt if professional players would be asked to subject themselves to such a rigorous regime. We were inviting trouble and we got plenty of it. Players will always pick up injuries but the scale of the problem had reached a new and frightening magnitude. When we played Dublin in the 2005 championship, we had eight players on the injured list. In 2004 there were eleven players injured. In 2003 the figure was ten. This may seem like sour grapes now, but they were the hands dealt to us.

I was disillusioned with the new club championship format from its inception and for three successive years I pleaded my case to the county executive: Pat O'Neill, central council representative; Barney Allen, county board secretary; Fintan Ginnity, chairman and Colm Gannon, treasurer. We were playing counties in the championship whose policy was not to start their club championship until the county's involvement was over – and here we were playing club under-21 championships (which started before 17 March), county under-21 championships, club senior championships, intervarsity championships and seven National League matches – all in the run-up to the inter-county championship. It was inevitable that the injuries would mount up and players would suffer burnout. It should not have been a surprise. If, for example, a club is playing Carnaross then the mantra will be: 'Hold Ollie Murphy (Carnaross's star player) and you will win!' Naturally, Ollie will come in for more attention. We will all support Ollie when he plays for Meath, but at club level it's another story … Similarly with all inter-county players. It could be an argument for a larger panel, but I don't like too big a panel. Every player on the panel should feel he has a chance of getting on the team, otherwise it is a self-defeating exercise. In my view, the county executive should have eaten humble pie and said this new format was not working. I don't think a reversal of the format would have taken from the club championship at all. I regret that the executive did not see things my way.

From 2001 onwards I stated my case each year in an interview for the position of manager. Each nominee was interviewed and then the executive put the names before club delegates for voting. I never doubted for a minute that I could do the job, given the time and conditions to nurture promising players. Otherwise I would not have wasted anyone's time, least of all my own. I found those interviews ultimately humbling. They were probably embarrassing for the executive too, but according to the bye-laws of the GAA it is the duty of the county executive to select the coach/manager. In my view they abdicated their responsibility by leaving the decision to the delegates, who had not heard my views nor those of any of the candidates. The executive should have said: 'This is the man for the job,' and stick with that. Instead they were putting candidates up against one another, which led to canvassing of votes – something I abhor and never practised. It was a case of divide and conquer, and it was not for me. If the executive had made a choice and it was not me, that was fine. After three years I decided I would not go for interview again but because Brendan Dempsey had now replaced Pat O'Neill on the executive and had not heard my views before, I relented. However, if I could not convince the executive, how could I convince the delegates? I was not an officer of the county board. I had no voice with the delegates. The crunch would come in 2005 ...

I remember the day with particular clarity, 31 August. It was the day of the funeral of the great Galway maestro, Sean Purcell. I travelled with my father-in-law, George Yeates, down to Tuam to pay my respects. It was a hugely emotional day for the family and the fans of this great but humble man, and asthe Galway people made us visitors so welcome. The meeting with the county board executive later that evening was obviously on my mind, and earlier in the day I was leaning towards having one more go at the managerial job. The more I thought about it, however, the more I felt I would be wasting my time going forward.

For three years I had spoken with the executive and nothing had happened regarding the club championship. I had no power to change things. About half an hour before the meeting I made up my mind. I would stand aside and let someone else have a go at the job. I rang Tina a few minutes before going into the meeting. Her reply was simple: 'Okay, if that's how you feel, that's fine.' I rang my good friend Tommy Reilly. His reply was similar. Out of courtesy I informed my co-selector Colm Coyle and asked him to tell the other selectors, David Beggy and Declan Mullen. I walked into the meeting and told the executive that if they felt changes could not be made, there was no point in my going ahead. 'What do we do?' Brendan Dempsey asked. 'Just say I'm not standing,' I said. It was as simple as that. There was no storm-out, no histrionics. It was not an ego thing, as some journalists have written. If it were, the time to walk away would have been after some major success. I just had an obsession with sport and found great satisfaction in helping young men achieve excellence in sport. Now it was over. An amazing twenty-three year journey had ended.

Despite being offered great hospitality in Tuam, George and I had not eaten, as we were rushing back to the meeting. We went to the County Club for a meal and did not get home until after eleven o'clock. Seán Junior and Ciarán (who should have been in bed for a very early start for school next day) were there to meet me with Tina. Seán ran to me and threw his arms about me. At the tender age of thirteen he knew the significance of the moment. The word spread quickly and early next morning Des Cahill rang me from RTÉ Radio. 'I can't believe this,' he said. 'You have been in management for as long as I have been in broadcasting!' As the morning wore on there was a stream of callers to the house: my sisters, neighbours, friends, and people who had worked with me over the years. Some people brought drink; others brought cakes and flowers. It was like a wake. The 'corpse', however, was fine. I had loved what I did, but if it was felt that I could no longer do it right, so be it. No regrets. I like to think I served my county well. It was a great honour and privilege to do so and those twenty-three years have been a fantastic part of my life.

I reflected on all those who had influenced me: my parents, teachers like Fr O'Sullivan and Fr Murray in Belvedere College, the great West Indian cricketer Frank Worrell (who was one of my first coaches in Belvedere), Jim McCabe and Sean Murphy in Clogher Road school, my childhood hurling hero Dessie Ferguson (whose sons I would later coach), great Dunboyne men like Brian

Smith and Paddy McIntyre. I was so lucky to rub shoulders with my heroes – all of them passionate men.

Who am I after all? I am just a guy who was asked to do his best to bring success to his county. That is all I am. I was never any greater than the man who carried the bags. I was never fortunate enough to play in an All-Ireland Final, but I was lucky enough to have a team in seven All-Ireland Finals and four National League Finals. I was blessed with the support of selectors, back-up team and the county board. I am thankful to my maker for the talents I was given. As a child I may have dreamed of lifting up the Sam Maguire Cup as Meath captain, but that is not the hand I was dealt. We all have our different talents. I just thank God for those that were given to me and that I had the opportunity to use them. It is hard to believe that a little leather bag of air, with 'O'Neills' written on it, could evoke such passion and endeavour, such goodwill when you were successful and the opposite when you made a mess of it ... But isn't it wonderful that it is so?

And, of course, the journey isn't quite over yet! In October 2006 I will be honoured to manage the Irish team in the International Rules series against Australia. A poisoned chalice, some might think. Like a number of others, I was offended by how the series went last year. I felt that there were deliberate intentions to hurt players and the essence of sport seemed to go out of the game at times. Maybe the Aussies had been taunted on their last visit here and saw this as pay-back time, who can say? Players were blamed but officialdom must take the blame too. There is obviously need for greater clarity in the rules and their interpretation. If there is an opportunity for me to iron out those difficulties, I will gladly take it, because these games are a great occasion for all the players.

Looking back on my career with Meath, it was quite simply a labour of love. Love of sport. Love of making it happen for willing young players.

Love of place and of what success did for your people – and being sorry as hell when it didn't happen for them! No matter which way it went, love was at the heart of it all.

And so Farewell – and Thanks!

In the weeks after the announcement of his retirement from football management, the letters and the postcards came to Seán Boylan in their hundreds. They came from ordinary fans, from current and past footballers, from team managers, from rival fans. Some letters had attachments: mass bouquets, a lotto ticket, requests for hurling final tickets and even a brochure on a 'twenty-acre farm for sale' that Seán might be interested in buying. All the letters were saying the same thing, thanks for the memories, but the following selection of excerpts illustrates the variety of their sources and the different ways in which Seán Boylan touched people's lives – ways that went far beyond football.

(John Quinn)

From Meath footballer, Darren Fay:
It was only on Thursday evening, sitting out at the back of my house with my wife Rhona, that I realised how much I owed you in life. I have a wonderful wife and two lovely kids, with another on the way. That certainly would not be the case had you not guided me so well or given me the opportunities that you did ... For the first nineteen years of my life I never had won a football accolade – not one. And then when I was twenty I won Young Footballer of the Year and an All-Star award, but most of all I had an All-Ireland medal ... I matured overnight and was able to appreciate what we had achieved as a

team ... That new personality helped me to plan my life the way it is today, because before that I was arrogant, immature and disrespectful to myself and others and would not be mature enough to be married with kids today. I thank you so much for that ...

From MJ McGearty and family, Ballivor, County Meath
Thank you, Seán, most sincerely, for twenty-three years of excitement, pleasure and pain and honest endeavour. We have been on a roller-coaster since the Centenary Cup in 1984!

From Pat Donnellan and family, Kilbride, County Meath
You helped make us part of what we are and you shaped part of our lives.

From Mikey Sheehy, former Kerry footballer
Well done on a fantastic innings in Meath football. You rank up there with the very best. Statistics don't lie! I will always remember the great welcome you gave John Dowling and my father many years ago in Dunboyne. You were always a true gentleman.

From Colm Corless, Dublin
Words will never explain the marvellous influence you have left in Gaelic Football. We will never see your likes again.

From Frankie Byrne, former Meath footballer
By your zeal, innate sense of fairplay, integrity, honesty and good humour, you have given hundreds of young men ideals to aspire to. Whether those ideals were embraced or not is irrelevant. Those young men were privileged to have been coached by you. This may ultimately prove to be a more lasting testament to your tenure as *Bainisteoir* of Meath Senior Football.

From Tommy Clarke, Navan
A big thank you for all the wonderful years. You gave us some wonderful memories and joy.

From Olivia Smith, Dublin

I want to thank you for a generation of excitement, euphoria and occasional heartache. I know in the context of world events football takes second place, but in the hearts and memories of Meath supporters it will always mean a little more.

From Lorcan Quinlan, County Kildare

As a Dub fan, going to Croke Park since 1983, I have screamed abuse at you and Meath for twenty-two years. But in that time I have come to realise what a huge contribution you and Meath have made to the GAA. The sheer determination of your teams never to give in broke my heart on a number of occasions. 1991 was remarkable and will go down in history. Because of you Meath will always be my second team (but I have to keep that quiet ...)
P.S. The Dubs might need you in a few years!

From the Lynch family, Trim

We hope you don't take on any other county. The Meath people would hate to be going up against you!

From the Murphy family, Smithstown, County Meath

Heartfelt thanks for looking after Cormac [former Meath player] so well.

From Peter Cassells, trade union leader

Thank you for the years of pleasure, fun and near heart-attacks you gave us over the years. In other walks of life, I keep quoting you as a great example of people-management.

From Deirdre

As a child I never knew what it was to have the Meath team bring the Sam Maguire to our school – but my children know, and for all that happiness and pride, a huge thank you.

From Liam Mulvihill, Director General of the GAA

You can feel proud of your outstanding achievements with Meath, and you have left a legacy which will be very difficult to emulate. On a personal level I want to thank you for giving such a positive image of the GAA and of the game – even when things were going against you.

From Cis
You are my hero and you always will be.

From Brian Talty, former Galway footballer
Thanks for the memories, Seán – some bad ones for me! As they said about Seánín Purcell, not alone were you a great football man, you were a pure gentleman and a joy to meet.

From Sister Marie Louise Moore, Navan
You brightened up our school the day you presented sports medals and you gave the children such an inspiring talk.

From Robbie O'Malley, former Meath footballer
    'And ever has it been
    That Love knows not its own depth
    'Til the hour of separation ... '
(Kahlil Gibran, Lebanese philosopher and, as far as anyone knows, not a regular follower of Meath's footballing fortunes in recent decades). Anyway, his profound observation will no doubt have been borne out this past few days as to the regard the people of Meath in particular and the Gaels of this county and beyond hold you ... Thank you for giving of yourself the way you have done and thank you for all the good example you have given to countless people. God bless and keep you – and enjoy your time with Tina and the clan. 'Those were the days, my friend ... '

From Tony and Madge McEntee, County Meath
A special thank you to Tina whose support allowed it all to happen.

From Conor Counihan, former Cork footballer

Congratulations on a tremendous career – not so much for the success you obviously achieved, but for the way you handled defeat. Of course from a Cork point of view you should have stepped down as manager in 1986 and then we might have a few more Celtic Crosses [All-Ireland medals] down here!

From Cathal Donohue, Athboy, County Meath

And all the time there was you. On your hunkers watching from the line. As gracious in defeat as you were generous in victory. A true sportsman. A true gentleman. A true Gael. Please God, some day I will be able to tell my children about our glory days, just like my Da told me of his.

From Bernie, County Westmeath

I would have cheered for your earlier teams – until this national contagious disease of begrudgery set in (do you have a bottle for that?). In latter years, you broke our hearts in Westmeath, so surely we are entitled to a little pleasure from 'hating' Meath!

From Paddy McDonnell, Dublin

There is no man to take your place. You are the greatest manager of all times. I will keep my fingers crossed that you will (still) keep the manager's job!

From Elaine Duffy, County Meath

You have inspired me to play for Meath Ladies in Croke Park. My ambition in life is to win an All-Ireland and experience for myself the wonder of playing in Croke Park and that winning feeling. My first memories of Croke Park are those four matches against Dublin in 1991 and the excitement and euphoria felt by the entire nation. As a nine-year-old I thought this is what life is all about!

From Pauric McShea, former Donegal footballer

I always admired the principles you brought to management: great tactical awareness, discipline and a great competitive spirit.

From Betty Heaney, Navan

My husband always thought you were the Messiah, so you will be sadly missed in our house!

From Kathleen, Frank and all the O'Connors

It was easy to raise the children – going to matches, meeting the cousins, picnics on the side of the road ... Simple but great times.

From Cliona Foley, sports journalist, Independent Newspapers

Like everyone else in the media, I will miss your courtesy, which was always a feature of our dealings ... With your motorsport interest, I will expect to meet you on a Harley or something (with Tina in a sidecar!).

From the Killian family, County Meath

Thank you for twenty-three years of heart-stopping excitement, tears and shouts of joy, dedication to the county – not just in sport but in every other way.

From Donal MacArtáin, former Down footballer

Many thanks for all you have done for Cumann Luthchleas Gael.

From John Horgan, Toronto

As an emigrant in Canada, you made me proud to wear my Meath jersey up to the park and to watch the games on television. I remember meeting you in Boston and how you marvelled at the fact that we had driven for ten hours to meet you guys. You were the reason for us doing that – restoring our faith in Meath football.

From Tony Davis, former Cork footballer

You brought such a good nature to the sport – something often sadly lacking. We had some good clashes and some bad results – but great memories!

From Kieran Weldon, County Meath

I can still remember my first trip to Croke Park, for the Centenary Cup in 1984. My granny's sister lived in Dublin and she had two stools and a sweeping brush on top to make sure our carpark space was secured ... Your team always conducted themselves with great pride, dignity and sportsmanship. It's ironic when you see the 'professional' soccer players across the water being paid ridiculous amounts of money and the terrible ways they conduct themselves off the field ...

From Patricia Redlich, psychologist

Football is not where we meet but I didn't want the occasion to slip by without comment. I saw the joy and enthusiasm in your face every time you talked about football.

From Patricia and Michael O'Brien, Navan

Our seven grandchildren are devastated at your retirement, as you always had the time to speak with them and shake their hands in Dalgan Park, Páirc Tailteann, or wherever they met you.

From Michael Meally, Maynooth, County Kildare

I will always remember a winter's night you travelled back from Leitrim to present medals to our under-16 team in Maynooth. You inspired us all that night.

From Tomás, Marc and Dara Ó Sé, Kerry

They will find it hard to fill your boots ... You gave the Meath boys many a great day ... You are held in the highest esteem in the Ó Sé house.

From Tom Burke, Drogheda, County Louth

You never sought to blame someone else, neither referee nor official, so for me you brought to Gaelic Football management a new dimension which will never even be equalled, much less surpassed.

From Gabriel Kelly, County Cavan

Even though you broke my heart when I was manager of Cavan, you always came to me after the game with words of encouragement and advice.

From Fr Willie Fitzsimons, County Westmeath

I am sure it will be a relief to watch the players from the stand. I just don't know how you endured the tension and the stress.

From Ailish Martin (mother of former goalkeeper Conor)

Thank you for the joy and the happy times you brought to our house and for always being so kind to Conor when he worked in London – and for keeping him on as 'No. 1'.

From Bill Halpenny (former Meath footballer) and Ann

Just to say thanks for all the pride and glory you brought to Meath and Meath football. Words alone cannot thank you.

From Ann and John Egan, Dunboyne

Thank you for all the ups and downs, going early to Croke Park, going to this little cafe for tea and tart; the joy of three best forwards – O'Rourke, Stafford and Flynn; Ollie Murphy's goals; draws with Cork and Mayo; hammering Kerry; and the four great games with Dublin.

From Jimmy Gibbons, Tara, County Meath

I don't know why Bertie Ahern had to import the American analyst Robert Putnam to advise the Government on 'Civic and Community Values'. He would not be in the running with your track record!

From John Bruton, EU Ambassador to Washington

Thank you for the joy and the pride you gave to me as a Meathman, a neighbour and a friend.

From Fiona Kelly, County Meath

I am seventeen years old. As I live near Dalgan Park, myself and my sister would always go to the Meath training sessions. I loved the buzz of seeing yourself and all the players preparing for big matches. When training was over I would get players' autographs on my Meath jersey. Then we would rush home and sit on the garden wall, waiting for all the players to pass on the way to Bellinter House for their well-deserved supper! We would wave our flags and would be delighted if the players beeped their horns.

From Mary

I heard you had stepped down and I found myself going into a trance of memories ...

From Dickie Kieran, County Louth

You broke our hearts as far as Louth were involved, but you gave us great pleasure with many mighty displays from your Meath boys.

From Ronan Gingles, Waterford

I feel as if I know you personally after all this time. People like me have never known any other Meath manager. Your sides have given Meath people great pride and have provided a huge sense of county identity to those of us living 'in exile.'

From Michael Smith, Bishop of Meath

Your greatest contribution was the manner in which you treated all the players who came under your care during that period of twenty-three years. Would that others would learn from your example.

From Jimmy Cudden

I write on behalf of Nan and myself – and approximately fifty loyal Meath supporters who have travelled on my bus since I started in the business in 1982. We travelled to every match and we would like to express our thanks for all those wonderful years. You have been a wonderful ambassador for our county.

From Jim Corkerry, Cork exile in Navan

In my twenty-three years in Meath, I could never be beaten in the pub quiz question about Meath managers! But, as we say in Cork, 'Could you not have done this in '86?' ...

From Peter McKeever, former Meath footballer

Your resignation was performed with the same integrity, honesty and charm which you have manifested throughout the twenty-three years you were in charge. You brought not only success but also great pride back to Meath football. I am grateful to have witnessed it and proud to have known you. I don't expect we shall ever see your like again ...

From Máiréad McGuinness, MEP

I bit my lip when I heard that you will no longer be managing Meath. My husband Tom stood to attention when the news was revealed on RTÉ Radio! Things will never be the same again!

From James Reilly, Meath county board

My time with you and the lads from 1995 to 2000 was a great experience. I learned a lot about management styles that I have been able to put into practice in my employment with the Health Service.

From V

You and the boys put a spring in our step. We could walk with the best and we did not feel inferior.

From Stephen Bray, current Meath footballer

Thanks for selecting me as part of the Meath football team. It was a life-long ambition of mine to be a Meath player. As a manager you have improved me as a player and you made me work on all aspects of my game. I wish things could have been different after all your efforts this year [2005].

From Joe Harte, a Meath exile in Cork
One championship match is all I missed during your term of office. I enjoyed driving the round trip from Cork to Belfast this year, as ever in my Kepak jersey ...

From Jo Jo Barrett, writer and sports journalist
I lived through your 'Golden Era' as a journalist and it was one of the great periods in the history of Gaelic Football.

From Rita and Gerry Beggy, parents of David 'Jinksy' Beggy
This is to say thank you for your contribution to making David the lovely man he is today.

From Fr Eoin Thynne, chaplain, Cathal Brugha Barracks
The Lord has a way of humbling us and Meath became experts at putting manners on the Dubs!

From David Hickey, surgeon and former Dublin footballer
Congratulations on your fantastic achievement of four All-Irelands and eight Leinster championships. It will be a long time before that is achieved by any other manager. In fact, it will never happen again.

From Seán Medlar, Castleknock, Dublin
All future successes will stem from the seed planted by you over the last twenty years.

From Dave Kavanagh, former Offaly footballer
One of my proudest moments was in 1988, winning the Railway Cup with Leinster. You were manager and I was representing Offaly ... You gave it some run over twenty-three years and you achieved great things, but the way in which you dealt with people is an even greater legacy than all the cups and medals you won.

From Brendan Hughes, Navan
Your smiling, jovial face will be missed around the dressing rooms.

From Ger Canning, television sports commentator
I cannot ever remember a moment, in victory or defeat, when you did not spare us a few valuable minutes to talk over a game and to recognise that the group you were really communicating with was the wider sports-loving public. Many others missed that point. You were well aware that I was from Cork and when Cork and Meath met in the late eighties, some dreadful stuff was being written about players you were close to, but I always had a huge admiration for the quality of Meath football. You played it the way football should be played.

From Leon Ó Móracháin, County Mayo
A letter from a Mayoman – someone you will hardly know, let alone remember ... In the 1996 Final, Meath beat Mayo by one point in a replay. In the dressing rooms, Meath were ecstatic, Mayo crestfallen. In speaking to your own team, you said: 'Just remember the team next door. They have been beaten in an All-Ireland Final by one point ... ' I have often said to players over the years – if it is hard to be a good loser, it is even harder to be good winners – really good winners. I want to remind you that you proved my theory to the hilt. Thank you for your generosity of spirit.

From Tom McGlinchey, former Tipperary football manager
I remember ringing you after Kerry had given Tipperary a trouncing in my first championship match as manager. Your words of encouragement and advice helped me get the show back on the road and I thank you for that.

From Louise Duffy, County Meath
Meath matches won't be the same for me as I've never known any different. You took over as manager the year I was born and have been there all my life until now!

From Ollie Bird, Athboy, County Meath

My late brother, Fr Jim Bird, was one of the many who used to go berserk at matches! Sad to say, quite a lot of Meath fans have departed this life. With the help of God, we will all meet again under a better referee in Heaven!

From Elma, Dowdstown House, Navan

You were truly a role model for adults as well as youth. Thanks for bringing the team here for meals these past two years. We were proud to have the lads here and to be associated with you.

From Brian Smith, former Meath footballer

Your gentlemanly attitude and concern have earned you the respect of GAA people throughout the length and breadth of the country and much further a field.

From Kate-Ann Gray, County Meath

What a bonanza of football over twenty odd years! Thank God I was able to attend every game. I was so lucky, thanks to you Seán and to your wife. She has to be a treasure.

From John O'Mahony, former Galway football manager

From one who sat in the opposing dugout on many occasions, thank you for the dignity and respect you showed to us all, whether it be in victory or defeat. You were always everything that is good about Gaelic Games.

From Anne Farrelly, County Offaly

When you came on the scene, it was a wilderness. Yet you have the special charisma for discovering hidden talent, cultivating it and waiting for it to come to fruition.

From Noel Dempsey TD, County Meath

You are a man who could wring greatness from anybody. It is the impact you have on people that is your magic.

From Owen McCrohan, County Kerry

Your dignity and good sportsmanship remain an abiding memory.

From Ciara Martin, County Meath (born in the year of Kevin Foley's goal!)

It's hard to imagine a Meath team without Seán Boylan. If you ever want to make a comeback, Rathkenny's arms are always wide open ...

From Jack Kiernan, Navan

The best years of our life – you made us so proud and gave us identity and a great loyalty to you and your teams.

From Jack Mahon, sportswriter and former Galway footballer

I regard you as one of the all-time nice men of the GAA. You were an absolute gem!

From Pat Duffy, County Meath

I can honestly say that the legacy you have left is infinite. More than anything else, I appreciate the respect and admiration you have achieved for Meath football.

From John O'Donoghue, Navan

I can think of no better tribute to your contribution to social and sporting progress in Meath than to quote Fidel Castro: 'When men carry the same ideals in their hearts, nothing can isolate them ... ' And nothing became you better than the manner of your departure ...

From Dom Gradwell, Drogheda, County Louth

What most impressed me was your graciousness and sincerity ... You were not one to gloat about victories – even though you had plenty of opportunities – nor to bury your head in the sand in defeat. Myself and my good friend Philip used to call you God. Once during a big match against Kildare in Croke Park in 1998, Philip noticed you pacing the line with a bottle of water in your hand. In his best north Meath accent he turned to me and said, as droll as you like: 'He'd better put that water down quick before he turns it into wine!'

From Frank Henry, Navan

My favourite memories from your term of office (in no particular order):

1. Colm O'Rourke's siege-lifting mighty point in the 1986 Leinster Final when we finally broke decades of championship domination by the dreaded Dubs!
2. David Beggy's 'slalom run' that led to a free and the equalising point in the last minute against a very strong Cork team in the All-Ireland Final of 1988.
3. Jody Devine's unforgettable extra-time performance against Kildare in 1997 – scoring four points that had to be seen to be believed.
4. The entire four-match series against Dublin in 1991, culminating in Foley's goal and Beggy's point. Victory has never been sweeter!
5. Colm Coyle's incredible equalising point against Mayo in the 1996 All-Ireland Final.
6. Ollie Murphy's brilliantly defiant goal, and celebration at the Hill end, in the 1999 Leinster Final against Dublin.
7. Graham Geraghty's logic-defying points at the Canal End in the Leinster championship against Dublin in 2005. As it transpires now, we were watching the dying embers of a Golden Era ...

From Kepak Management's statement on the ending of their sponsorship of Meath football, 26 September 2005

Seán Boylan has been a super ambassador for Kepak, Meath and the GAA at large. His contribution has been immense.

For the Record

Meath's championship record under Seán Boylan.

1983 **Leinster Championship**

| First Round: | Meath | 2-8 | Dublin | 2-8 |
| Replay: | Dublin | 3-9 | Meath | 0-16 |

1984 **Leinster Championship**

First Round:	Meath	2-15	Westmeath	1-5
Quarter-Final:	Meath	1-12	Louth	0-10
Semi-Final:	Meath	3-15	Laois	3-10
Final:	Dublin	2-10	Meath	1-9

1985 **Leinster Championship**

| First Round: | Meath | 0-13 | Kildare | 0-7 |
| Semi-Final: | Laois | 2-11 | Meath | 0-7 |

1986 **Leinster Championship**

First Round:	Meath	1-15	Carlow	1-12
Semi-Final:	Meath	1-17	Wicklow	0-11
Final:	Meath	0-9	Dublin	0-7

All-Ireland Championship

| Semi-Final: | Kerry | 2-13 | Meath | 0-12 |

1987 **Leinster Championship**

First Round:	Meath	1-11	Laois	2-5
Semi-Final:	Meath	0-15	Kildare	0-9
Final:	Meath	1-13	Dublin	0-12

All-Ireland Championship

Semi-Final:	Meath	0-15	Derry	0-8
Final:	Meath	1-14	Cork	0-11

1988 **Leinster Championship**

First Round:	Meath	3-13	Louth	0-9
Semi-Final:	Meath	0-19	Offaly	0-10
Final:	Meath	2-5	Dublin	0-9

All-Ireland Championship

Semi-Final:	Meath	0-16	Mayo	2-5
Final:	Meath	0-12	Cork	1-9
Replay:	Meath	0-13	Cork	0-12

1989 **Leinster Championship**

First Round:	Meath	1-15	Louth	0-13
Semi-Final:	Meath	3-11	Offaly	0-9
Final:	Dublin	2-12	Meath	1-10

1990 **Leinster Championship**

First Round:	Meath	3-15	Longford	0-12
Semi-Final:	Meath	4-14	Laois	0-6
Final:	Meath	1-14	Dublin	0-14

All-Ireland Championship

Semi-Final:	Meath	3-9	Donegal	1-7
Final:	Cork	0-11	Meath	0-9

1991 **Leinster Championship**

Preliminary Round:	Meath	1-12	Dublin	1-12	
Replay:	Meath	1-11	Dublin	1-11	AET
Replay:	Meath	2-11	Dublin	1-14	AET
Replay:	Meath	2-10	Dublin	0-15	
First Round:	Meath	1-9	Wicklow	0-12	

Replay	Meath	1-12	Wicklow	1-9
Semi-Final:	Meath	2-13	Offaly	0-7
Final:	Meath	1-11	Laois	0-8

All-Ireland Championship

Semi-Final:	Meath	0-15	Roscommon	1-11
Final:	Down	1-16	Meath	1-14

1992 Leinster Championship

First Round:	Laois	2-11	Meath	1-11

1993 Leinster Championship

First Round:	Meath	1-12	Laois	0-7
Semi-Final	Dublin	1-10	Meath	0-12

1994 Leinster Championship

First Round:	Meath	0-20	Laois	2-10
Semi-Final:	Meath	4-14	Wexford	2-6
Final:	Dublin	1-9	Meath	1-8

1995 Leinster Championship

First Round:	Meath	1-15	Offaly	1-5
Quarter-Final:	Meath	4-15	Longford	0-10
Semi-Final:	Meath	3-14	Wicklow	0-9
Final:	Dublin	1-18	Meath	1-8

1996 Leinster Championship

First Round:	Meath	0-24	Carlow	0-6
Semi-Final:	Meath	2-14	Laois	1-9
Final:	Meath	0-10	Dublin	0-8

All-Ireland Championship

Semi-Final:	Meath	2-15	Tyrone	0-12
Final:	Meath	0-12	Mayo	1-9
Replay:	Meath	2-9	Mayo	1-11

1997   Leinster Championship

First Round:	Meath	1-13	Dublin	1-10	
Semi-Final:	Meath	0-12	Kildare	1-9	
Replay:	Meath	2-20	Kildare	3-17	AET
Replay:	Meath	1-12	Kildare	1-10	
Final:	Offaly	3-17	Meath	1-15	

1998   Leinster Championship

First Round:	Meath	3-10	Offaly	0-7
Semi-Final:	Meath	0-15	Louth	1-11
Final:	Kildare	1-12	Meath	0-12

1999   Leinster Championship

First Round:	Meath	2-10	Wicklow	0-6
Semi-Final:	Meath	1-13	Offaly	0-9
Final:	Meath	1-14	Dublin	0-12

All-Ireland Championship

Semi-Final:	Meath	0-15	Armagh	2-5
Final:	Meath	1-11	Cork	1-8

2000   Leinster Championship

First Round:	Offaly	0-13	Meath	0-9

2001   Leinster Championship

First Round:	Meath	2-12	Westmeath	1-14
Semi-Final:	Meath	1-16	Kildare	1-11
Final:	Meath	2-11	Dublin	0-14

All-Ireland Championship

Quarter-Final:	Meath	2-12	Westmeath	3-9
Replay:	Meath	2-10	Westmeath	0-11
Semi-Final:	Meath	2-14	Kerry	0-5
Final:	Galway	0-17	Meath	0-8

2002   Leinster Championship

Quarter-Final	Meath	1-12	Westmeath	0-11
Semi-Final:	Dublin	2-11	Meath	0-10

All-Ireland Championship

Qualifier 1:	Meath	3-8	Louth	2-9
Qualifier 2:	Meath	1-15	Laois	0-7
Qualifier 3:	Donegal	1-13	Meath	0-14

2003   Leinster Championship

Quarter-Final:	Meath	2-13	Westmeath	2-13
Replay:	Meath	1-11	Westmeath	0-5
Semi-Final:	Kildare	0-15	Meath	1-11

All-Ireland Championship

Qualifier 1:	Meath	2-10	Monaghan	0-12
Qualifier 2:	Fermanagh	1-12	Meath	0-9

2004   Leinster Championship

First Round:	Meath	2-13	Wicklow	1-8
Semi-Final:	Laois	1-13	Meath	0-9

All-Ireland Championship

Qualifier:	Fermanagh	0-19	Meath	2-12	AET

2005   Leinster Championship

Quarter-Final:	Dublin	1-12	Meath	1-10

All-Ireland Championship

Qualifier 1:	Meath	5-12	Antrim	0-13	
Qualifier 2:	Meath	1-12	Leitrim	1-8	AET
Qualifier 3:	Cavan	1-8	Meath	1-6	

Total games played: **95**

Won: **61**

Drawn: **11**

Lost: **23**

AET = after extra time.